THE INNOVATION

MANUAL

THE INNOVATION
MANUAL

Integrated Strategies and Practical Tools for Bringing Value Innovation to the Market

David Midgley

A John Wiley & Sons, Ltd., Publication

Other Wiley Editorial Offices

John Wiley & Sons Inc., 111 River Street, Hoboken, NJ 07030, USA

Jossey-Bass, 989 Market Street, San Francisco, CA 94103-1741, USA

Wiley-VCH Verlag GmbH, Boschstr. 12, D-69469 Weinheim, Germany

John Wiley & Sons Australia Ltd, 42 McDougall Street, Milton, Queensland 4064, Australia

John Wiley & Sons (Asia) Pte Ltd, 2 Clementi Loop #02-01, Jin Xing Distripark, Singapore 129809

John Wiley & Sons Canada Ltd, 6045 Freemont Blvd, Mississauga, ONT, L5R 4J3, Canada

Wiley also publishes its books in a variety of electronic formats. Some content that appears in print may not be available in electronic books.

Library of Congress Cataloging-in-Publication Data
Midgley, David.
    The innovation manual : integrated strategies and practical tools for bringing value innovation to the market / David Midgley.
        p.   cm.
    Includes bibliographical references and index.
    ISBN 978-0-470-72453-8 (cloth : alk. paper)   1. Technological innovations—Management.   I. Title.
    HD45.M476 2009
    658.5'14—dc22

                                                                                            2008053891

British Library Cataloguing in Publication Data
A catalogue record for this book is available from the British Library

ISBN 978-0-470-72453-8 (HB)

Typeset in 11.5/15pt Bembo by SNP Best-set Typesetter Ltd., Hong Kong

To my wife, Véronique

CONTENTS

PREFACE

I have lived innovation for over two decades. I consult on innovation with firms for business objectives, I teach innovation to executives and MBA students, and I research it for academic journals. Over that time I have met thousands of business people on three continents. Many have innovation agendas. They can be executives who want to improve the speed and quality of their firm's innovation, or to shift its focus from products to services and business models. They can be managers who need to understand a particular method or tool used in innovation development, or to customize it to their industry. The experience of talking to them has been enjoyable, intellectually challenging and personally rewarding. Innovation is *the* most interesting topic in business. But the contrast between what we know about innovation and the practical challenges of business people leads me to conclude that we can do innovation much better. If we can apply our knowledge more effectively we can improve the way firms deliver innovation to the market. And that will benefit not only shareholders and managers, but also society as a whole. My motivation for writing this book is to bridge the gap between the latest research, best practice, and the practical challenges that managers face in a typical firm. The book focuses on five key tasks I think executives and managers need to perform for innovation to succeed, and it provides the supporting tools that managers can use to carry out each task well.

I think this specific focus is important because the literature on innovation is vast and offers many differing opinions and recipes for success. What's more, many innovation experts take the perspective of one discipline or business role and fail to integrate their solutions with other parts of the organization. This makes it hard for managers to form a sense of priority across different solutions, or to see an overall picture of a good approach to innovation for their firm. Fragmentation also makes it difficult for them to identify and apply important lessons from research and best practice in their organization.

The supporting tools are also important. The executives and managers I teach increasingly demand to see the 'how' behind an idea; they want to see how they can apply it to their organization, with its own unique challenges and circumstances. They are looking for a sort of toolkit or instruction manual that adds depth to the ideas it contains, and provides practical guidance for customizing ideas and tools to their firm. This book aims to supply this practical guidance, within the overall framework of the five main tasks.

There are many people I need to thank for helping me put this book together. These include the publishing team at John Wiley—Claire Plimmer, Jo Golesworthy, Michaela Fay, Julia Bezzant, Samantha Hartley and Natalie Girach; the team at Cambridge Editorial Partnership—Sally Simmons, Carole Pearce, Jemma Carter and Fraser Pettigrew; and my assistant at INSEAD, Joelle Fabert. I also owe a big debt to the numerous INSEAD colleagues who influence my thinking on innovation, with special thanks to Markus Christen, Hubert Gatignon, Chan Kim, Jean-Claude Larreche, Prashant Malaviya, Renée Mauborgne and Jens Meyer. Thanks should also go to those at other business schools who have helped me develop my ideas, notably Lee Cooper, George Day, Tim Devinney and Jordan Louviere. And to those in industry who supported the project in other important ways, especially John Atkin, David Marshall, Steve Mayer, Bruno de Monplanet and Pierre Pringuet. Most of all I thank my wife, Véronique, for making it possible, and our children, Edward, Alexandra, Ellen and Solène for their patience and support.

CHAPTER 1

THE THREE CHALLENGES OF BUSINESS INNOVATION

THE OBJECTIVES OF THE BOOK

This book empowers managers to deliver breakthrough innovations successfully into the new world of business. Firms are under increasing pressure to make major innovations in products, services and business models. Whether through competitive pressure or shareholder expectations, they need to create significantly more value. That means moving away from the cautious approaches of the past to embrace the challenge of major innovation. Many firms are trying to grapple with this challenge. They are trying to shift the mind-set of their managers from the old world of R&D and products to the new world of services, business models and customer value. This book focuses on the manager and provides the essentials he or she needs to know about this new world.

Who are the managers this book is for? They are those responsible for bringing their firm's innovation to market. They work in roles such as business development, marketing, R&D and information technology. Or they are senior executives charged with innovation strategy, governance and leadership. They understand their current role thoroughly, but their work schedule leaves them little time to study new approaches or to take a broader view of innovation.

And as the nature of innovation changes, their current management practices are no longer satisfactory. Product innovation is still necessary but incremental changes are no longer enough to achieve the firm's growth and profitability targets. Instead, the firm must seek major growth through breakthrough innovations in products, services and business models. To bring these successfully to market, managers need new knowledge and practices and they need to develop skills that are different from those of the past.

This book has two objectives that set it apart from others on the topic. First, it seeks to address the changing nature of innovation and its implications for managers and management practices. Second, it seeks to provide an integrated and practical approach to bringing innovation to market.

First Objective: Address the Changing Nature of Innovation

The new knowledge and skills that managers need for major innovation are many and diverse. For executives, developing major innovation requires that they set a clearer direction for the firm, introduce better governance and use different leadership styles. For managers, it means working in new sorts of innovation teams and developing new skills in creativity and collaboration. It also needs new approaches to understanding customers and new ways of managing complex projects. Delivering the resulting innovation to the market often requires widespread changes to the organization and so innovation teams also need change management skills to achieve this. This is because teams often face resistance from within their firm, and the greater the innovation the more resistance they can expect.

The set of skills needed to manage change is valuable to corporate innovators. Building the market for a major innovation also needs a longer term, more sophisticated approach to strategy and marketing than the typical manager is familiar with. Managers and firms need to shift their perspective from the annual plan and budgeting cycle to a flexible strategic plan spread over many years and campaigns. And they need to plan from a thorough understanding of how new markets develop. Meeting the first objective of this book therefore has two parallel and supporting themes. The first is to redefine the idea of innovation to include major changes to products, services, business models and organizations. The second is to identify the management knowledge and skills that are necessary to achieve such major changes.

Firms can innovate by creating an offer to the customer or a business model that has never been seen before. Or they can innovate by significantly improving what customers buy now, or how they go about buying it or how the firm delivers on its promise. All such innovations pose the critical organizational and managerial questions that this book seeks to address. How can firms create innovations that add value to their customers and shareholders? How can they develop these innovations from idea to reality both effectively and speedily? How can they change their organization and people to deliver the innovation and build the new market? Answering these questions requires perspectives from more than one business discipline so ideas from strategy, leadership, marketing and organization all play a prominent role in the chapters to come.

The last decade has seen great advances in our understanding of major innovation. From the fields of psychology, sociology and marketing comes a better understanding of how customers accept innovation. From the fields of strategy and organization studies come better ways to think about customer value and better ways for firms to organize to deliver it. From studies of team performance come new ideas for selecting, organizing and managing the project teams that must develop innovation. From marketing and technology come new ideas on how these teams can get breakthrough insights from customers. From studies of organizational change come new principles for successfully changing the firm. And, finally, from marketing and economics come better perspectives on how to build and compete in new markets.

The challenge is to bring all this knowledge to bear more effectively and so improve the ways firms manage innovation. I hope that this book does distil and prioritize this knowledge in a useful way. In particular, I hope that it explains the essentials clearly and links them to the decisions that managers must take.

Second Objective: Provide an Integrated and Practical Approach to Managing Innovation

There are thousands of books on innovation containing many interesting ideas and suggestions. But ideas in and of themselves are not especially helpful. What managers need is far harder to get. Time pressures and the scarcity of talent in the workforce mean that managers need to focus on the few ideas that really do work. Ideas that are isolated from one another, and that are thus limited by the perspective of one business discipline or role are also not useful. Instead, managers need ideas that are organized into clear business tasks. Such tasks should form an overall approach to innovation, preferably one drawn from best practice and tested theory.

An approach that shows managers what they should do, when they should do it and how they might go about doing it is also inadequate. Managers also need practical tools for carrying out these tasks. Such tools bridge the gap between abstract ideas or recommendations and the steps they need to carry out in their daily work. And managers need to know how to adapt both recommendations and tools to the widely varying business circumstances they find themselves in. The second objective of this book is to provide such an integrated and practical approach.

Thus, the content of the book ranges from the conceptual to the practical. Conceptually the book identifies five key tasks that managers must complete to bring major innovation to the market successfully. It discusses the best way to tackle each task and links these tasks into an integrated overall approach to innovation.

However, as well as general recommendations, the book also covers various tools that managers can use. A tool can be a method for collecting relevant data, a set of criteria for decision-making or a way to manage an innovation team. There are many tools already available in some areas of innovation development. Where these exist the task will simply be to select the key tools that managers need. Yet there are no tools for some of the newer and equally critical areas of innovation development. Here the tools have to be invented. But whether old or new, they need to be tools the managers themselves can use. An important lesson from best practice is that managers cannot delegate these tasks to others. Each chapter thus identifies the practical steps that a manager can take or provides criteria for important decisions.

Further, the nature of the market, the industry or the firm might give one approach or tool advantages over another. Many prescriptions for better innovation management ignore the differences between industries and firms. This is not useful: we need to identify where a specific industry or firm will find that one approach is better than another or that one tool is more applicable to the circumstances. This book recommends how managers might adapt best practice to the unique circumstances of their firm. Similarly, the nature of the innovation itself strongly influences what the best approach or tool should be. Different innovations need different management techniques. Here again the book recommends approaches and tools and identifies the particular challenge set by each innovation by placing them a new framework. The next section develops this framework.

I hope that this content is both novel and of real benefit to managers. The focus on key tasks provides them with a sharper and more usable understanding of the existing knowledge about successful innovations. The tools enable them to apply this knowledge in their company. By customizing the recommendations, I also hope managers will be able to apply both the knowledge and tools to their own circumstances.

ADDRESSING THE CHANGING NATURE OF INNOVATION

The first part of this section illustrates the changing nature of innovation, while the second develops a clearer picture of the challenges inherent in this change. The final part examines the consequences of these challenges for managing innovation within the firm.

The Changing Nature of Innovation

In the recent past innovation was synonymous with product innovation. Even today much of the way firms think about and manage innovation comes from lessons about new product development. Yet over the last decade there has been a shift in this thinking in at least four important respects. The first three of these concern the nature of customer value and the fourth concerns the nature of the business model the firm uses.

First, there has been a shift to thinking about innovation as the total value offered to the customer. With that perspective, while products remain important, there are many circumstances in which other elements of the offer are of equal or greater importance. Typically these other elements involve services. For example, there are many portable music players whose product technology is similar to Apple's iPod. Yet iPod is the runaway leader in that market. Why? Many argue it is because of the seamless integration of the iPod, the iTunes software and Apple's online music store. This service provides value to customers because it makes building up and enjoying their music collection simple. A business–to–business (B2B) example of the same trend is Otis Elevator. Most of Otis's revenues now come from services around elevators rather than the physical elevators themselves.

Second, many managers now realize that large numbers of customers are often unwilling to buy a product or service simply because firms lack the vision to provide the right benefits. The classic example here is the Cirque du Soleil. Before the Cirque du Soleil came into existence the circus was a declining industry, appealing to shrinking audiences of families with small children. The Cirque reinvented the circus and broadened its appeal to many other audiences. This example also concerns value to the customer, but in this case providing value to customer segments not currently served by the industry.

Third, many managers also accept that firms sometimes offer too many features or benefits for certain customer segments. This includes the many examples of successful low-cost providers such as Southwest Airlines, Formula 1 hotels or Nucor in sheet steel. These providers sell to customer segments that do not need the full benefits currently on offer by their industry, and they have also reinvented their product or service.

Fourth, many managers now realize that an equally important consideration is the business model their firm uses to profit from the innovation. Apple largely adopted the existing business model of the music industry for iTunes. They did this by making the iTunes music store another reseller buying songs at wholesale prices from the record companies. These companies then give out royalties to other parties in the traditional manner. That this online model was not as threatening to the record companies as other models may be another important reason for Apple's success. A B2B example here is Dow Europe's selling industrial polyesters through the Internet. Dow's online offer is standardized, with a fixed size, no extra services and a competitive price. The offer targets a segment of the market that resellers do not want to serve. It also slows down the entry of generic products that erode the margins of both Dow and the resellers.

The first three of these points broaden the idea of innovation from product features to all the elements that offer value to the customer. They show how important it is to understand the target customer and to use that understanding to select the right offer. The fourth point seems self-evident – surely all firms want to make a profit from their innovations? However, there are many examples where competitive pressures led to firms adding unnecessary and costly features to their innovations, thus eroding their profits. That is why Kim and Mauborgne's *Blue Ocean Strategy* is so instructive.[1] This work shows managers how to think about value broadly and creatively, and how to make an intelligent trade-off between the customers' priorities and the firm's profits.

Now, managers know these examples or others like them as well. The point here is that, while the examples are known, many firms do not incorporate these lessons into their innovation development practices. Indeed, firms often manage innovation poorly. Typically, the worst firms do not set guiding principles; their culture and incentives do not support innovation; their strategies are simplistic; their projects lack resources and the firm pays inadequate attention to the customers' needs. But even in the firms that manage innovation well there is a significant gap between current practice and the challenge of major innovation. Too often firms see innovation as an incremental extension of the past; narrowly focusing on refining an existing product or service.

As a first step they need to define innovation more broadly. Innovation is first and foremost about the total value that firms provide to customers. But it is also about how creatively they configure their business model and organization to deliver that value profitably.

Defining Innovation through the Eyes of the Key Constituencies

In discussing innovation it would be useful to have a classification scheme that distinguishes between the many different types and degrees of innovation seen in products, services and business models. This scheme would provide a common terminology for discussing which management approaches might be best for different types of innovation. A useful scheme would also allow firms to assess the degree of challenge they might face in completing a specific project. This is important for both resource allocation and risk management.

Unfortunately no such scheme currently exists. Indeed, on the contrary the literature has many alternative descriptions and classification schemes. There are incremental, radical and disruptive innovations. There are non-customer innovations, low-end innovations, bottom-of-the-pyramid innovations, architectural innovations and format innovations. Garcia and Calantone point out there are over 20 different schemes in the product innovation literature alone.[2] They point out that many of the differences between these schemes result from the differing perspectives of the authors. These perspectives can differ so much that what in the eyes of one author is an incremental innovation becomes a radical innovation in the eyes of another!

An example they mention is the Canon digital photocopier. Some authors see the capacity to store or send digital images as marking a radical discontinuity in the market. Others see this as just an incremental or architectural development of existing laser photocopier technology. This simple example shows both the confusion in the literature and the danger of relying on external observers, however skilled or well-meaning. Surely it is better to understand an innovation as the degree of change it represents for all those it impacts on? These include those who must develop it, those who must deliver it to the market and, most critical of all, the customers who may buy it. If all these people see the innovation as being a major development from current solutions then it probably is. These are the key constituencies that must learn about the innovation, change their behaviour and accept the innovation if it is to succeed. Understanding their perceptions of the innovation is central to developing and marketing it successfully.

Another problem with the existing literature is that it largely ignores innovation in services. Even where authors do recognize services they view them as pseudo-products. Yet, as every service practitioner knows, services differ from products in their intangibility, inseparability, variation and perishability. Many services are also produced in that moment of truth between the customer and the employee, not in the factory or the office. Creating a service innovation is therefore not the same as creating a product innovation. It needs much more attention to people and organization. And in the many product firms that add services as a way to grow, every manager needs to understand these differences.

The literature also pays inadequate attention to innovation in business models. Afuah defines a business model as 'which activities a firm performs, how it performs them, and when it performs them as it uses its resources ... to create superior customer value and put itself in a position to appropriate the value'.[3] It is the last phrase 'put itself in a position to appropriate the value' that is important because it sets up a new challenge. Innovation is not just about creating superior customer value: it is also about ensuring the firm takes its fair share of that value. Understanding how the firm can use organizational or process innovation to capture value should carry equal importance to understanding end customer needs. There is no point in innovating if some other party in the value network captures all the newly created value.

Taken together, recognizing that innovation is broader than products and examining its impact on key constituencies provides a better scheme for assessing the firm's challenge. How new is the innovation in the minds of the target customers? How new is it in the minds of those developing the product or service? And how new is it in the minds of partners and others in the value network? A true breakthrough innovation in this framework is the one that involves a major change for all three constituencies. An incremental innovation is one that involves only modest changes for each constituency. But the main goal here is not to label innovations. No, the goal should be to assess the degree of change the firm must achieve by calibrating the gaps between the innovation and current solutions. From this perspective, we can see the challenge of a business innovation as three distinct challenges. These are:

1. developing the innovation and its delivery system;
2. getting the customer to adopt the innovation;
3. appropriating a fair share of the new value.

Each of these aligns with a key constituency; that is, the firm itself, the customer and the value chain or network. Exhibit 1.1 shows the new scheme, with examples of the issues that each challenge might involve. These examples are on a scale from a low to a high challenge, with the higher challenges to the right-hand side of each. For example, meeting latent customer needs is inherently harder for the firm than meeting existing or proven ones better, if only because latent needs are less well understood.

Notice that the point of reference for the degree of challenge is relative to the firm and its constituencies, not to some absolute standard. The challenges are therefore unique to each firm.

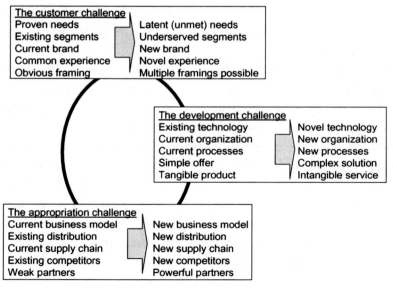

Exhibit 1.1   The three challenges of business innovation.

In this scheme, innovations such as Apple's iPod, Nintendo's Wii or Sony's PS3 fall somewhere in between the crude stereotypes of breakthrough and incremental. They are challenging in some dimensions but not in others. And it is precisely the dimensions in which they are novel, and those where they are not, that is most informative. The technology in Apple's iPod did not represent a great challenge since it involves repackaging well-understood hard disk technologies. Customers also have a proven need for mobile music, as seen in the sales of previous product technologies such as Sony's Walkman. What is more challenging is the iTunes business model of pay-per-downloadable songs plus the seamless efficiency of the downloading service.

The technology of Nintendo's Wii is also not especially challenging. Although it may be a little more novel than the iPod because of the motion controller, Nintendo built it mostly on existing gaming technology. Its business model follows the well-worn path of retail distribution and game royalties. What is more challenging is taking this innovation to non-customers – people who do not consider or use game consoles, such as families or fitness addicts.

Finally, Sony's PS3 aims at just the opposite customer from the Wii, namely gaming enthusiasts. It uses the same retail distribution and game royalty model. What is challenging is the new Cell processor, which seeks to take gaming to new levels of realism and excitement. This processor is not a simple extension of previous processor technology. All three of these innovations are combinations of products, services and business models and all provide personal entertainment. But they also differ in important respects, especially in the management challenge that each of these firms faced.

For that reason the overall challenge of business innovation needs reformulating as follows. Given the perceptions of the three constituencies, what critical challenge does the firm face in delivering the innovation successfully? Apple's critical challenge was more political and institutional than technological. They had to develop a download business model acceptable to the music industry. Without this iTunes would have failed, as several other music services indeed did. This challenge does not fit the traditional view of product development, which pays little attention to such broader issues. Nintendo's challenge was to convince the mainstream family customer that gaming has value. This is the difficult marketing challenge of crossing the chasm from enthusiasts to mainstream. Here technology and business models are secondary to marketing skills. Sony's challenge was different yet again. It was to deliver PS3 technology that worked to a group of customers who were waiting for it. They also did this using a well-established go-to-market strategy and games royalty business model. This latter example is the closest to the traditional view of product innovation, since the focus is on improving product performance through the Cell processor technology.

In summary, trying to impose arbitrary classifications on innovation is a pointless exercise. From a management perspective it is better to examine the three key constituencies and form an assessment of where the critical challenges lie. In Apple's case this was politics, in Nintendo's marketing and in Sony's technology. This is not to understate the challenges each firm faced in the other areas, but simply to point to the areas where they most needed resources, clever strategy and good management.

Implications of Taking a Broader View on Innovation

There are two straightforward implications of this broader view of innovation, and a deeper conclusion that goes to the foundations for success. The two implications concern using customer insights to develop and launch the innovation and changing the organization to deliver it. The deeper point concerns the idea of advantage to the customer.

Using Customer Insights to Develop and Launch the Innovation

Broadening from product to service and business model innovation immediately adds to the challenge the firm faces in developing the innovation. Developing services and business models needs good insight into the customer because these are inherently abstract ideas, not products. For example, services exist in the moment in which customers consume them. This makes early discussions with customers around potential ideas for innovations more difficult than for products. Discussing new business models poses the same problem with both customers and potential partners. For both services and business models it is also harder to get accurate reactions to prototypes later in development. Customers can see and touch products, but they experience services. So any prototype needs to simulate the real experience for customers. This is not to say that some product innovations are not equally challenging. They are challenging, especially when they involve the latent needs of the customer or undeveloped segments. These are also difficult to discuss at the idea creation stage and it is harder to get accurate reactions to them later in development. The implication here is that, as ideas of innovation change, so must the methods that firms use to get customer insight during innovation development. And the most recent and effective solution to these challenges is to co-create the innovation with customers as partners.

Once created, services, business models and product innovations targeting latent needs are also abstract ideas that firms must communicate to customers. Designing effective launch campaigns needs good customer insight as well. And, of course, the customer is the final arbiter of success. Technology, service and business models need to come together to deliver an effective value proposition, but marketing needs to give the customer a reason to adopt the innovation. One of the lessons of the last decade is that success in the market is just as much about perceptions as it is about the novel features of the innovation itself. Good marketing cannot save a poor innovation from failure, but many good innovations fail because of poor marketing, especially if managers do not understand how to build new markets. The implication here is that not only must methods for getting customers' insight change, so must the underlying understanding of how new markets are built. Building new markets for major innovations is different to launching incremental product innovations.

Changing the Organization to Deliver the Innovation

Broadening from product to service and business model innovation also adds to the challenge the firm faces in getting the organization to deliver the innovation. Studies have shown that most service innovations involve changes to firm processes and organization.[4] For example, the firm may reorganize or build new business units. Employees may need new skills and the training that will lead to this. Managers must communicate the reasons for the change to people both within and outside the organization. Indeed, part of the appropriation challenge involves explaining to, and persuading, partners in the value network to support the innovation. Similar comments hold true for product innovations that meet latent needs or address undeveloped segments of the market. For all these reasons, major innovations often also involve major organizational change and thus require those developing them to have good skills in change management.

Creating Advantage Is the Foundation for Success

Creating customer value is the first goal of any innovation project. However, new value in and of itself is not enough. To adopt, customers must perceive an advantage over what went before it, otherwise the innovation will fail. More importantly, typical customers perceive that they will lose much more from dropping what went before than they gain from adopting the innovation. For a major innovation, the customers must perceive a compelling advantage for them to adopt it. It is the word 'perceive' that is critical.

Advances in social sciences over the last decade have deepened our understanding of how customers perceive and evaluate advantage. They show that for many customers advantage is at least partially a social construction, formed from the many local influences that weigh on them as they consider the innovation. These local influences include the marketing efforts of the firm and its competitors but also other customers and third parties. Thus, to be successful firms need to provide a good platform for building advantage in the eyes of customers alongside the purely technical development of the innovation. This requirement has become more pressing with the broader concept of innovation. It is harder to design and communicate advantage when the innovation has more abstract or intangible benefits or where the target segment is undeveloped.

Chapter 2 provides the foundation for the rest of the book by reviewing all these advances in our understanding of how to build advantage in the market. The title of the chapter – *Creating Advantage in the Minds of Many* – points to the goal of all innovation projects; namely widespread acceptance by customers. First, using advances in cognitive psychology, the chapter looks at customers as individuals. As individuals, they do not see advantage in absolute terms but as relative to some frame of reference. The choice of the frame of reference for the innovation is one of the most important decisions for the innovating firm. Most customers are risk averse and happy to stick with the status quo unless given a strong motivation to change. Understanding what might motivate acceptance is another important consideration in development.

Second, the chapter reviews advances in personality psychology to understand how individual customers might vary in their predispositions towards innovation. To extend this foundation to B2B markets the decisions made by groups are also examined. Understanding these differences between customers is important in building new markets. Third, it looks at customers as social beings, using advances in sociology, especially computational sociology and models of the way peer influence spreads through markets. Encouraging peer influence is central to overcoming the status quo bias of many customers. Finally, it reviews advances in economics and marketing to understand how the supply of influence can help to develop the new market.

The basic principles behind creating advantage and building new markets are well-known. However, the recent advances reviewed here both extend these principles and destroy some common myths about them held by managers. For that reason, the chapter ends with a new model of adoption and action steps that point out how management practices need to change. The model highlights the role of the innovating firm in setting the agenda for change and providing the right platform for customers to construct advantage. As a result, firms should co-create their innovations by partnering with certain types of customer early in development, and all types of customer later. They should also involve customer-facing managers from the start of the project. Firms and their project teams should also devote more effort to visualizing what the mass market might look like. While this may be several years away, their early actions can shape the mass market and it is where they can make the most profit. Current management practices in many firms pay lip-service to these ideas but lack the depth of understanding and tools to carry them out effectively. Chapter 2 tries to provide this understanding, which the following chapters both expand and provide the necessary tools for.

THE FIVE KEY TASKS

There is no doubt that innovation is an important topic for firms. Study after study shows that innovation is one of the least well-managed areas in most firms. For example, from their well-known surveys the management consultants Booz, Allen and Hamilton argue that it is not the effort that firms put into innovation that decides success.[5] They find little correlation between levels of effort and the firm's performance. Instead, it is the way firms go about doing innovation that decides their success or failure. In particular, how well the various parts of the organization collaborate on key tasks is decisive.

The book focuses on five key tasks the firm needs to manage well to be successful. They have been chosen for their known high impact on overall success. As a result the book omits many other topics, not because they are unimportant, but because they have a lower impact on success. Unless the firm manages the key tasks correctly doing other tasks well will not lead to a successful innovation. These five key tasks are:

1. chartering innovation within the organization;
2. selecting, preparing and supporting the right team;
3. co-creating the innovation with customers;
4. changing the organization to deliver the innovation;
5. building the market for the innovation.

This list of topics is the core of a general management prescription for innovation. These are tasks that any firm needs to do well to be successful with innovation, in the old world as well as the new. What is different is how these tasks have changed for the new challenge of a major product, service or business model innovation.

Some brief comments on the five tasks may be useful as context before I provide a synopsis of each. The five tasks together form the central sequence for developing and bringing a major innovation to market. Doing these five tasks well is also an ambitious but feasible stretch target for busy managers. Especially when they need to change their management practices to meet the broader definition of innovation.

The five tasks span several business roles and topics. These tasks do not fit into neat functional boxes and to succeed managers need to approach them from the perspective of the organization as a whole. Apart from the fact that the enemies of innovation are narrow perspectives, in the end the whole organization has to deliver the innovation to the market. That is why this is not a marketing book, a strategy book, or a change management book, but a general management book on innovation, which incorporates the best from each of these areas.

There are many excellent books and studies on each of these individual topics, whose ideas and expertise this book cites and builds on. For example, taking each task in turn one can think of Mourkogiannis' *Purpose*,[6] Lencioni's *The Five Dysfunctions of a Team*,[7] Kelley and Littman's *The Ten Faces of Innovation*,[8] Kotter's *Leading Change*[9] and Golder and Tellis's *Will and Vision*.[10] And many others from authors like Christensen, Gladwell, Larreche, Moore, O'Reilly, Rogers, Tushman and Zaltman.

However, this book introduces new ideas to integrate the key lessons in each area or discipline into an effective innovation process. The fragmented state of our knowledge makes this necessary. In some ways writers and researchers on the topic of innovation are also in silos, mostly looking at this topic through the lens of a specific business function or academic discipline. The other reason is perhaps more controversial but also driven by fragmentation. When one starts to integrate key lessons from different knowledge silos it becomes obvious that innovation management practices need a marked rethink. The conclusion I make in more depth later is that many recommendations about innovation management ignore the latest thinking in important respects. Meanwhile, as a preview of the chapters to come, here is a synopsis of the five key tasks.

Task One: Chartering Innovation within the Organization

Chapter 3 first sets up business objectives and governance guidelines for the firm's innovation programme. Together these provide an Innovation Charter that lets everyone know where innovation fits and how to do it. The charter should define a programme involving a stream of potential projects, not simply a one-off event. For sustainability and to exploit success firms need a stream of innovations. Alongside the business objectives run the governance guidelines. What freedom has been given to the innovation teams to act? Who will decide to scale up or drop projects and what criteria will they use? How will the firm reward success and failure?

Without clear objectives it is difficult to evaluate potential innovations and to keep innovations coming in at a competitive rate. Without clear guidelines it is difficult for innovation teams to carry out their task. Worse, any lack of clarity can undermine and frustrate new projects, especially ones that threaten existing business. Chapter 3 provides a template for both parts of the Innovation Charter.

The second part of this chapter looks at setting up a specific innovation project, especially defining the right objective for the project team. This part of the chapter focuses more on tools than on big picture frameworks. It examines three complementary tools that can help define project objectives. These are the strategy canvas, scenario planning and discovery-based planning. The chapter ends by noting that clarity of direction and flexibility of organization are important to success. By implication this means that different types of innovation need different types of leadership.

Task Two: Selecting, Preparing and Supporting the Right Team

Firms use project teams to develop most innovations, so having the right team is an important ingredient of success. Chapter 4 looks at how to select, prepare and support this team, and addresses two main topics.

The first part of the chapter examines how the various types of team that firms use in innovation perform. These types of team include multifunctional, autonomous teams, X-teams and separate business units. More importantly, it also looks at the fit between these types of team and the new world of service and business model innovation. Of particular interest is the increasing need for effective collaboration with the rest of the organization.

The second part of the chapter uses lessons from the first to set up the principles for selecting, preparing and supporting innovation teams. This section focuses mainly on the role of the core team in the front end of development. It addresses issues in selecting the project sponsor, team leader and team members. It also addresses criteria for selecting these members, such as getting a diversity of viewpoints, collaboration skills, the particular focus of innovation, and the experience and expertise necessary. The chapter ends by suggesting how firms can best invest in developing their teams and supporting their progress. Chapter 4 also includes tools for selecting teams, setting the agenda for their first meeting and checking their development as a functioning team. The main conclusions of this chapter are that team membership, responsibilities and development should reflect as closely as possible the nature of the innovation they are creating.

Task Three: Co-Creating the Innovation with Customers

Leading firms now co-create innovations with their customers. Co-creation means working with customers and users as partners throughout development. Not just when the firm has an idea to test, but at every step of the way from defining the project objective to launching the innovation. Co-creation begins with a thorough understanding of customer needs, continues by generating novel ideas from customers, and ends with testing prototypes with them. Where the innovations involve services, firms use learning experiments with customers to adapt and improve as they scale-up from prototype to full launch.

The novelty of Chapter 5 is in explaining how to use the right customer with the right tool at each step along the way. Advances in psychology tell us that customers may not always be able to explain their needs. Lessons from the study of creativity tell us not all customers can provide good ideas and research on how to build new markets tells us this is not a representative process. Some customers play a bigger role than others. Managers can be much more successful if they select the right customers and the right tools according to the goals of each stage of development.

Chapter 5 divides into three parts: when to involve customers, which customers to involve and how to involve them. Thus, it has a strong emphasis on tools, including the tools for selecting the right customer, and the tools for simulating the impact of local influences during the launch. The latter is important for understanding what typical customers may decide about the innovation.

Task Four: Changing the Organization to Deliver the Innovation

Chapter 6 starts by contrasting the principles of change management with the organizational demands of major innovations, especially those involving services or business models. This identifies the five decisions that firms face whenever an innovation calls for a significant change to the organization. These decisions are:

1. the role of the firm's leadership in innovation;
2. the role of the innovation team in change management;
3. the relationship between the team and the rest of the organization;
4. how to manage large, complex projects involving many parts of the organization;
5. whether there should be a separate business unit to develop and deliver the innovation.

The chapter examines each of these decisions in depth to decide how to manage innovation projects and the preconditions for their success. The preconditions concern the actions of the firm's leadership in supporting the Innovation Charter. For example, has the CEO, CIO or VP of Innovation built a powerful guiding coalition to support innovation?

However, the rest of Chapter 6 chiefly focuses on the decisions that various levels of management must take at different stages of innovation development.

Here the main conclusion is that the innovation team should be responsible for developing and carrying out the change strategy. While the leadership can direct and support the innovation, the team is in the best place to understand the changes the firm needs to make to deliver the innovation. Chapter 6 also provides tools that can help the team assess the scale of organizational change they face.

Task Five: Building the Market for the Innovation

Most of Chapter 7 follows the same three-part sequence that a firm will use in building a new market. First, the firm chooses the right customer innovators to target and designs an offer and message that will attract them. Second, the firm gets sales moving by engaging these innovators through the media and other channels of communication, including the new media. However, launching the innovation immediately makes it visible to friends and foes alike. So Chapter 7 also looks at the impact of competitors entering the market, and how to deal with any third-party criticism. Third, the firm needs to reach the take-off point where mainstream customers start to buy. To ensure this happens the firm will need to change its marketing campaign, both to complement the social buzz and to make it easier for a typical customer to adopt. It may often also require adapting the innovation to meet the needs of various mainstream segments. Chapter 7 also includes tools for designing the new market, positioning the innovation and dealing with criticism.

Chapter 7 builds on the ideas in Chapter 2. While the basic ideas are well-known, recent advances in our understanding of how customers come to perceive advantage have major implications for building new markets. Similarly, improved understanding of competition and the time it takes to develop new markets also has implications here. In particular, these suggest that firms should rethink their approach to business planning and pay more attention to management development.

HOW TO USE THE BOOK

Next follows Chapter 2 – *Creating Advantage in the Minds of Many*. This chapter provides the foundation for the five chapters discussing the key tasks, so it is important for the reader to read Chapter 2 before going much further. Chapters

3 to 7 deal with the central sequence of innovation from chartering innovation within the organization to building the new market. Finally Chapter 8 – *Putting It All Together* – looks at how firms can be more successful with their major innovations. Chapter 8 uses the main conclusions from each preceding chapter to recommend better practice for firms in six areas of innovation management. This chapter also discusses how these recommendations might change for different innovation challenges.

Each chapter (Chapters 3 to 7) has roughly the same five-part organization. A brief discussion of why the particular task is important is followed by a more extensive review of current knowledge and management practice. That review leads to identifying what works and what does not. It also identifies gaps or inconsistencies in practice, or where we need to go beyond current knowledge, either to reflect recent advances in understanding, or to suggest new perspectives on management practice. Third, the chapter sets out the action steps that should follow from this review. These are the major conclusions and recommendations on each task, including how these might differ by market, industry and firm. Fourth is a discussion of how this task links with others in the main chapters, including the implications of the action steps for other tasks. Finally the chapter ends with a separate section – the Toolkit – that outlines the essentials of the two, three or four tools that best allow managers to put the ideas of the chapter into practice.

Once the reader looks at Chapter 2 there are three possible ways to read the rest of the book. One is to read it from front to back in the traditional manner. Another is to look first at the action steps of each of the five chapters, before going back to look at any of these chapters in more depth. A third is to look at the final chapter. This provides a summary of the book but as it builds on the conclusions of preceding chapters, and assumes some familiarity with the tools, this way is not recommended. Similarly, it is not recommended to look at the tools associated with each chapter without familiarizing yourself with the contents of that chapter. The details of how to do things do not always make sense if you have not gone through the underlying ideas.

CHAPTER 2

CREATING ADVANTAGE IN THE MINDS OF MANY

INTRODUCTION

Creating advantage in the minds of many is the most important task for the innovating firm. Unless customers perceive advantage in adopting the innovation it will fail. So understanding just how customers evaluate advantage is an important part of innovation development, not just for marketing managers but for every manager in the project team. Deeper understanding, building on recent advances in several fields, leads to two lessons that change the way in which firms should approach innovation development.

First, the firm should *co-create* the innovation with its customers. Effective development places customers at the centre of development from the start of the project. And not just from the existence of an idea or prototype as is commonly done by many firms. Also, effective development treats customers as active partners in the endeavour, and not simply passive participants in market research. Co-creating the innovation maximizes the chance the firm will produce the innovation customers want.

Second, *start from the end*. The firm should define the innovation project to meet its strategic goals. In particular, the profile of the new market the firm wants to build, and the position in this market it wishes to achieve. During the launch marketing plays a crucial role in conveying advantage to customers, maximizing the chance they will adopt, and the new market built to plan. But marketing can only build on the platform the innovation itself provides. Thus the firm needs a view on how it can best build the market and what this implies for the design of the innovation. In that sense there is a need to start from the (desired) end.

Both these lessons are important and both support each other. Success requires the right innovation with the right advantage to communicate. And achieving both requires deeper understanding of how customers adopt innovations. Therefore the ideas in this chapter precede those in the chapters that follow. The ideas here provide the foundation to all the recommendations and practical steps that are to come in later chapters.

The first section of this chapter outlines the standard model of innovation adoption that is familiar to many managers. The middle section examines recent developments in fields such as psychology, sociology, economics and marketing. This material is likely to be less familiar. However, these developments have revolutionized our understanding of adoption and provide the basis of the new model summarized in the third section of the chapter. This third section also sets out the action steps that flow from the new model while the fourth and final section shows how the ideas here link to other chapters.

THE STANDARD MODEL OF ADOPTION

To create advantage the firm must ensure that customers see a clear benefit to adopting the innovation. For example, in believing their lives will be better if they can carry all their music wherever they go in an MP3 player. The firm must also convince them the firm's offer is the best of all competing offers based on the same product technology, service delivery platform or new business model. For example, convincing the customer that Apple's iPod is better than Creative's Zen.

Convincing the Customer to Adopt

Customers adopt an innovation readily if the benefits clearly outweigh the costs and risks. This could be because the innovation is better than any existing solution to their needs or because it extends this solution into new areas. Or it could represent a worthwhile new direction to their life or business. Most innovations replace existing solutions or extend these solutions to new areas. For example, high-definition television replaces low-definition television, hybrid cars replace non-hybrids, and web-enabled portable phones extend communication.

Occasionally, innovations create new needs. For example, personal computers for home use or, going further back in history, cosmetics. Marketing philosophers argue whether innovations do create new needs. Surely, they say, human beings had a need to count before personal computers were developed, or to decorate themselves before cosmetics were invented. Indeed, there is plenty of historical evidence for such arguments. But from the perspective of the market and the customer these debates are irrelevant. It is much more useful to ask how customers solve their problems in the present and how big a change the innovation represents to them at the time they first meet it. Changing from a non-web-enabled portable phone to a web-enabled phone is a relatively small degree of change, while for most people a much bigger change took place the first time they set up a personal computer in their home. Similarly moving from simply washing the face to applying cosmetics each morning also represented a marked change in customer behaviour during the 1920s, when firms such as L'Oreal and Elizabeth Arden expanded their product range. Remarkable as it may now seem, before that time only actors and the rich applied make-up.

One can find similar examples in business-to-business products and services. For example, for most companies the recent shift to outsourcing support functions of the business to service providers is a major innovation and change. This is so even though some functions of businesses have been outsourced for decades (for example, advertising to advertising agencies). Thus innovation managers do not need to distinguish between what is and is not really new. Instead, they need to know how customers solve their problems today and what degree of change their innovation represents in the eyes of these customers. This is not a trivial step. Managers and firms often fail to see this trade-off objectively[1] or to understand fully how their customers perceive these costs and risks of change. Many of the tools in the rest of the book exist to help the firm hear the voice-of-the-customer clearly.

History is useful in showing that the greater the degree of change, the longer it will take to prove an advantage in the minds of most potential customers. For example, today most people take the advantages of their portable phone for granted. Yet it took eight years to sell the first million portable phones and several more years before the product took off.[2] The vignette *The humble phone becomes upwardly mobile* provides a short history of how this market developed from 1946 to today.

The humble phone becomes upwardly mobile[39]

The commercial history of mobile (cell) phones extends back to the 1940s. In 1946, AT&T and Southwestern Bell introduced the first American commercial mobile radio-telephone service. The mobile phones used car radio-telephone licences granted to Southwestern Bell by the Federal Communications Commission (FCC). One of the biggest problems back then was the limited number of channels made available by the FCC, which meant that only 23 cellular phone conversations could occur simultaneously in the same service area.

Phone-equipped cars were introduced in Stockholm in the 1950s; the first users were a doctor on call and a bank on wheels. The equipment was powered by the car battery, and the phones were reported to devour such an incredible amount of power that it was only possible to make two calls before the car battery lost all charge. These first car phones were too heavy, cumbersome and expensive to use, with just a handful of subscribers.

In 1968, the FCC decided to 'increase the cellular phone frequencies allocation, freeing the airwaves for more mobile phones'. In every city where a mobile telephone service was introduced, waiting lists developed and grew year on year. By 1976, 545 customers in New York City had mobile phones, but 3700 more customers were on the waiting list. Across the United States, around 44 000 Bell subscribers had mobile phones, but 20 000 people sat on a 5–10 year waiting list.

Despite the obvious demand, nearly 40 years elapsed between the launch of the first mobile phone in 1946 and their widespread introduction after the FCC finally sanctioned a commercial cellular phone service for the US in 1982. The first cellular phone was marketed to the public in 1984, when Motorola introduced the DynaTac 8000X, which weighed in at a hefty 2 lb (~1 kg) and cost $3995. Even in 1991, the lighter Motorola MicroTac Lite still weighed 7.7 oz (~220 g) and cost $1000. Although there were 1 million subscribers in the US in 1987 and 11 million in 1992, at this stage, the bulky and expensive to use phones seemed destined to be a toy for the wealthy.

As technology advanced, however, phones became smaller and more affordable, network coverage widened and became more reliable, and new features were added. The general demand for mobile phones grew … and continues to grow. Modern mobiles are more than just telephones. They come equipped with cameras, video recorders and MP3 players and users can access the Internet and send and receive emails from them. With worldwide sales in 2009 estimated at 1041 million, the companies involved in the early days of cellular technology could not have begun to imagine that these products would grow to be the global phenomenon that they are today.

Worldwide mobile terminal sales, 1997–2009 (millions of units)

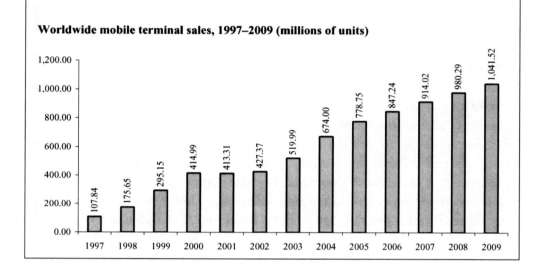

Similarly every business office has a fax machine. Yet this category of product also took decades to take off, despite phone networks already being in place and the low cost of this innovation. Why does it take customers so long to accept innovation?

The Role of Information in Creating Advantage

On most occasions the potential customer has to make a trade-off between the benefits of the existing solution (the status quo) and those of the innovation. This trade-off is often more complex than it first appears. For example, it seems obvious that it is worthwhile to carry music on an MP3 player. After all, most people have a CD player at home with a collection of music they often play. This makes it easy for them to see the player as a simple extension of existing technology. However, customers need more than this. They also need to see situations in their daily life where it makes sense to play their music on a *portable* player. After all, it cannot compete with their existing audio system for volume or quality, so there needs to be some compensating or added advantage above and beyond this status quo. Customers also need to understand how to get their music from the CD to the portable player, or buy new music on the Internet and organize it in the way they like and so on. In short, they need to think about how the MP3 player might add to their life and whether they can use it. And customers need to have enough information on these topics that they are confident to buy.

Such information comes in part from the marketing campaigns of the suppliers of the innovation but also from seeing and talking to other people like themselves. For many people the knowledge that others like themselves are benefiting from the innovation is an important, even critical piece of evidence for adopting it. Information may also come from comparing competing players on the Internet or when the potential customer takes time during their weekly visit to the shopping centre to talk to a salesperson. Many potential sources and types of information are relevant to these decisions. And although some people may buy on impulse, the typical customer needs this information before they buy. The *information environment* surrounding the innovation becomes critical to its success.

Thus, it is not surprising that it takes customers time to understand and recognize the benefits of an innovation. Nor is it surprising the more significant the behavioural change the innovation demands, the longer it takes to get this recognition. If creating advantage for a significant innovation in a supermarket category can take one or two years, then doing the same for innovations that change the business practices of firms can take one or two decades.

Showing Your Version is Better

To create advantage you must also show that your innovation is the best one to adopt. On some occasions several firms launch the innovation close together. More commonly one launches, then several others will enter the market before mainstream customers start to adopt. Competition is the norm in innovation just as in other areas of business. So the customer has to make a second trade-off: is brand A better than brand B? Again, this trade-off can vary in complexity.

The choice can sometimes be simply one between different branded variants of the same technology (the MP3 player example above). Or it can be between two different technologies providing roughly the same benefits (Blu-Ray versus High Definition DVD) or between different visions of the future (mySAP versus Oracle E-business in ERP systems). Again, it is also easy to imagine the more complex this trade-off is, the more information and thought the typical customer will need to decide between the alternatives. This conclusion holds irrespective of whether this customer is an individual or the decision-making committee of a large business.

This trade-off will be between the relative advantages and disadvantages of the alternatives *as the customers perceive them*. These perceptions will depend in part on what marketing messages customers receive direct from the supplier. But they also depend in part on what information customers receive from seeing or talking to other customers, independent sources and retail salespeople. Competing marketing messages may also influence what these sources say or do, creating indirect influences on the focal customers.

The marketing battle for attention and persuasion is at the heart of this trade-off and the outcome of this battle is perhaps even more important for innovations than for products in a mature market. This is because customers are learning what is good about the innovation and marketing can have a significant influence on the criteria customers use to choose between alternatives. Thus marketing can shape preferences towards the firm by defining these comparisons in particular ways.

To summarize, so far the chapter simply outlines the standard model of adoption, and normal marketing practice. In this model customers weigh up the costs and benefits of the innovation and decide whether to adopt or not. They use various marketing and non-marketing sources to get the information they need for their deliberations and they differ in their attitude to risk. Some are happy to take risks and adopt early, using their own judgement; while some need confidence the innovation has shown benefits to others like themselves. The first elements of this model were sketched out by Tarde in 1903. However, it is best associated with the *Diffusion of Innovation* books by Rogers,[3] ideas which Moore has popularized more recently in *Crossing the Chasm*.[4] Firms compete to gain a share of the new market through carefully executed marketing campaigns that convey clear messages to the target customers. These messages will include the main benefits of the innovation as well as what is different about the firm's version.

ALTERNATIVE MODELS FROM PSYCHOLOGY AND SOCIOLOGY

Many managers know and accept the standard model of adoption but it is now thoroughly out-of-date. Our understanding of human decision-making has advanced significantly in the last two decades, especially through the work of cognitive psychologists. Cognitive psychology now provides a clearer picture of how people decide and what influences them. It also now links decision-making to the underlying organization of the brain, as identified and studied by neuro-scientists. These advances are also well-known, through books such as Pinker's *How the Mind Works*,[5] but they are yet to be incorporated into models of adoption.

What is perhaps less well-known is that personality psychology and computational sociology have also made as much progress. Personality psychologists understand the differences between people better and computational sociologists understand the impact of social networks better. All four areas: cognitive psychology, neuroscience, personality psychology and computational sociology, are important in bringing the standard model of adoption up to date. Adoption involves decision-making by individuals (cognitive psychology and neuroscience) who are different from one another (personality psychology) and who influence one another through social networks (computational sociology). Recent work in all these areas is therefore relevant to better models of adoption.

Lessons from Cognitive Psychology: Decisions Can Be Influenced

Gains and Losses are Subjectively Perceived

For cognitive psychology the place to start is prospect theory, as developed by Kahneman and Tversky in the 1980s.[6] Prospect theory is a theory of choice between alternatives. In brief, this theory states that people prefer certain outcomes to uncertain ones, they focus on what is different between alternatives, and they weigh up what they will gain and lose by choosing one. Prospect theory has two main implications. First, customers see their gains and losses relative to some reference point that makes sense to them. For innovation, the reference point is often what they are doing before the innovation appears. So far, this is similar to the standard model of adoption where what matters is the *relative* advantage of the innovation over the current idea.[7] Second, customers do not treat comparably sized gains and losses in the same way. Instead, losses have a greater impact than gains in their decisions. If people value their gains and losses differently their choices will not follow the standard model.

Preferences are Subject to a Status Quo Bias

Since its introduction there has been a good deal of research which supports prospect theory and its successors. Particularly relevant to adoption are two outcomes of the theory, the *status quo bias* and the effects of *framing*. The status quo bias refers to the strong tendency of customers to keep using their existing product or service because they perceive the losses incurred in dropping it are greater than the gains from adopting an innovation.

A simple example will explain this point. Suppose an objective observer is able to value the gains from adopting the innovation at $100 and the losses from dropping the existing product at $50. An economically rational customer should adopt the innovation as they would expect to gain $50. However, evidence from studies on prospect theory suggests that typical customers overvalue losses against gains by a factor of three.[8] So, in the example given, they perceive their loss from dropping the existing product to be $150 and they do not adopt the innovation since, in their mind, they would lose $50.

Status Quo Bias Also Applies to Non-customer Innovations

These are innovations addressing totally new markets with no pre-existing product or service for the target customer to buy. The name *non-customer innovation* comes from the seminal work of Kim and Mauborgne.[9] The name itself appears a little awkward until you understand its origins – non-customers are those multitudes of customers that industries ignore because of their blinkers on what provides value. Kim and Mauborgne document many examples where creative individuals and firms have launched non-customer innovations and reshaped their industry.

At first glance prospect theory does not apply to this case. What is the status quo reference point? In fact the status quo bias the innovation must overcome is doing nothing. However, doing nothing has value! It allows the customer to spend time or money on their other needs. And the customer may value the loss of these relatively more than the gains from the innovation. So in reality there is status quo bias that non-customer innovations must also overcome.

Framing Influences Choice

The second outcome of prospect theory, the effect of framing, arises from the theory's assumption of a reference point. Typically the product or service the customer currently uses is the reference point from which to evaluate the innovation. However, people are sensitive to how the decision is described to them. Indeed in experimental studies minor changes in the words describing alternatives can produce different choices in people, simply because they invoke different reference points. Thus, the way the marketer presents the decision to people – the way it is *framed* – can influence their choice.

At first glance the status quo bias and framing effects might contradict each other. If the customer sees little benefit in giving up an existing product, how can any form of words about the innovation persuade them to adopt? Well by carefully choosing how to describe the innovation, marketers can try to influence which reference point the customer applies to their decision. The vignette *And you thought this was just another microwave* sketches the challenge LG Electonics faced introducing its revolutionary light wave oven SolarDom™. Should they frame this breakthrough innovation as a better microwave oven (one reference point)? Or should they frame SolarDom as a better fan oven (another reference point)? Or should they frame SolarDom as an entirely new category of oven (thus inviting the customer to develop a new reference point)? Each marketing strategy would influence the customer to think along different lines and therefore to make different comparisons. Status quo biases might still exist in all three cases but the perceptions of losses and gains, and thus their decisions, would be different. As the vignette shows, LG Electronics chose different framings in different countries, building on its local understanding of these markets.

And you thought it was just another microwave oven ...[40]

LG Electronics was set up in 1958 and is now a global company that develops and makes home appliances such as radios and TVs. In 2003, LG launched their range of SolarDOM light wave ovens. This oven uses a powerful halogen lamp to cook food quickly but in a more natural way than microwave ovens. Although the oven has the same features worldwide, the framing of this product in different markets shows how firms often adapt their marketing according to the psychology of the target customers.

In the United States, the emphasis is on innovation and convenience. The SolarDOM is promoted alongside other LG home appliances under the strapline 'Convergence in home appliances' and is positioned as part of LG's 'home network'. This system connects appliances so they can exchange information through the Internet. For SolarDOM, this means that customers can use their mobile phones to ensure that meals are ready when they arrive home.

Innovation and convenience are also features of the marketing in the United Kingdom, where LG targets household cooks who strive to be world-class cooks while saving time and effort. Features that make cooking easier, including programmes such as e-cook book and autochef, are highlighted. The speed of cooking is compared with that of LG's own superfast conventional oven − 'LG's newest built-in oven cooks twice as fast as conventional ovens. And its SolarDOM is even faster than that.' SolarDOM's product brochure uses phrases such as 'The future of innovative cooking' and 'The latest in cooking innovation and sophisticated design' to appeal to design-conscious customers looking for state-of-the-art products.

Fast cooking is the main emphasis in Malaysia, where LG Electronics uses the strapline '18 minutes roast chicken (guaranteed!)' in the product description. This is also a feature of the marketing in Singapore, although promotional materials also add further benefits such as reduced energy consumption and ease of use. Indian marketing materials also mention energy efficiency, alongside ease of cleaning and space-saving design. The literature also targets Indian consumers by mention of the programmable 'Indian Auto Menu option'. High nutrient retention is another feature of LG's Indian marketing, but this idea is the focus of the strategy in Kuwait, where LG promotes the SolarDOM as one of a range of health-friendly product lines. Indeed, the Kuwaiti literature points out that because the SolarDOM cooks four times faster than conventional ovens, the food's nutrients, including proteins and carbohydrates, and taste are kept intact while harmful ingredients such as cholesterol and fat are eliminated.

The third case, creating a new reference point, is more intriguing. Research suggests that customers naturally associate any new idea with existing categories of ideas in their mind, particularly more elaborate categories based on their prior experience.[10] Thus a customer who often cooks in the traditional manner might see the SolarDom as a subcategory of fan ovens. While one who only reheats frozen food might see it as a subcategory of microwaves. Encouraging them to form an entirely new category is an unusual and difficult task, about which we know little. But if an association with existing categories is disadvantageous to the innovating firm they will need to develop powerful marketing messages to overcome this natural association.

Local Cues and Emotions Influence Choice

The final lesson from prospect theory is therefore that marketing is critical to the successful launch of an innovation, especially in its choice of message. Subtle differences in presenting persuasive arguments can have a great impact on the success or failure of the innovation. Indeed, prospect theory is only one example among several streams of research in cognitive psychology and behavioural economics that all point to the same conclusion. Namely, informational cues in the local environment heavily influence choices.[11] The way marketing frames the message is one such cue. But there are many others, such as the sights and smells when buying food at the market, the store surroundings when considering a major purchase, or the way the chairperson runs the meeting when managers are considering a new IT system. These and other local cues can significantly influence the customer's decision. They are *local* because they are unique to the customer and the time and the place of the decision. The information environment that matters is the one the customer experiences at the point of decision. And customers at least partly build their preferences for different alternatives from this local environment.

Lessons from Neuroscience: Uncertainty Reduces Advantage

Emotions Guide All Decisions

One reason for the power of local influences lies in the emotions. While cognitive scientists were exploring local influences, neuroscientists were discovering that emotions play a central part in all human decisions. Here evidence comes from brain imaging studies, in particular those seeking to understand what happens when people face competing alternatives. The most striking finding from these studies is that pleasure or happiness or other emotions are not goals; they are signals that move us to act.[12] This may surprise economists or marketers who think of pleasure or satisfaction as the goal of customer choice. But evolutionary scientists point out that our abilities evolved to ensure our survival and reproduction, not to make economic choices. It is therefore not surprising the brain has some modules that signal what the right action should be. And these modules now play a role in economic choices. Indeed, emotions are sometimes more important and accurate guides to such decisions than logical thinking. Researchers can show that, in certain circumstances, people make worse choices when the experimenter forces them to think about it rather than when they follow their emotional reaction to the alternatives.[13] Here interference from the cognitive modules in the brain – the modules associated with conscious logical thinking – reduces the quality of the decisions made. Neuroscience also shows that a part of the brain automatically processes events; events that we are not consciously aware of, nor have much control over.

Grasping the nature of these logical and emotional modules and controlled and automatic processes are useful aids to understanding the choices we make. However, the biggest lesson from neuroscience is that all these modules and processes interlink in complex ways, but not in the sense that logical thinking captains the ship, although we may like to think it does.[14] Instead, the many modules of the brain sometimes collaborate with one another but sometimes they compete. And often the job of the captain (our conscious, logical and sequential thinking) is to make sense of what happened after the decision! This complexity is relevant to innovations because customers decide about these in a state of uncertainty. And uncertainty evokes not only logical thinking but also emotional and automatic processes which interfere with logical thinking.

Risk and Ambiguity Lower the Chances of Adoption

To the potential customer, any innovation can have uncertain outcomes. When, for example, farmers are invited to adopt a crop protection innovation, the supplier claims it will improve the yield and quality of their crop. According to the prospect theory the farmers analyse their decision by looking at the gains and losses from their reference point, namely their current crop protection solution.

However, a limitation of prospect theory is that it assumes the farmer can accurately predict what these gains and losses are. This may be true in some circumstances but not in all. The farmer may think there is a risk the innovation will not work in their fields. Equally they may lack information about whether the quality improvement will result in getting higher prices for their crop. The farmer's uncertainty thus has two parts. The first is the risk the innovation does not work for them. The second is the ambiguity which comes from poor or missing information making it hard to estimate their gains accurately. This dual aspect to uncertainty is often the case with innovations, especially major ones.

Risk and ambiguity are two factors that invoke conflict between modules of the brain. The cognitive modules are trying to do the right thing and rationally process the risk and return ('there is a 50% chance I can add $100 000 to my cash flow so I expect to gain $50 000'). But as these cognitive modules process the information they notice that some is missing, or of poor quality, and pass this conclusion on to other modules. At the same time the emotional modules that keep us safe – the vigilance modules – are warning that survival is threatened (fear of failure). This warning always occurs when uncertainty is present. And all these signals come together in the brain's integrative modules, whose job is to reach a compromise and take the decision. One of these integrative modules concerns the anticipation of gains and, given the presence of emotional warnings, it adjusts for missing or poor information by lowering the individual's perception of their gains.[15] Thus the eventual compromise is to make adoption even less likely. Innovations that customers perceive as risky and ambiguous are unlikely to take off fast and may need lengthy persuasion campaigns by their proponents.

Cognitive psychologists and neuroscientists are interested in the general functioning of the brain and, while they recognize individual differences, they do not study these in depth. However, the way brain modules work, individually and together, differs between people. Since these differences are critical to the market accepting innovation, it is useful to look at the lessons from another area that deals with individual difference. This is the field of personality psychology.

Lessons from Personality Psychology: People React to Uncertainty and Influence Differently

The purpose here is not to review the vast area of personality psychology, but to show that people differ on the dimensions that matter to innovation adoption.

In particular, they react differently to the uncertainty associated with innovations, and use different mixes of local influences to resolve this uncertainty. These differences are essential to the overall way in which a market adopts an innovation. Indeed, without them the market would not work as effectively as it does in separating innovations with value from those without.

Genetic Makeup Influences Personality Traits

Personality psychology, the study of the psychological dimensions on which people differ, experienced a rebirth in the 1990s. Scholars now agree the most important traits are the so-called Big Five of extraversion (social orientation), emotional stability, conscientiousness, agreeableness and openness to experience.[16] Further, studies show that these traits influence behaviour over a series of decisions or life outcomes, not so much for any one decision by itself. Within any one individual these traits are stable over time and, while they are not frozen, they are slower to change when a person is past adolescence. Studies of twins show individual traits contain a strong genetic component. The consensus is that about half the differences between people on the Big Five are the result of differences in their genetic makeup.[17] Striking international studies show the genetic basis of personality is the common heritage of all humans and does not depend on birthplace or culture.[18]

Early Experiences Play a Role in Personality Formation

But genetics provides only a partial explanation of differences in personality. Equally important are early childhood experiences that may lead to choosing different life strategies, enduring situations leading to long-term adjustments or the outcomes of specializing in one activity or another. All of these can create a focus on some traits at the expense of others. Neuroscientists are beginning to understand the brain modules behind these traits. Their work provides the links between specific brain processes and the genetic and environmental influences that shape them. For example, openness to experience connects with cognitive modules, including some that education clearly influences. Extraversion connects with emotional reward modules that are more likely to be hereditary.

Agreeableness connects to cognitive and automatic modules which may have both genetic and environmental bases.[19]

From studying these connections, DeYoung proposes that the Big Five is made up of two categories of traits, each driven by a specific system of brain modules.[20] These two categories are (1) *stability*, which associates with agreeableness, conscientiousness and emotional stability and (2) *plasticity*, which associates with openness to experience and extraversion. He speculates the brain modules that regulate swings in emotion and behaviour, notably the serotonergic system, drive stability. The brain modules that govern exploratory behaviour and cognitive flexibility, notably the dopaminergic system, drive plasticity. Individuals display significant differences in both these systems. It is also worth pointing out that stability has connotations of conformity – fitting in with the crowd. On the other hand, plasticity has connotations of individualism – sticking out from the crowd.

Personality Psychology Helps to Understand Broad Individual Differences

To connect the Big Five directly to innovation adoption is not easy. Few studies have tried to do this and so far they have not been done with enough rigour. Besides, this may not be the best way of thinking about the issue. Personality psychology looks at the whole gamut of human behaviour, not simply innovation, and examines high-level traits. No one would contend that because, for example, some individuals are open to experience they will necessarily adopt every innovation that comes their way, or that they will always be among the first to do so. There are many local influences intervening between a trait and a single instance of behaviour.[21] However, if we view personality psychology as suggesting broad differences in how individuals react to new ideas and where they may seek information to help in decisions then it is useful. Some individuals are more likely to take risks and some less likely to do so, just as some individuals are more likely to listen to others and some are less likely to do so. Local influences will still play a big role but they will influence different people differently. And to understand the role these local influences will play in the overall evolution of the market it is important to know the underlying mix of different types of people. So what do we know about this mix?

Model of Personality Predispositions and Market Segments

Exhibit 2.1 shows a simple two-by-two matrix of stability and plasticity and the connection between these characteristics and the market segments of an improved adoption model. The exhibit also shows rough estimates of the proportion of potential customers in each cell of the matrix. Some studies suggest the biggest segment of people is in the top right cell, called the *mainstream* here (and the well-adjusted or confident in the psychological literature).[22] That is, most people are cautious about novelty, risk and ambiguity and need convincing before they will adopt an innovation (lower plasticity). More critically, social signals about the acceptability of the innovation are an important part of the local influences for these mainstream customers, driven by their need to conform (higher stability). The mainstream customer would best fit findings of the prospect theory outlined previously, with status quo bias, in particular. The other cells would also fit the prospect theory model, but the way these individuals perceive gains and losses would differ from that of the mainstream customer.

Innovators clearly have a more positive perception of the gains and losses equation, while *laggards* have an even less positive one than the mainstream. But both are less socially involved and are less conformist. Therefore, social signals play a lesser role in the local influences on their decision. Finally, the *connectors* are an interesting group, being open to innovation but also more socially involved and more conformist. We can speculate that they are akin to swinging-voters. If they like what they see and hear about the innovation, it is likely to succeed as they will influence mainstream customers to adopt. If they do not

	Higher plasticity *More open to experience* *More extraverted*	Lower plasticity *More closed to experience* *More introverted*
Higher stability *More agreeable* *More conscientious* *More emotionally stable*	Connectors 10%	Mainstream 70%
Lower stability *Less agreeable* *Less conscientious* *Less emotionally stable*	Innovators 10%	Laggards 10%

Exhibit 2.1 Personality predispositions and segments of potential adopters.

like what they see and decide to reject the innovation, then adoption may never spread from the innovators to the mainstream. The role of the connectors will become clearer once we discuss the lessons from sociology.

Individual Versus Group Decisions

At this point the discussion requires qualification. The new model of innovation adoption is, to this point, chiefly one of individual decision-making. This makes sense for many markets, both business-to-consumer (B2C) and business-to-business (B2B). Clearly, however, there are markets where decision-making occurs in groups. These include decisions by households and by organizations, such as a capital equipment purchase. Less is known about these markets. Studies show that they follow similar patterns at the macro level. For example, the spread of adoption has the same overall pattern, although it is typically slower than for markets with individual decision-makers. Research shows that local influences still include social signals, that is, information that passes between households or firms (including competing firms). But how the characteristics and opinions of various group members combine to reach a decision is not well understood. This interaction between group members will shape reference points and perceptions of gains and losses.

For organizational decision-making, conscientiousness plays a greater role, and this may explain in part why adoption is often slower in B2B markets.[23] The need to be conscientious implies more systematic information collection, greater deliberation and consensus building, all of which takes time. Further, work on organizational culture consistently shows that firms differ on three dimensions.[24] These dimensions are whether they are entrepreneurial or not, whether they are bureaucratic or not and whether they support their employees or not. All of which suggests a broad analogy to the other traits of Exhibit 2.1. Firms do differ in their approach to adopting innovation, just as individuals do. Finally, the decision-makers in these environments are still human, so the lessons above still apply to the way each individual approaches the decision to adopt. The general framework of the model is thus likely to be valid, while some of the details of interaction within the decision-making group are missing.

The new model of innovation adoption is not yet complete. Thus far it is a sketch of how perceptions of gains and losses may vary from customer to customer and how social signals play a greater or lesser role in local influences. To flesh out this sketch it is necessary to examine the way signals propagate through society and to do so we need to take on board lessons from computational sociology.

Lessons from Computational Sociology: Social Networks Create Common Knowledge, Common Knowledge Resolves Uncertainty

The Small World of Social Networks

Many managers are familiar with some of the conclusions arising from the large body of knowledge about social networks. The first conclusion is that of the small world — everyone on the planet is only separated from everyone else by six interpersonal links.[25] ('I know someone who knows someone who knows someone …'). These links are clearly mostly weak ones. By the time the message reaches people two or three steps removed from the originator they are complete strangers to one another. Perhaps the more interesting conclusion is that, for relaying novel information or new opportunities, the weak links are often more important than the strong ones.[26] This is because your family and friends or closer workmates and professional contacts largely know the same things as you do. Through talking to them you may not learn much that is new. Weak connections between social groups, for example, between individuals who may have a passing acquaintance with someone in another group, serve as links through which novel information can pass from one group to another. Some individuals also act as brokers between groups, bringing together otherwise unconnected individuals.

Indeed, for innovations to take off and reach mainstream customers, Gladwell points to the importance of connectors, mavens and salesmen.[27] Connectors are those members of society who span different worlds, mavens are those who gather and share knowledge and salesmen the enthusiasts who advocate the innovation to others. But the role of all these stereotypes is to spread the message from the innovators to the mainstream.

By themselves the innovators will not exert enough influence to achieve this take–off. The innovators are inherently a small segment of the market and are not especially socially oriented. They are also spread across the thousands of local social networks that form the foundation of any market. Roughly in any local network of 150 people (relatives, friends, workmates and acquaintances) there may only be a handful of adopting innovators. An even smaller number of these innovators may be advocating the innovation to others. This is such a low incidence that most of the local network will be unaware of the innovators' opinions. The members of this network who are mainstream customers then lack the confirmation they need to adopt, even if they are aware of the innovation from the media. And members of other, weakly connected, networks would, of course, also lack this confirmation. Similar analogies and conclusions hold for B2B markets, although the local networks may be smaller or larger depending on industry. What needs to happen is for the message to spread, and that is why the role of these connectors, mavens and salesmen is so important.

The market research agency GfK Roper characterizes these people as the 'few who act for many'. They are individuals who make an effort to learn, and like to share what they have learned with others.[28] Indeed, they have opinions, they like others to ask about these and they take pride in being able to give an informed and useful answer. They are also open to many sources of information and new ideas. Roper's characterization of these messengers is closer to the ideas here than Gladwell's stereotypes. The *connectors* of Exhibit 2.1 are high on both plasticity and stability (or their organizational equivalents for B2B markets). Like the innovators they are more open to new ideas. However, they have higher stability than the innovators, which means they are more socially agreeable, conscientious and emotionally stable. All of which are characteristics that enable this group to have better personal relationships with more people than the typical innovator. Thus if the connectors hear about or see an innovation that *works* they will share the message with many others, as well as add force to the message through their own adoption.

Social Influence and the Creation of Common Knowledge About the Innovation

To most marketing managers and many experts, social influence stems from one person talking to another. This need not necessarily be an adopter talking to a potential adopter. The speaker can also be relaying the experience of someone else they know who has tried or heard about the innovation. Equally, indirect knowledge that other people are doing something can also be powerful. Knowing that other people enjoy some activity, service or product can lead individuals to a more favourable opinion of that activity.[29] But in the common view, social influence comes through one person speaking direct to another. That is not surprising; direct word-of-mouth is fun to talk about and easy to study in surveys.

However, the sociologist Chwe points out there are multiple levels to thinking about such messages.[30] Simply receiving the message may not be enough; the receiving individual also wants to know that other people got the same message. Otherwise they may run the risk of reacting to a mistaken or misleading message. And to be confident to act they also need to know not only that other people got the same message but that these other people also know that others got the same message. In other words, that many people are equally confident it is a good idea to adopt the innovation. If that is the case they can adopt and not run the risk of looking different because they were in the minority or stupid because the innovation did not deliver. If everyone adopts and the innovation works that is great. If everyone adopts and it turns out to be a bad idea then everyone just made the same mistake. So it is not just the messages passing from individual to individual (or firm to firm) that is important to building confidence; it is also the knowledge held in common by many. Positive *common knowledge* within the local network is thus the key to successful innovation.

Chwe focuses his thinking on 'social goods', roughly products and services which are either consumed with, or whose consumption is visible to, people outside the customer's household (or business). Depending on the particular market these people might be friends, acquaintances or other businesses, both competing and partners. The critical point here is that, for connectors and mainstream customers, *all* innovations are social goods. These market segments need confidence that others are likely to adopt. There are two major outcomes of Chwe's view of social influence as developing common knowledge.

First, strong links between people (or organizations) are better at forming common knowledge.[31] It is true that weak links spread information quicker and further than strong links; however strong links are more influential. Strong links imply that my friends are also likely to be your friends, and that I am more likely to care about what they think. Thus knowledge about the innovation is more likely to be held in common between groups of people who have strong links. In contrast, weak links imply acquaintances that are less likely to know one another, less likely to care about what the other thinks and thus less likely to have shared beliefs. To summarize, weak links help beliefs about the innovation reach many local networks, strong links help form common knowledge within those networks.

Second, from the common knowledge perspective, advertising and other media influences become, paradoxically, more important. This contradicts the widely held view that advertising and social influence are independent of each other. In fact advertising can help build common knowledge. To take a simple example, advertising the innovation during the Super Bowl or the World Cup. Yes, this tells the potential customer the firm's positioning message. And it may also be a signal of quality – the firm believes strongly enough in their innovation that they are willing to spend money on this advert. However, because this advert appears during such a popular event it is also telling potential customers that many other people now know about the innovation. That is one step toward building common knowledge. This idea cannot, of course, be taken too far. If the messages about the innovation circulating between people are negative the advert will not help.

Do Not Confuse Connectors with the Obsolete Idea of Opinion Leaders

The idea of an opinion leader is common in business and marketing practice.[32] An opinion leader is a customer who listens to the messages of the innovating firm and then shapes the beliefs of other customers. There are also many market research agencies searching for them, some of whom provide lists to firms. Some authors even extend this notion to redefine market mavens as those opinion leaders who influence the beliefs of others across several product or service categories.[33] All of which is likely driven by a strong need for marketing managers to feel in control. If they can target these leaders, they can influence the outcome of the innovation launch.

Unfortunately, this idea is a hangover from a now obsolete part of the standard model of adoption – the *two-step flow* of communication. In this two-step flow, influence is thought to pass from the mass media to opinion leaders who in turn influence everyone else. This is where computational sociology and its lessons enter the picture. Recent work in this field shows the two-step flow in general, and opinion leaders in particular, are unnecessary for explaining patterns of innovation adoption. Connectors and common knowledge explain these just as well or better.

The Multi-step Model of Influence

Computational sociologists – those who use computer simulations to look at problems – have been examining a *multi-step flow* model. In this model individuals exert direct influence on some people but they may also influence others indirectly, for example, at one, two or three steps removed. So their indirect influence continues to spread as their opinions travel beyond their local network.

That leads to the question of how people connect. Studies have revealed some characteristics. In general, only a few people can exert direct influence over any one individual, simply because this individual is not in direct contact with all the other people in the market. Instead, the indirect influence of these other people filters through the connections of the individual, their immediate group and the connections of this group to the larger network. These connections are partially structured and stable but also partially unstructured and random. The best analogy is probably one of many communities or local networks loosely connected to each other.[34] This is true in B2B markets as well.[35] To simulate the spread of *novel* information between and within groups, such as that about an innovation, computational sociologists use various approximations to real networks. These simulations also incorporate a rough approximation to Chwe's common knowledge. They do this by requiring individuals to adopt only when the number of adopters in their local network reaches a critical threshold. For example, 'three people I know bought the innovation'. By varying the average number of other people that each individual connects to, and by using various levels of threshold, the researcher can produce different outcomes to compare to real data.

The Importance of a Critical Mass of Customers Ready to Listen

The lessons from these simulations provide us with a different perspective on the spread of information and influence. In particular, the work of Watts provides strong evidence the ideas of the multi-step flow model are more likely to be correct than those of two-step flow and opinion leaders. First, the key to the spread of adoption is the existence of a critical mass of sufficiently vulnerable individuals. Simulations show that adoption does not spread in networks where each person connects to only a few others, or where the thresholds for adoption are too high. For adoption to spread there need to be enough links between individuals whose thresholds are low enough to allow the resulting influence to lead to adoption. What is surprising in these results is that it is not influence that matters, but vulnerability to influence. Watts argues that it is therefore better to think of success resulting from easily influenced people influencing other easily influenced people than it is to imagine opinion leaders.[36]

Watts further argues that when market researchers identify 'opinion leaders' they are fooling themselves by drawing conclusions from random events. After the fact it looks like someone was an opinion leader but this was because they were in the right place at the right time as the novel information spread. Their opinion then spreads through indirect links to others outside their local network to make them appear influential. However, for a second innovation they might not even receive a message about the innovation. Or there might not be enough common knowledge in their local network for them to adopt or be confident to recommend the innovation to others. Any seeming act of 'opinion leadership' is thus just an accidental by-product of the way novel information and influence spreads.

In real networks the connectors provide the greater number of links to others. It seems likely that without such a group the innovation would fail to reach the mainstream customers. So Roper is right in saying these connectors are the 'few who act for many'. Similarly these mainstream customers provide the critical mass of 'easily influenced' people.

Care needs taking with Watts's statement though. 'Easily influenced' does not mean weak or malleable. For mainstream customers to adopt requires first that they have reached the point where they can decide. Second, common knowledge in the local network must tell them that many people with whom they have strong links are also considering adoption or have adopted. These are high requirements for decisions, so in that sense the phrase 'easily influenced' is misleading. 'Ready to listen' is a better way of putting it. Common knowledge just provides the last piece in the complex jigsaw that is an adoption decision.

Although the models of computational sociologists are brutally simple, they offer good explanations for the role of social influence in the market transition from innovators to the mainstream. Further, by highlighting the short-lived and random nature of social influence they show that elaborate marketing strategies for targeting individual customers are unlikely to work. However, these models too have limits; in particular they focus on messages spreading among customers once adoption starts. They thus ignore where this message first came from and how it tried to frame the innovation.

This brings this discussion of innovation adoption to a crucial point. All the work above, be it by cognitive or personality psychologists or by computational sociologists, fails to explain the content of the information about the innovation and who supplies this content. The economist Glaeser points out that, while cognitive psychology shows that framing influences decisions, the more interesting question is who supplies the framing and influence.[37] And on that question both psychology and sociology are silent. The question of the supply of influence is the territory of economics and marketing and it is to those lessons the discussion turns.

THE SUPPLY OF INFLUENCE

Exhibit 2.2 shows the broad set of influences at work during the launch of any innovation. These are the local influences that can impact on customer decisions. The top of the table shows the potential sources of influence. These divide into

Potential sources of influence	
Marketing influences	**Non-marketing influences**
TV, print and poster advertising	Social influences
Promotions	Family and friends
Displays	Co-workers
Direct marketing	Indirect influences
Websites	Third-party influences
Store formats	Editorials and reviews
Salespeople	Comparison and testing services
Support personnel	Independent experts
Potential content of influence messages	
Benefits of innovation	Advocated reference group
Costs and disadvantages of innovation	Authority endorsement
	Evidence of claims
Uncertainty of benefits and costs	Observation of others using and
Advocated reference levels	valuing or not valuing

Exhibit 2.2   Local influences on decisions.

marketing sources – those used to promote the innovation – and non-marketing sources. The latter include the social influences just discussed, as well as other third-party sources of influence on adoption decisions. The bottom of the table shows the potential content of influence messages. These are in a single list as a potential adopter can receive any of them from any source. This list is not exhaustive but the table shows that influence messages can be complex and subtle. It also shows that many are not social or random; the innovating firm supplies them.

Framing Messages to Encourage Adoption

The marketer of the innovation will try to use some or all the marketing sources in Exhibit 2.2 to encourage adoption. This they will do through positive messages about the benefits of the innovation. Negative messages are more likely to come from non-marketing sources, especially adopters who have had a bad experience with the innovation. And this bad experience can come about not just because the innovation fails to meet customer needs but also because framing sets the wrong expectations.

Negative messages are common, especially for major innovations that are often not fully worked out when they launch. This is not because the innovating firm has been hasty or their managers inept. It is because it is difficult to predict all the ways in which customers will use major innovations. Laboratory or pilot testing results often do not translate to the real market. Thus, some adopters may have an unsatisfactory experience or some third parties may raise doubts. Besides, the status quo bias suggests that many potential adopters will resist the innovation initially, creating social reinforcement for the status quo. This does not necessarily mean the innovation will fail. Potential customers balance the various messages they see and hear. If most innovators have a bad experience failure is likely. But in other circumstances the impact of negative messages is more complex, depending on *who* is saying *what* and (as seen from computational sociology) *when* they say it.

The impact of positive messages also depends on who is saying what and when. This is where marketing enters the picture. The positive messages coming from sources under the control of the innovating firm play a crucial role in framing the debate about the innovation. The analogy with debates and election campaigns is useful here. Major innovations often produce groups that support the innovation and groups that are initially against it. The first job of marketing is to frame the debate into areas where the positive benefits of the innovation will outweigh the losses of giving up the old solution. That will get adoption growing among the innovators. Done skilfully, so a clear view of the innovation emerges early on, it becomes more difficult for opponents or sceptics to shift the debate onto negative territory. More importantly, the innovators are adopting with the right expectations and, if the innovation delivers on these, positive social influence will start to spread via the connectors. Note that this clear view can both influence those customers who receive it direct and frame indirect social influence on others. As knowledgeable customers interact with other potential customers, the debate will then include the positive benefits the marketer wants to get across.

Chapter 7 – *Building the Market for the Innovation* – looks at these marketing issues in more depth. All that needs saying here is that success largely depends on the skill of marketing managers in creating advantage in the mind of the customer. This in turn depends on their understanding of innovation adoption, together with the strength of the platform the innovation itself provides. Firms may fail to create advantage because they do not create an innovation that meets customer needs. But they may also fail because their marketing managers:

- do not understand which mental category to connect the innovation to;
- do not fully recognize the cost to the customer of giving up the familiar product;
- choose the wrong attributes of the innovation to promote; and
- promote to an inappropriate segment of the market.

All these and more can rapidly lead to the failure of the innovation, either by not overcoming the status quo bias or through allowing too much negative social influence to appear early in the launch.

Realizing that Customers Don't Always Think Hard About Decisions

However, another aspect to influence needs mentioning. Put succinctly, this is the extent to which the customer thinks about the decision. It is tempting to consider this as simply a matter of the scale of the innovation and the potential risk in adopting it. For example, a firm adopting a new robotic assembly line faces a bigger decision than an individual consumer in adopting a new form of dental hygiene. So the firm may collect information from more sources and evaluate them more thoroughly than the individual consumer. In general this is true and partly explains why B2B adoption spreads more slowly than B2C. But this also depends on the situation the customer faces and the local influences acting at the time. Sometimes firms and individuals follow the systematic approach to decision-making, reaching a balanced conclusion on whether positive or negative messages are more convincing. However, sometimes they decide at a time dictated by external circumstances, with the outcome depending on whatever sources of influence are active at that time. And when the innovation starts to reach the mainstream market, competition between firms can make the choice of which variant to adopt huge. It is often difficult for the customer to be fully informed on all of these. The vignette on *Digital differentiation* illustrates this point.

Digital differentiation[41]

First introduced in 1997, digital audio players (DAPs) are portable electronic devices that store, organize and play audio files. Apple's iPods, the first generation of which was launched in 2001, are the most well-known among the public and have become synonymous with digital audio players, but many different devices are available. As well as stand-alone devices, DAPs are increasingly being incorporated into various other electronic products – from mobile phones to stun guns.

Apple's iPods dominate the market, and a swathe of iPods is now available, each with its own unique selling points. Apple's success has encouraged other companies to try for a bite of the apple, and as more companies bring new DAPs to market, they must find ways to differentiate their player from others. This has created a competitive market in which consumers are faced with a dizzying array of features as manufacturers compete to win their favour. As with most products, there is a trade-off between features from one product to another.

Different DAPs use different storage media: hard drive-based devices have higher capacities, while flash-based players have a lower capacity but require less battery power and may be more resilient to hazards such as dropping.

Capacity is often a major selling point. The iPod Classic can store up to 20 000 songs and boasts the user can carry their entire music and video collection in their pocket, although the large capacity also comes hand in hand with larger size and weight. Apple's iPod Nano can store only up to 2000 songs but is a sleeker, lighter model than the iPod Classic. The Creative Zen is the size of a credit card. According to Creative this is the first player that allows users to 'enjoy a media storage capacity previously only supported by hard disk-based media players, together with the skip-free content playback stability of a flash memory-based player'. It weighs little more than the iPod Nano, has a maximum inbuilt capacity of about 16 000 songs and has the further advantage that consumers can add extra memory.

Compatibility and usability are also important when a customer selects a DAP. The iPods work with both Apple computers and PCs but require the owner to use Apple's proprietary software – iTunes. Neither Walkman nor Zen are compatible with Apple computers, but they do not require a proprietary link. The Walkman is compatible with Windows Media Player and users can easily 'drag and drop' media from their PC to their Walkman.

The iPod Nano's main selling point has been its ability to play TV shows, movies and video podcasts on a large, bright display designed to provide excellent picture quality despite the device's small size. Nowadays, however, most players play video as well as audio, and some will display photographs. The Zen and Walkman both support a wide variety of video and music formats, including unprotected music tracks which people can buy from the iTunes store. The iPod Classic can support a wide range of digital photo standards, while both the Zen and Walkman can only support the jpeg format.

On top of these key selling features, manufacturers use add-ons – from the useful to the quirky – to capture a customer's interest. Across its range, Apple has looked to the global market by providing a choice of languages for their display and navigation interface. The iPod Classic has a lengthy list of extra features, including a phone book, a calendar and variable playback speed. The Zen has an FM radio and voice recorder, while, true to its musical origins, the Walkman has clear bass sound effects. The iPod Nano comes in a choice of five different colours. Indeed, for some consumers, the product's design and looks are more important than their functionality – one DAP even comes complete with its own make-up mirror!

Reality is more random, less systematic and less informed than the standard model of adoption suggests. Equally not all decisions are so important to the customer that they warrant systematic and fully informed decision-making. Both firms and individuals take shortcuts to less important decisions, and use simple heuristics when the costs of mistakes are low.

Thus intelligent marketing campaigns can exert a powerful influence over events. Marketing can shape and mould the debate to favour adoption by creating advantage in the mind of the customer. It does this by ensuring the right information has every chance of being present whenever potential customers arrive at their decision. And it does not matter whether this information comes from marketing or non-marketing sources, or whether it is direct or indirect. All that matters is that potential customers frame their decisions so gains unambiguously outweigh losses, and risks are acceptable.

Understanding the Asymmetry Between Market Influence and Customer Susceptibility

Indeed, evidence from economic studies shows an asymmetry between the power of marketing to supply influence and the relative susceptibility of customers to such influence. Suppliers always try to use their power to persuade customers. Is this wrong? Not necessarily. Customers understand this and accept it, particularly in markets where the costs of mistakes are low or where they gain some reward for accepting influence.[38] Where the stakes are high they will counter the influence, either by collecting more information or by devoting more thought to their decision.

For major innovation, framing the decision to create advantage is important, but taking this idea too far is a mistake. Behind the framing must be some real benefit to a significant number of customers. If there is none, there are enough checks and balances in the market to make the innovation fail. These checks and balances come from several interrelated sources. One source is the different approaches customers have to adoption decisions. Some will think harder about their decision than others and may decide the innovation has no benefit, or some will realize their adoption was a mistake quicker than others. Another source is social networks. These networks will communicate negative opinions and experiences to others, often at several steps removed. So, while a few customers can be manipulated to adopt innovations without real benefits it is hard to see that a supplier can persuade a whole market to do so. This conclusion is consistent with the evidence that many innovations fail.

ACTION STEPS: THREE STEPS TO CREATE ADVANTAGE

The first step is to understand the new model of adoption that emerges from these lessons. A better understanding of how customers adopt major innovation is a precondition for improving innovation management. Especially as many current practices and normative prescriptions ignore what happens in the market. So the first part of this section summarizes the main features and conclusions of that model. The new model shows the innovating firm has significant power to influence customers by carefully developing and framing the innovation and its advantages. But to do so effectively the firm needs to take two important steps to improve its innovation management. These are to co-create the innovation with its customers, and to start from the desired end.

Step 1: Understand the New Model of Adoption

The new model that emerges out of all these lessons has three threads. The first of these is the role of the innovating firm in creating the information environment in which customers will evaluate the innovation.

The Innovating Firm Frames Advantage

If the innovation meets important needs of these customers and the firm chooses its messages carefully, the firm can have great influence. In particular, influence over how customers see, discuss and evaluate the innovation. With skill the firm can frame the decision so most of the target audience sees advantage in adopting the innovation. This message of advantage will then spread further through the many forms of social influence, as well as the marketing campaign itself. This is a major difference between the new model and the standard model of adoption. The standard model largely ignores the economic actions of firms that build markets.

Customer Decisions are Subject to Local Influences

Customers are willing to accept the firm's influence provided the innovation has value, a value they discover either direct or through the actions of other customers. This second thread differs from the standard model chiefly in that it recognizes that mainstream customers are more open to local influences and less likely to evaluate the innovation systematically. Human societies are quick to accept innovations seen as valuable. However, if the innovation does not have value then countervailing and powerful social checks and balances will settle its fate. Some early adopters will kill the innovation through their words or actions and in doing so they perform an important role for others. Human societies resist ideas they see as having little value. But the main conclusion here is that what is valuable or not is a *social construction*. A construction partly determined by the innovating firm's message, partly by the views and actions of some customers and partly by social networks and common knowledge. Innovators and connectors play the key roles in deciding what value is and what message will pass to the mainstream.

Common Knowledge Builds in a Semi-random Way

Finally, the third thread is the manner in which influence and adoption spreads. This is far less structured and more random than the standard model suggests. In practice it is impossible for the innovating firm to know which local influences are acting on an individual customer at a particular time, or how social messages pass from one customer to another several steps removed. Nor, in most circumstances, is it possible to know how common knowledge will build in each local network. Elaborate targeting strategies seem unlikely to succeed. Instead, the goal should be to make sure the framing message is omnipresent through the multiple sources the firm can control. Similarly, in many circumstances it is not possible to identify which particular customers will be innovators. Trying to target them direct through mailings or personal selling also seems unlikely to succeed. For any chosen target market there will be enough customers with higher plasticity and lower stability. If they receive the framing message and it is sufficiently compelling in its own right they will adopt. And if their experience with the innovation is satisfactory, they will start the spread of social influence, encouraging others to follow by adding positive social messages to the mix

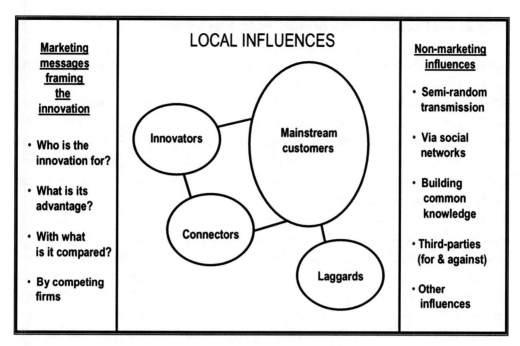

Exhibit 2.3   The new model of adoption.

of influences these other customers are already receiving. And creating common knowledge in local networks that supports the innovation. Exhibit 2.3 summarizes the main features of the new model.

There are also the connectors to put into this picture. They are socially involved and open to new ideas. The innovating firm's messages may directly influence them to adopt but they also need the social confirmation of the innovators. The confirmation that others are adopting is an important part of the mix of local influences in their decision. However, because of their social involvement they pick up on these positive messages quickly and, if they adopt, this adds to the growing momentum of the innovation.

More importantly, the connectors form the connection between the innovators and the mainstream, relaying the message to many others. The innovators are less social. So without the connectors there would be no critical mass of links to others, nor would the necessary common knowledge build in local networks. The innovators are also atypical, so it is also likely the mainstream finds the message of the socially attuned and typical connectors more convincing. Finally, the mainstream starts to adopt, at which point the market takes off.

Step 2: Co-Creating Innovations with Customers

Developing a successful innovation needs empathy with the potential customers and their view of the world. What are the unmet needs of the target customer? Which potential innovations might address these needs? What gains and losses do different types of customer see in these potential innovations? What is the best design to select for the innovation? To answer these questions well, the firm needs to understand its customers from the start of the innovation project. That way development goes in a good direction, resulting in an innovation that meets the needs of the customer.

The best way to gain such an understanding is to involve customers throughout development. This cuts out unnecessary filters and anchors the development process in the market place. Customer involvement is an essential part of good development practice, from the first analysis of customer needs to the final forecast of launch demand. Constant dialogue helps identify the best innovation design to aim for and ensures the final innovation delivers what customers expect. This is not to say that customer preferences should be the only consideration in firm decisions; clearly there are other considerations. But involving the right customers in the right ways improves the chance the firm will focus development around the innovation that works best for the target market.

One major implication of the new model of adoption is that different types of customers should play different roles at different times during development. For example, innovators and connectors should be more open to new ideas and thus easier to involve productively at the start. They can co-create innovations and their views will be influential in the market place. Mainstream customers can and should play a role, but later in the development process when a more concrete innovation prototype emerges. The role of the mainstream customer in co-creation is more to corroborate the viability of the final innovation. And to suggest where changes or variants of the innovation might better fit the needs of different mainstream segments.

Thus what is new here is not customer focus; that is an old idea, although one often poorly performed. Rather what is new is involving customers in ways that follow from advances in our understanding over the last decade. Most firms have yet to reflect this new understanding in their development practices. In particular this approach is in complete contrast to standard market research practice with its emphasis on the typical customer. To make co-creation work effectively, the representative samples, focus groups and surveys of traditional market research have to give way to more selective samples and subtler methods.

Step 3: Start from the End

The firm should define the innovation project to reflect the revenue and profit trajectories it needs to meet its strategic goals. In turn, revenues and profits depend on the profile of the new market the firm wants to build, and the position in this market it wishes to achieve. During launch marketing plays a critical role in framing the adoption decision in the mind of the customer. Proper framing, and the marketing campaigns that deliver this, maximize the chance that a critical mass of customers will act, and the new market be built to plan. Proper framing also maximizes the chance of achieving the right price point and profit levels. But framing can only build on the platform the innovation itself provides. Without the right platform proper framing may not be possible, leading the innovation to under-perform or fail. For major innovations this is an important issue because the firm can often develop the creative idea in many directions, each direction meeting customer needs in different ways and allowing different framings. Thus the firm has not only to be clear on the needs of the target customers. It also has to have a view on how best to release the potential of the new market. Again achieving all of this builds on customer understanding and the new model of adoption, but in a different sense to co-creation. Here the firm is forming a view on how it will build the market and then working back to what this implies for the design of the innovation. In that sense there is a need to start from the (desired) end.

As a result marketing also has to play a major role in the project from the start. Many leading companies of course do this. However, there are still major companies that do not involve marketing until the prototype is ready, or send junior marketing people to join innovation teams. Instead senior marketing executives, familiar with ideas here, should work alongside other team members from the start. These executives are the champion of the voice-of-the-customer and of a clear focus on customer needs rather than technological possibilities. They also understand what it takes to build a new market and how to design the innovation to best achieve that.

LINKS TO THE FIVE KEY TASKS

The ideas of this chapter provide the general foundation for all the remaining chapters in this book. Two chapters pick up and build on these ideas directly. That is Chapter 5 – *Co-Creating Innovations with Customers* and Chapter 7 – *Building the Market for the Innovation*. Both of these extend and recast the ideas here into effective management methods and provide the practical tools to support these. However, the ideas here also shape the other chapters. These links are worth mentioning because they show how the foundation underpins *all* five key tasks of Chapter 1. For brevity the text here only mentions the most important link. Many other links are mentioned in the chapters themselves.

Links to Chapter 3 – *Chartering Innovation within the Organization*. The firm's rules and procedures for developing innovations need to change to reflect the new model of adoption, especially where major innovation in services and business models is the goal. The traditional Stage–Gate™ method needs adapting to meet these new challenges. Chapter 3 provides suggestions on the necessary changes.

Links to Chapter 4 – *Selecting, Preparing and Supporting the Right Team*. Co-creating innovations with customers has implications for the membership of innovation teams. It is important the team pays attention to and involves customers from the start and this implies the team having the right people to do this. Chapter 4 looks at the consequences for team selection and training.

Links to Chapter 6 – *Changing the Organization to Deliver the Innovation*. The way new markets are built has implications for firm organization and employee skills. The timescale of adoption and the differing demands on the firm during the development, launch and mainstream phases of market building suggest significant changes to organization and people. Chapter 6 looks at how to manage the necessary changes.

All the chapters, from Chapter 3 to Chapter 7, of course look at other topics and issues. But the ideas of Chapter 2 drive many of the recommendations for how to improve innovation management that those chapters put forward.

CHAPTER 3

CHARTERING INNOVATION WITHIN THE ORGANIZATION

INTRODUCTION

Developing a stream of successful innovations is one way a firm can survive, grow and outperform its competitors. To be successful, managers need to know in which markets to innovate (strategic direction), and how to go about developing the necessary innovations for these markets (operational guidelines). To have both good direction and effective guidelines firms need to approach innovation systematically. It is wrong to leave these tasks to the R&D laboratory or ad hoc managerial inspiration. A systematic approach to innovations does matter and studies show that most firms are ineffective at developing such an approach. In their series of major studies on innovation, the consultants Booz, Allen and Hamilton show that successful innovation does not depend on money, effort or luck. In brief, their studies show two main characteristics distinguish the better firms from their less successful rivals. First, they set a direction for innovation that aligns with their strategy and strengths. Second, they manage development effectively, especially in the ways they collaborate across the firm[1] and listen to the customer throughout.[2]

The typical firm is poor at both tasks. Measuring return on investment as new product sales for every dollar of R&D investment, Booz Allen and

Hamilton show the best performers consistently get twice the return of the industry average. That is a big difference. For example, in consumer healthcare the typical firm gets $2 in new sales for every $1 it spends on R&D. The best performer gets $4. It does not take many years for such differences to add up to real competitive advantage for the firm that manages innovation more effectively.

This chapter sets up the business objectives and operational guidelines for developing the innovations the firm needs. As a first step, firms should document and communicate both to their employees. Here objectives and guidelines are called the company's Innovation Charter, using the word 'charter' to mean a licence given to someone to act in certain areas.

The charter serves several purposes. First, it directs innovation activities towards strategically and economically important areas and away from areas that are likely to have less impact on the growth and sustainability of the firm. Second, it sets out the guidelines for developing innovations of various sorts. These guidelines specify the key decisions managers should make, the basis for making them and the roles and responsibilities of the various people involved. A clearly defined and communicated charter ensures that everyone in the organization knows the direction of innovation and his or her own role in it. This clarity is essential for success.

It is important to note the Charter is the formal, strategic and rational component of a systematic approach to innovation. The cultural and emotional side of the organization is the other, equally important component. A systematic approach to innovation will not work unless the culture of the organization supports this. Chapter 6 looks at these issues of culture and shows how the behaviour of the firm's leadership team is critical to encouraging innovation.

This chapter is in five sections. The first section introduces the idea that innovation is a planned, programmatic activity not a one-off event. The second section looks at setting the direction for this innovation programme; including making sure it achieves the firm's purpose, managing risk and return and issues of resources and organization. The third section looks at decision-making during development, particularly experience with stage–gate methods and the lessons from this experience. This section includes criticisms of current methods and suggestions on how to improve these to reflect current thinking on strategy, as well as the ideas of Chapter 2. The fourth section addresses the key task of setting up specific innovation projects and defining their objectives. This section also identifies three tools that can help ensure the objective is both customer-focused and realistic. These tools—the strategy canvas, scenario generation and discovery-driven planning—are detailed in the Toolkit for this chapter. The final fifth section looks at some of the implications of the chapter and its links to other chapters and tasks.

INNOVATION IS A PROGRAMME, NOT AN EVENT

A common metaphor for innovation development is a funnel. Creative employees produce many ideas for possible innovations, either alone or in brainstorming sessions. These ideas pour into the top of the funnel and continue to develop from embryonic idea toward finished innovation. However, at decision-points the funnel narrows as managers evaluate all the ideas in progress, discarding some and refocusing their efforts on the ones they think have more promise. Eventually a single commercial success emerges from the bottom of the funnel.

This metaphor is useful up to a point. In a well-run organization with capable people, ideas are plentiful and the job of the development team is to identify and develop the best. It is also good practice for the team to create alternative solutions and use customer data and systematic procedures to focus firm resources on the best of these. However, at another, strategic, level this metaphor is misleading. It implies that innovation development is a one-off, stand-alone exercise and that innovation development is somehow different from normal business. It also implies that innovation is more of a creative than strategic exercise.

These implications are wrong. Innovation development should connect to, and draw on, the organization as a whole. It is an integral part of normal business, driven by strategic objectives just like any other activity. Creativity is an important part of this, but innovation development is not creative in the random, inspirational sense of the word; creativity is just one part of a systematic programme for achieving strategic objectives.

Innovation Strategy as Part of Overall Strategy

There are several reasons for seeing innovation development as a programmatic and strategic activity. The first of these concerns strategy. Innovation plays a major role in achieving a firm's growth objectives. To meet these the firm needs to plan the contribution that innovation will make to this growth.

All firms have a reason for existing; a purpose that defines their vision and scope of activities, as well as capabilities that enable them to fulfil this purpose rather than another. They therefore need to think carefully about the areas in which they need innovation, and those in which they do not. They need to do this from the perspective of both the purpose of the company and from the way the innovation fits what they are doing or would like to do in future.

Finally, most firms realize that their existing businesses have a use-by date, not necessarily through obsolescence but though falling returns. Markets mature and as they do competition often increases and prices and profits fall. As well as planning for new profit opportunities, firms need to consider their portfolio of existing businesses to identify emerging profit gaps and plan for innovations that replace these. In summary, identifying where the firm needs to innovate is a strategic activity driven by its purpose, financial goals and existing businesses. For these reasons, innovation is also an integral part of normal business; just one part of the firm's vision and plans.

Commercial Development can be Programmed

The second reason concerns the programmatic nature of innovation development. While breakthrough scientific research may be difficult to programme, commercial innovation is not. Indeed, commercial innovation is development, not research, since it mostly involves applying known techniques to solving customer problems. It is therefore open to systematic procedures designed to deliver a stream of innovations that fit the strategic direction of the firm.

This is not the same as saying the firm knows the eventual form of these innovations in advance or that it can predict their market impact accurately. In reality the more radical or disruptive the innovation is for customers, the less well the firm can know its form in advance or predict its impact. The same is true for innovations that involve major developmental or appropriation challenges. Nevertheless, firms can set up systems that focus innovation in the best areas; reject bad solutions and make sure the right development skills are available. On average, these systems create successful innovations. They are not perfect: some projects will not work out and some launches will still fail. However, systematic approaches to innovation yield major improvements in a firm's effectiveness over rivals who improvise.

Taking a Strategic Perspective on the Innovation Programme

Two perspectives are in play in developing innovations, that of the firm and that of the project team. Since the purpose of innovation is to fill strategic gaps in the firm's revenue growth path, and since the outcome of each project is not certain, the firm needs to manage its innovation programme as a portfolio of projects. Each of these projects will target an area of business the firm identifies as important and each will have a team of managers and other employees responsible for its execution. These teams will each focus on their area of innovation and the objective the firm gives them. Each team will try to achieve this objective by filling their funnel with suitable ideas and working towards turning the best ones into a commercial innovation. Good teams provide the firm with focus, dedication and execution. However, by its nature the team has a narrow view of the whole innovation programme.

In contrast, the firm's executives have to make two decisions. First, they must decide whether the innovation each team proposes is both feasible and valuable to the firm. Second, they must judge whether it is this innovation project or another in the programme that is most likely to meet the financial goals of the firm. Development funds are usually finite, and the executives are responsible for choosing the best investments for the firm as a whole.

Because of these needs for both focused execution by the team and careful selection of investments by executives, the best innovation development practices combine the passion of project teams with executive judgement. The first step for the executives is to set the overall direction for the innovation programme.

SETTING THE DIRECTION OF THE INNOVATION PROGRAMME

Project Types in the Innovation Programme

If firms need a programme of innovation projects, we need to examine the nature of this portfolio. How many projects, of what scale, and sorts of innovation should the programme contain? Chapter 1 defines three challenges that executives need to consider here; the customer challenge, the development challenge and the appropriation challenge. Each project will differ in the degree and mix of these challenges, and the job of executives is to ensure balance across the portfolio. For discussion, we can outline four stereotypes.

The first is an *incremental innovation* project. This innovation builds on the firm's existing knowledge, skills and operations. Here it does not matter which mix of the three challenges the project entails because the firm is building on what it already does. What matters is that the degree of challenge in any area is only moderate for the firm. In addition, it is likely employees, partners and customers will readily understand and accept the innovation. Note this does not mean this is an easy project. Simply the degree of challenge it entails does not imply breakthroughs in development (including organizational change), business models or customer understanding.

The other three stereotypes each represent a bigger challenge on one of the three dimensions. Thus, we can talk about a project that needs a *development breakthrough*, one that needs an *appropriation breakthrough* or one that needs a *customer breakthrough*. By assumption, the degree of challenge on the remaining two dimensions of each stereotype is only incremental. What does a breakthrough entail? Essentially the firm lacks all the necessary knowledge and skills at the start of the project. Nor does the project build on anything the firm is already doing. Appropriation and customer breakthroughs also imply that partners or customers will not understand and accept the innovation without major effort by the firm.

Incremental innovations are what most firms do regularly.[3] These innovations are continual and significant improvements to existing products or services in established markets. They are necessary to keep a competitive edge, improve margins, up-sell customers or fix flaws in existing offerings. Without incremental innovations, firms start to lose their market position to more proactive competitors. Unfortunately as existing markets mature and price competition increases, incremental innovation, while still necessary, becomes a cost of staying in business instead of a contribution to profit growth. Thus, firms need to balance incremental with breakthrough innovation if they are to achieve financial growth targets. Balancing exploitation (of existing forms of business) and exploration (of new forms of business) is among the most difficult decisions a chief executive has to make.[4] Today's profits come from the existing businesses that they understand; tomorrow's profits come from new businesses that they do not.

Moreover, breakthrough innovations are difficult for large firms. Development breakthroughs need new technologies (products) or new organizations (services). Appropriation breakthroughs need a business model that is capable of beating the existing one in the medium term. They also represent major political and economic threats to existing industry structures. Customer breakthroughs need unusually open minds amongst employees and a willingness to explore new opportunities. The customers themselves may need to learn new skills or see benefits in a different way.

For all these three breakthrough stereotypes, market potential and growth trajectories are much less predictable than for incremental innovations. In addition, the firm must move away from its current core competences and existing organizational procedures and structures. There are significant risks in all three, but the returns are potentially much greater than for incremental innovations. Therefore, for any firm the real choice is not between incremental or breakthrough innovations; it is to balance correctly both types of innovation to meet its growth targets.[5] While incremental innovation projects will likely be the most common, the firm will also need some more radical projects to sustain growth.

How should it choose the areas for these projects? The important criteria for making this decision are the firm's purpose; risk and return; and capability and culture. However, since the firm's purpose largely determines its approach to both risk and return and capability and culture, purpose becomes the primary criterion to meet.

Projects Must Meet the Firm's Purpose

All organizations have a purpose. As Mourkogiannis notes the purpose is not to make a profit, which is the result of being good at the purpose. It is their reason for existence.[6] The basic purpose of an airline is to move people from A to B, the purpose of a bank to look after people's money and so on. In addition, organizations usually define their purpose to include the kind of airline or bank they seek to be, as encapsulated in slogans like Southwest's '*Freedom to Fly*' or HSBC's '*The World's Local Bank*'. This seems trite but it is fundamental. The innovation programme should contain only projects that meet the intended purpose. Being clear about the purpose of the company provides a benchmark against which to judge whether projects make sense or not. More importantly, a statement of purpose can allow creative and radical projects to flourish. The firm's purpose is less constraining than its specific objectives for the near future. Thus, addressing purpose can bring about more forward-looking perspectives than statements bound up in the technologies of today. A good statement of purpose allows the company to evolve through relevant innovation, both incremental and breakthrough.

A specific example of purpose is Toyota's emphasis on giving customers value for money. Value for money is essentially an altruistic purpose arising from the founder's concern for 'ingenuity in craft'.[7] Such ingenuity yields elegant, simple solutions that provide value for customers in their everyday life. Another example is Sony's emphasis on useful innovation. Again, this purpose originates from Sony's founder, but the core elements here are the joy of technological innovation and open-mindedness about what provides value.[8] This purpose is more one of discovery than altruism, although there is no doubting the customer focus of both companies.

Both purposes provide guidance on the areas of innovation these firms should pursue. Both also have implications for the risk the firm wants to take on and the capabilities they need to develop for the future. A firm aiming at discovery, such as Sony, may want to take on more risk and develop newer capabilities at a faster rate than a company aiming at altruism, such as Toyota.

This is a useful contrast. Currently many commentators see Toyota as one of the world's most successful firms, while delays in the Play Station 3 and other problems have tarnished Sony's image. However, between the 1950s and 1980s Sony launched no less than 12 breakthrough innovations.[9] During the same period, Toyota launched none. This shows there is no right or wrong method. Toyota's purpose defines it as chiefly an incremental innovator and it is possibly the world's best incremental innovator.[10] Sony's purpose, at least for three decades, defined it as a breakthrough innovator and it was possibly the world's best breakthrough innovator during those decades. Each purpose defines which innovation projects to fund, what level of risk and return to take on, and capabilities to nurture. Both firms were successful because they had a clear purpose and tailored their innovation to achieve that purpose.

The vignette *Making innovation an objective* shows how purpose leads to general and specific objectives for the innovation programmes of two firms.

Making innovation an objective[33]

Innovation is a risky business, and firms can benefit from having a set of innovation objectives to inform the actions people take. Firms will usually have a set of general objectives that fix the mix of innovation activities they wish to follow. These general objectives normally derive from their overall purpose as a firm. A set of specific objectives will then define what the firm wishes to achieve by product, process, service or business model innovation. A firm may run several innovation projects under any one or more of these specific objectives.

Saint-Gobain is involved in the design, production and distribution of materials for the construction, industrial and consumer markets and is Europe's largest distributor of building materials. The firm's range of products includes insulation, timber, plumbing materials, tiles and glass. Saint-Gobain's purpose is to 'specialise in transforming these materials into advanced products for use in our daily lives; as well as developing the materials of tomorrow'. This purpose translates into four general objectives for innovation, namely to:

- invent new processes
- create new products
- develop new applications
- invest in the future.

The first of these objectives covers both product and process innovation. Saint-Gobain defines this further through five *specific* aims. These are to expand the basic knowledge of materials and processes, and to integrate scientific and technical progress on a continuing basis. In addition, to perfect production processes to make them more competitive and maintain the group's technical lead, to improve product properties and reliability, and to invent new, more effective, processes.

The second and third objectives both concern product innovation. The firm further defines the second by the specific objective of creating new products for traditional markets or that meet new needs (usually products derived from the firm's base materials). In addition, these products should bring about a change in the market because of their innovative functions. Saint-Gobain further defines the third objective as conquering new markets in close collaboration with marketing teams and looking for new applications for the firm's materials outside their traditional markets. The fourth objective ensures the firm invests in research that supports its other goals.

In contrast, the purpose of Demohouse is sustainable renovation of the existing housing stock in Europe. This consortium of construction firms and research institutes undertakes research and innovation activities to reduce energy consumption for heating, cooling, ventilation and hot water in renovations. Demohouse has six main objectives for innovation:

* develop minimum standards for sustainable renovation
* develop decision-making tools to improve sustainable renovation
* create management structures to implement sustainable renovation
* guarantee ongoing communication and training concerning sustainable renovation
* develop and demonstrate technological solutions to reduce energy consumption
* develop a multidisciplinary approach to sustainable renovation.

As with the objectives of Saint-Gobain, each of these translates into specific objectives that precisely define how the organization will work to achieve these objectives. And these specific objectives then lead to innovation projects. For example, pilot demonstrations in renovated housing or a decision support tool for housing associations.

Although the two organizations have a different purpose in pursuing innovation – Saint-Gobain's being materials in daily life and Demohouse's sustainable renovation – their general and specific innovation objectives will guide and steer both organizations towards achieving their purpose.

Managing Risk and Return to Reach Growth Targets

Exhibit 3.1 shows a commonly accepted set of statistics on the risks of various types of innovation, shown here on the classical dimensions of market and technology. Risks increase as the company moves away from its present markets and technologies to adjacent or new markets and technologies. The figures represent the likelihood of failure.

The shape of the various risk bands confirms what was said above, that incremental innovation (existing technology and markets) is far less risky than breakthrough innovation (new technology and markets). However, what the figure does not show is the financial return. The return is far less from a successful incremental innovation than from a successful breakthrough one. Breakthrough innovations can create new markets or take away existing ones from

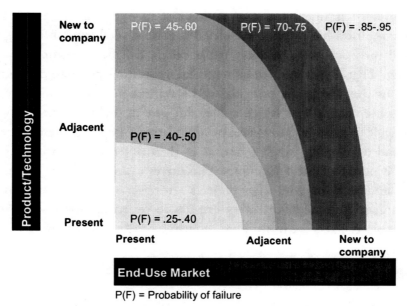

P(F) = Probability of failure

Exhibit 3.1   Balancing risk and return along the growth path.
Source: G. Day, Closing the Growth Gap: Balancing 'Big I' and 'small i' Innovation, Working Paper 06-004, Marketing Science Institute, 2006, p. 6. Reprinted by permission of George S. Day.

incumbents while incremental innovations gain a share, but no more than a share, of an existing market.

The real strategic decision concerns the level of risk and return the firm needs to achieve its purpose and its financial growth targets. A clear purpose defines the space in which innovation will occur and sets the general stance toward risk and return for the firm as a whole. Stakeholder expectations will also influence what the financial growth targets should be and what levels of risk and returns can be set. Out of which considerations flow guidelines to the balance of project types in the innovation programme. However, this is not portfolio management in the quantitative sense of managing an investment fund. As soon as the firm thinks about projects outside its present markets and technologies, it becomes difficult to forecast outcomes with any precision. It is better to decide that existing businesses and incremental innovations will provide a certain share of the growth target, leaving a shortfall for other types of project to fill. It is also possible to forecast the contribution that existing businesses and incremental innovations will make, leaving the shortfall for breakthrough innovations to fill.

However, it is much less easy to forecast how to fill the gap remaining. Essentially the firm has to place calculated bets on several breakthrough projects. Some will turn out to be winners while others will never complete or fail in the market. That is also true for incremental innovation projects. The important difference is that the profit potential of breakthrough innovations may not be clear for some time. All of which makes this part of the innovation programme more difficult to manage. However, by articulating a need for these more radical projects and developing rough estimates of their potential the firm gets a sense of where it needs to direct its efforts. Executives can also use these estimates to build an argument for why such projects are necessary for meeting the firm's growth targets. Arguments that they can use to overcome the resistance breakthrough projects often get from those in charge of existing and more predictable businesses.

Relating the Programme to Your Resources and Culture

Alongside purpose, risk and return are issues of capabilities and culture. Which capabilities does the company need to support the chosen direction for innovation? How does the company culture support or not support this direction? What is the best organizational structure for delivering these innovations to the market? The answer to these questions for incremental innovation projects is largely obvious: it is what the company is already doing. For breakthrough projects, the answer is less obvious, and for that reason executives also need to take into account capabilities and culture.

Just because an innovation project meets the organization's purpose, and has a desirable risk and return profile within the innovation programme, does not mean the firm can deliver it to the market. It may need to develop, buy or outsource new capabilities. Equally, some directions for innovation may get support from the existing culture, while some may meet with apathy or even resistance. Finally, some innovations may fit neatly into existing organizational structures while some may not. And all of these capability and culture considerations take on more force for innovations involving service or business model changes.

So even for a firm that has a clear idea of its purpose leaders face a difficult trade-off. On one side is the logical, quantitative consideration of risk and return and on the other the emotional, qualitative consideration of capabilities, culture, structures and people's lives. For the mythical organizations that have strong cultures of innovation, great leadership and flexible and skilled people with a willingness to change, this is no problem. Next year the firm will look very different. Unfortunately, most organizations are not like that. Instead, change is difficult and slow and often fails to meet expectations or fails outright. Major change is not something that a firm should undertake lightly.

Thus in setting directions, the firm's leaders have to consider how far the organization can develop in the short to medium term. For success, break-through innovation may need a different mind-set from employees, handing over key tasks to partner organizations, or even creating a new business unit. If the chances of carrying out such steps with success are low then the organization should not take this direction. Instead, it should direct its more radical projects into areas where it is more confident it can bring them to market successfully.

Comments like this could be taken as demanding 'focus' from the firm, or asking that it 'sticks to its knitting'. That would be an oversimplification. Tightly focused firms do well for a while but then run out of growth opportunities and displease the stock market. Unfocused firms also run into trouble in other ways, chiefly through not placing enough resources behind their winners. Neither extreme is desirable. Research shows there is a happy balance between break-through and incremental innovation, which produces consistent growth and keeps the stock market happy.[11] The other oversimplification of the idea of focus is to stress the hard strategic criteria for choosing projects. Soft considerations of organizational change also have an important role to play in choosing innovation projects.

The Innovation Charter

The Innovation Charter is an internal document that sets out the leadership team's thinking about the firm's innovation programme. It has two parts, one concerning strategy, the other concerning governance. The purpose of the Charter is to guide employees in creating the innovations the firm needs to meet its growth targets.

Part One: The Strategic Roadmap

The strategic part of the Charter captures the leadership team's thinking on the overall shape and form of its innovation programme. Indeed, it is best to think of this part of the Charter as an important extension of the firm's strategic plan, an extension that links more global objectives and strategies to the specifics of the innovation programme. Hence this part of the Charter is also a living document because as the overall strategy of the firm evolves, so too will the innovation programme. Some people call this part of the Charter the *strategic roadmap*.[12]

The strategic part of the Charter deals with purpose, growth targets and the role of innovation in meeting those targets. It sets out the relative emphasis on incremental and breakthrough innovation, as well as the risk and return profile the firm seeks to achieve across its innovation programme. The Charter also comments on the way the firm sees its capabilities, structures and culture evolving, and at what rate it expects this to occur. Finally, and most critically, the strategic part of the Charter provides clear guidance on the areas of innovation the firm will support and those it will not. In due course, executives can translate this guidance into specific objectives for project teams responsible for innovation in each of these areas. Each team should receive its own individual charter setting out the objective the firm expects the team to achieve and the resources available to them. There is a definite art to setting these *project objectives*. They should neither be too broad that they are unworkable, nor too narrow that they stifle creativity. Chapter 5 – *Co-Creating Innovations with Customers* – looks at project objectives in more detail because setting them effectively also requires customer insight. For these reasons project objectives are not part of the Charter, although they follow its guidance. Instead, they are outcomes of discussions between executives and project team members and should not become final until both parties have more information on the target market. The vignette *IBM charters its plans for innovation* shows an extract from the strategic part of an innovation charter.

IBM charters its plans for innovation[34]

An innovation charter is a set of organizational objectives, policies, guidelines and limits. Although innovation charters are an offshoot of a firm's strategic planning, they are an essential part of development activities, as findings show that they are important for a firm's performance.

The global corporation IBM has been using innovation to shape the future for its customers since well before its incorporation in 1911. IBM now boasts five Nobel laureates, eight research laboratories, 3000 scientists and 38 000 patents worldwide. Originally known for hardware, IBM now makes most of its money through software and services. In particular, hundreds of thousands of firms around the world run critical enterprise, e-mail and messaging applications using the firm's *iSeries*™ platform for integrated business solutions.

IBM developed a charter that documents and guides the continued, multiyear investment the company is making in iSeries. The charter considers three areas: innovation, solutions and partnership.

Principles and future strategies for iSeries™

Innovation	Solutions	Partnership
• Exploit over $1 billion spent in the past two years on iSeries commitment to innovation • Secure iSeries leadership as the most complete business solution to simplify information technology environments • Enhance the value of customers' and IBM Business Partners' existing investments	• Broaden and enhance iSeries portfolio of industry-specific solutions in local markets • Support a broad range of most popular open and traditional applications and tools • Promote and jointly market innovative business solutions that leverage iSeries offerings	• Provide the skills and expertise to design, develop and deploy on-demand solutions • Stimulate partner teaming that encourages investment in new skills and solutions • Increase incentives to deliver reward commensurate with value delivered

The charter also defines an iSeries Initiative for Innovation. IBM intends this to speed up its efforts on behalf of thousands of independent software vendors and tool providers and deepen its relationship with them. IBM expects the resultant open collaborative effort to fuel innovation in iSeries solutions.

Part Two: Innovation Project Governance

The second part of the Charter concerns governance. How will the firm manage innovation projects? What are the principles and procedures by which the firm makes decisions to fund or discontinue them? However, before looking at this part of the Charter it is necessary to look at best practice and research on the governance of innovation.

COOPER'S STAGE–GATE™ METHOD

To bring an innovation to a chosen market the project team needs to work through a series of steps or stages from first idea to final commercialization of the innovation. As each stage completes the firm's executives also have to respond to the team's requests whenever they need more resources for the project to advance.

In fact, most innovation development follows the same basic template for stages and decisions, which is often called the stage–gate method after Cooper's work in synthesizing best practice.[13] Exhibit 3.2 shows his basic Stage–Gate™ model with five stages and five 'gates', or executive decision points. In this exhibit, the stages are: (1) scoping; (2) build business case; (3) development; (4) testing and validation and (5) launch. The gates are: (1) idea screen; (2) second screen; (3) go to development; (4) go to testing and (5) go to launch.

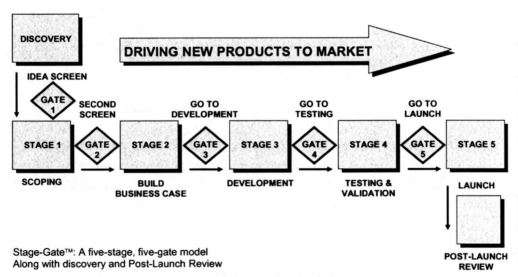

Stage-Gate™: A five-stage, five-gate model
Along with discovery and Post-Launch Review

Exhibit 3.2 The typical Stage–Gate™ model.

Source: R. Cooper, *Winning at New Products*, Cambridge, Mass: Basic Books, 3rd edition, 2001, p. 130.
Reprinted by permission of BASIC BOOKS, a member of Perseus Books Group.

The Stage–Gate™ Method

The Stage–Gate method is simple in concept. During *Discovery* the team creates several alternative ideas that might fit the objective the firm gives them. Or else the team gets these ideas from other sources internal and external to the firm. These ideas are then subject to a first screen, Gate 1, to identify those that are worth taking to Stage 2 – *Scoping*. At Gate 1 executives decide whether it is worth the cost to develop these ideas further. Here this is more of an issue of management time than budget. If the answer is yes, then during Stage 1 the team conducts preliminary assessments of the market, technical and financial prospects for the idea. If these look encouraging at Gate 2 they will gain approval to build a proper business case for the innovation, which is Stage 2. The main difference between scoping and building a business case is the latter will include thorough market and technical research, testing of the innovation idea with customers and a detailed financial and business analysis. The business case will need a modest budget, either because the research involves external agencies or because the team needs work by other parts of the organization. However, the first major commitment of investment funds is usually at Gate 3, where executives review the business case and decide whether the idea should advance to *Development*. This financial commitment then increases at Gate 4 and Gate 5 as the team gains approval to test and validate the innovation and then launch on the market. *Testing and Validation* includes customer tests of the completed innovation, test markets and trial production runs. *Launch* includes all the activities necessary to commercialize the innovation. After launch, the firm needs to track performance and decide whether the innovation merits further investment or whether to withdraw it from the market. The firm takes that decision at *Post Launch Review*.

A major element in the successful application of the stage–gate method is the separation of roles between the project team and executives. The team focuses on finding the innovation that will best meet their project objective. The gate decisions are the province of executives who are responsible for making the best decision for the firm. At each decision, these gate executives will look at the relative merits of various projects and try to manage the overall programme of innovation for the best impact. In this manner, the stage–gate method combines motivation and focus – the project team – with objectivity and a broader perspective – the gate executives. Having the right people in each role is also a significant determinant of success.

You can observe many different forms of stage–gate method, from the simple to the complex, in leading firms. The number of stages can vary considerably, as can the definition of the stages themselves. In service industries, the emphasis is more on people, and so stages appear such as team formation and personnel training. In product industries the emphasis is more on design and building new manufacturing plants. More recently, firms have tried to speed up development by simplifying the number of stages. Consultants and researchers have also tried to understand what matters in all of this. From such research, three main lessons emerge.

Lesson One: Recognizing That Different Stages Need Different Capabilities

The capabilities needed for being effective during the earlier and later stages are different. Idea generation needs creativity but also market knowledge. It should also involve working closely with selected customers. Building the business case requires financial and marketing skills, and the ability to make realistic projections or sketch scenarios of an uncertain future. Developing the innovation itself requires skills in rapid prototyping and project management, especially in delivering the innovation to the market on schedule. For new services and business models, development teams also need to be able to work across functional silos and to put change management strategies in place. Finally, commercialization requires everything pulling together effectively, needing skills in tactical planning and implementation as well as strategy.

Research shows the typical firm has problems in all these steps, mainly because they do not get the right people working together at each stage.[14] Taking this conclusion further, as it is unlikely all team members have the right skills for every stage, team membership should evolve as the demands of the stages change. Personnel management and effective team development are thus important to success.

Lesson Two: Using Gates to Select the Best Ideas for the Programme

While doing each stage effectively is important to the success of each *project*, the right gate decisions are critical to the success of the innovation *programme*.

Several authors note the problems the typical firm has with the gates.[15] These include allowing weak ideas to receive funding, using criteria that are too narrow and failing to take the programme/portfolio perspective. By not applying a rigorous and well-thought-out process of governance, they do not put their investments where they will deliver most return. Governance is also an important part of developing innovations, especially in running sustainable and effective innovation programmes.

From a project perspective, the idea generation and screening stages are critical to the progress of the project. The team needs to identify at least one robust idea for an innovation. Once the team identifies that idea, they can manage the later stages much more easily. This is because their task then becomes one of developing the idea in a logical and effective manner, a task at which most managers are good. Nevertheless, without at least one robust idea, the gate committee is likely to reject the project. Research suggests the best way to avoid failure is to create as many ideas as possible at the start. Note the word *idea* here does not mean a bullet point on a flip chart. It means a well-thought out and well-described concept for an innovation that adds value to customers in the target market. Both research and best practice suggest that teams need at least seven good ideas to deliver one success in the market.[16]

From a programme perspective, the job of the gate executives is different. They are managing teams with different objectives to meet overall growth targets and to preserve the right risk and return profile for the firm. Yes, gate executives need to assess each team's ideas against its set objective, and, if the team produces more than one robust idea, decide priorities for further funding. However, they also need to manage the overall programme. That means making comparisons across projects and stopping some, because either they judge them weaker than other projects, or they believe the risk and return profile requires them to allocate funds elsewhere. This is why governance is so important to successful innovation. Everyone, especially innovation team members, needs to understand the rules and believe the gate executives decide in a fair and objective manner. Evidence suggests many firms do not manage their programme effectively, partly because gate executives avoid hard decisions. They often allow weak ideas to pass into development, or worse yet into the market. Equally, they fail to allocate development funds for the best overall result. Part of the solution to such problems lies in the criteria the firm applies to gate decisions. If these are clear and suitable, it helps everyone, gate executives and teams alike. But what are suitable criteria?

Lesson Three: Mapping Appropriate Assessment Criteria at Each Gate

The criteria executives use to assess projects at each gate warrant careful consideration and should change from gate to gate. Exhibit 3.3 lists the typical criteria companies use.

How do these criteria differ, gate by gate? Whether the idea fits corporate strategy is important at Gate 1 (first screening) but not after that, as only ideas with a good fit should advance. For similar reasons it is important to assess the market opportunity early, so at least by Gate 2 everyone has confidence an opportunity exists. In contrast, technical factors are chiefly important at Gate 3 (allowing the innovation to go to development). Before that gate, these factors are hard to evaluate and afterwards the company has to invest to develop the idea. Technically flawed projects should therefore not reach the development stage. Assessing likely customer acceptance is important at every gate, but the

1. **Customer criteria**
     a. **Customer acceptance**
     b. **Customer satisfaction**
2. **Financial criteria**
     a. Break-even time
     b. Internal rate of return or return on investment
     c. **Margin**
     d. **Profit objectives**
     e. Stays within budget
3. **Market criteria**
     a. Marketing chance
     b. **Market potential**
     c. **Market share**
     d. **Sales growth**
     e. **Sales in units**
     f. **Sales objectives**
4. **Strategic criteria**
     a. Introduced in time
     b. Intuition
     c. **Product uniqueness**
     d. Time-to-market
5. **Technical criteria**
     a. **Product performance**
     b. **Quality**
     c. **Technical feasibility**

Exhibit 3.3   Example gate criteria for industrial firms.
Source: Adapted from a survey of 166 Dutch and UK industrial firms by Hart, Hultink, Tzokas and Commandeaur[32] with the criteria in bold being the more commonly used.

team's ability to measure customer acceptance improves over the project as the innovation takes more shape.

Expected profit is difficult to assess during the early stages but it becomes an important criterion for Gate 5 (allowing the innovation go to launch). There are differences in firm practices though. Many firms apply rigorous financial projections at Gate 3, before the firm gets into the development stage.[17] However, a contrary view is that until the innovation takes shape during development any assumptions made in financial spreadsheets at Gate 3 are likely to be wrong. Some experts even take this view further. They argue that trying to estimate the profit of an innovation too early kills good ideas and is harmful to the long-run health of the firm.[18] This debate turns out to hinge on the sort of innovation the gate committee is considering.

Researchers have studied the impact of the gate criteria on innovation success and examined how this differs for breakthrough versus incremental innovation.[19] They argue that for customer breakthroughs it is difficult to assess market opportunity, customer acceptance and expected profit at the early gates. It is much easier to assess these for incremental innovations. A similar conclusion probably holds for development and appropriation breakthroughs. This helps clarify the debate above. Application of financial and other gate criteria needs to reflect the innovation type and stage of development. It is possible to make a reasonable projection of the market and financial impact of an incremental innovation much earlier than for a breakthrough innovation. Firms with programmes that include both also have to handle this tension in their governance procedures.

Criticisms of Current Models

Are the Stages and Tasks Right?

In many ways stage–gate thinking originates from product innovation and does not yet fully reflect the trend to service and business model innovation. This trend increases the need for personnel training and, for services that need reorganization or business model innovation, effective change management. From now on, stage–gate sequences that include training and change management considerations are likely to become more common.

Service experts also point out that firms do not launch services in the same way as products. One reason for this is that going to a full launch of an innovative service is risky: it puts huge pressure on systems and employees and produces adverse publicity if anything fails. The other reason is that customers and employees co-produce many services in real conditions. This makes them harder to pre-test than products. More often firms scale up their new services from smaller beginnings to full operation, adjusting them along the way. Indeed, some organizations have deliberate strategies to check assumptions and resolve problems as the service scales up. The vignette *Navigo Pass – scaling up the testing process* illustrates one example of this.

Navigo Pass – scaling up the testing process[35]

Innovations designed for individuals are relatively straightforward to test with samples of customers trying various prototypes, either in simulated or real-life environments. But what if tens of thousands of customers will use an innovation at the same time? How can you test such a scenario in a laboratory or test facility?

This was precisely the problem faced by the Parisian public transport authority RATP in the late 1980s. RATP wanted to replace the ageing automatic ticket barriers in every metro station with a new magnetic pass card system – the Navigo. This pass card also had to be usable on the city's bus network. The new technology brought with it a new payment method, which needed to coexist with conventional paper tickets. All in all, there were enough technical and user challenges that RATP thought thorough testing essential before the Navigo pass went 'live'.

One test passenger can activate a prototype gate easily, but this does not reproduce typical use. How do you test performance at evening rush hour in the Châtelet-Les Halles metro interchange? What if passengers misunderstand how to use the system? How will RATP's own station assistants cope?

RATP's approach was to scale up the testing through a succession of trials, gradually increasing the demands placed on the Navigo system. Testing began in 1992 with technical feasibility studies in laboratory conditions. The following year 900 RATP agents tested the cards on station access gates in a real metro line. In 1994 RATP installed 200 checkpoints at their offices and 2000 employees simulated a crowded metro station. A further 4000 staff tested payment methods at dummy ticket booths around the city.

By 1997 the testing was scaled up to 40 000 employee agents. Then, for the first time, RATP recruited 1000 real metro users to test the pass in a special area using two access gates. RATP planned this experiment to last six months, but ended up running it for much longer. They also used professional actors to impersonate commuters. These actors created problems to test the training (and patience) of the station assistants.

Having challenged the practical aspects of the technology, RATP finally shifted their focus to payment methods in 1999. This they did by running tests involving 2000 real commuters in 50 metro stations. Here, RATP were able to balance customer preference against issues of cost, delay and fraud in the final design. The Navigo pass finally went live with annual pass subscribers in 2001, rolling out to other commuters in 2002, 10 years after the first tests began.

While firms can test and retest many innovations in closed environments before releasing them to customers, this would never have worked for the Navigo pass. Each phase of testing contributed changes that RATP incorporated into the next scaled-up level, with real customers introduced in stages and in greater numbers until every part of the system was proven. To have done otherwise would have risked chaos.

Another criticism is that many stage–gate sequences ignore the central importance of the project team. In contrast, some make team formation a distinct stage in the process.[20] These models are better because when the firm makes team formation explicit executives are more likely to take it seriously. If team formation is just implicit or an afterthought it is often not done well. Without the right team, successful innovation is unlikely.

Finally, the recent trend in innovation is to involve potential customers from the start and not to postpone 'serious' market research to the middle stages. Some experts argue that market research is not critical until the middle, especially for breakthrough innovations.[21] However, drawing on extensive experience with innovation projects, Kuczmarski argues for work on the intensity of needs as early as possible.[22] He makes the point that the team needs confidence the customer need they are proposing to meet is genuine. In addition, this need should be sufficiently intense and motivating that customers will adopt if the firm provides an innovative solution. Kuczmarski's argument fits well with increasing interest in research techniques for uncovering latent needs.

The basic stage–gate method remains the accepted procedure for developing innovations but there is clearly a need to adjust both stages and tasks to reflect greater knowledge and the changing business environment.

The Need for a Thorough Competitive Analysis

Turning to gate criteria the first significant criticism of current models is that they may underplay competitive analysis, mainly because they treat such analyses as just another section of the business case. Now it is true the gate criteria in most firms include competition, but they often do so in an oversimplified way. In many circumstances, the thorough analysis of a well-trained corporate strategist would be better. That is, an analysis including, among other considerations, who is likely to capture the profits from the innovation and what the firm's order-of-entry strategy might be. Both of these considerations concern the appropriation challenge the firm faces with its innovation.

Teece argues the ability of a firm to capture the profits from its innovation depends on two factors, inimitability and complementary assets.[23] High inimitability means that a competitor will have difficulty in copying the innovation. Low inimitability means it will be easy for the competitor to copy the innovation. Complementary assets are all the assets, other than the innovation itself, the firm needs to deliver the innovation to the customer successfully. These include assets such as distribution channels, relationships with customers or complementary technologies. Taken together these two factors point to the competitive scenario the innovating firm faces. In one scenario, it is easy for the firm to capture the profits; in all others, it is harder. The easy scenario is where competitors find it hard to copy the innovation, and complementary assets do not matter or are freely available. However, if competitors can readily copy the innovation they can take money away from the firm, and if another party holds complementary assets that are important, then that party can take money away from both the firm and its competitors. (This is because the third party will play multiple suppliers of the innovation off against one another.) Where there is a stand-off, namely, the firm's innovation is difficult to copy, but another party holds complementary assets that are also important, the outcome depends on relative bargaining power.

Competitive analyses should include such scenarios, alongside the more standard analyses of who might be a competitor and what their likely strengths and weaknesses will be. These deeper analyses have important implications for judging which innovation projects should go to development. Not least because, while it is important the innovation meet the needs of the customer, it is also important the firm, and not other organizations, capture fair value from this.

Who Will Be First to Market, Your Competitors or You?

Another consideration in judging the profitability of projects is what the order-of-entry strategy will be. Is the firm striving to be the pioneer of a new product or service category? Alternatively, is the firm content to let some other organization be first and then follow them into the market if it looks like this market will take off? Pioneering and follower strategies have different financial outcomes for the firm and imply different speeds of development and commercialization of the innovation. Typically, managers express the goal to be first, yet the evidence suggests this has mixed benefits. Yes, the pioneer has the market to himself for some time but the pioneer also takes on more risk than followers do. Followers may also learn from the pioneer and produce better innovations or more effective business models.

In an extensive historical analysis of 66 markets, Golder and Tellis found the median duration of the pioneer's market leadership is around five years.[24] That is, half the pioneers lost their early market share leadership in five years or less. More strikingly over longer-time perspectives, few, if any, pioneers keep their market leadership. In fact, for only six of these 66 markets is the pioneer still the leader today. The norm is more for leadership to change hands several times and, while there are firms who lead for long periods, these usually enter the market several years after the pioneer.

Of course, market share is not the same as profit. However, other studies show that pioneers suffer from long-run cost disadvantages that lead to lower returns on investment in 10 to 12 years.[25] These cost disadvantages arise from the followers learning better ways or the pioneer being reluctant to improve their methods. Overall, the picture that emerges is one where the pioneer has enough advantages to lead in market share and profits for around five years. Advantages that include the impression the pioneer makes on the minds of customers and the pioneer being ahead of its competitors on the learning curve for this innovation. However, five to ten years out from launch competitors begin to erode these advantages, eventually to the point at which they are lost.

Note that all these studies are of *successful* pioneers, since they look back at markets that became economically important. No one knows what the risks of the pioneer failing are. People throw around statistics like '80% of new products fail' but these statistics fail to distinguish between minor incremental innovations and breakthrough innovations. In contrast, studies of pioneering look at innovations that clearly add value to customers. Possibly the risk of failure is lower for such innovations but it is still not zero. Thus, the pioneer has an extra disadvantage the follower does not. Namely, the pioneer takes the risk the market will not take off; the follower can wait and see.

Now none of this is necessarily an argument for or against either pioneering or following. No, it is more an argument for the firm being clear on the outcomes of the strategy it adopts. If this is a pioneering strategy, the innovation team needs to think about how to maximize the customer and learning advantages of being first, and how to minimize the longer-run cost disadvantages. They also need to think about the next generation of the innovation to forestall the competition that will inevitably emerge. On this point, Golder and Tellis argue that the big challenge for the pioneer is the transition to the mainstream market, a step that many fail to foresee and take. On the other hand, if it is a following strategy, the team needs to think about how to learn from and better the pioneer, or how to capture the mainstream market before them. Yet again, all of this discussion of order-of-entry implies deeper analyses and more sophisticated gate criteria than typically is the case.

Gate Criteria Need to Reflect Market Dynamics

The second significant criticism of current approaches is that, astonishingly, gate criteria for market opportunity and customer acceptance often ignore knowledge of innovation adoption and market dynamics (as set out in Chapter 2). This ignorance might not be a problem for incremental innovations, but it is potentially dangerous for breakthrough innovations. For these firms routinely ask the wrong questions and involve the wrong customers, and so make poor estimates of market potential and likely adoption.

Chapter 2 gave some of the reasons for this, including the impact of status quo bias, framing and the local information environment. Because of factors like this, during early market research many customers cannot predict their likely acceptance with any degree of accuracy. For similar reasons traditional market research methods do not work for breakthrough innovation. There are newer methods that suit breakthrough innovation, and Chapter 5 details these, but as yet most companies do not use them.

Even if firms choose suitable methods, in the early stages these methods work best for customers who are innovators. Obtaining useful evaluations from mainstream customers typically requires developed innovations rather than early concepts. Further, market researchers should collect such evaluations while exposing potential customers to a similar information environment to the one they will experience during launch. Otherwise, the resulting projections will not hold when customers make real adoption decisions. 'Information acceleration' techniques exist to simulate this exposure and Chapter 5 looks at these.

Similarly, current stage–gate models do not separate the early launch phase with adoption by innovators and connectors from the point of take-off when mainstream customers start to adopt. Current models put these two phases together under the one heading of 'launch'. Yet, the marketing and organizational demands of the two are different. Overall, stage–gate methods need to reflect better what we know about adoption.

Towards Better Stage–Gate Methods

Exhibits 3.4 and 3.5 build on the trend to service and business model innovation and try to overcome these criticisms by suggesting stage–gate methods that might be more fitting in the future. Exhibit 3.4 deals with the stages, Exhibit 3.5 with the gate criteria.

Taking Exhibit 3.4 first, this adds a first stage for *Project Setup* and a sixth and final stage for *Broaden to the Mainstream*. *Project Setup* recognizes that it is important to select and develop the right team and prepare for the project adequately. This preparation should include assessment of the nature and intensity of the target customers' unmet needs. The new Gate 1 which Exhibit 3.4 associates with this stage recognizes that executives need to agree the final project objective once this preparatory work is complete. Having a separate stage – *Broaden to the Mainstream* – recognizes the distinction between the early market of innovators and connectors and the mainstream to follow. The fifth stage – *Commercialization* – now deals solely with the early market.

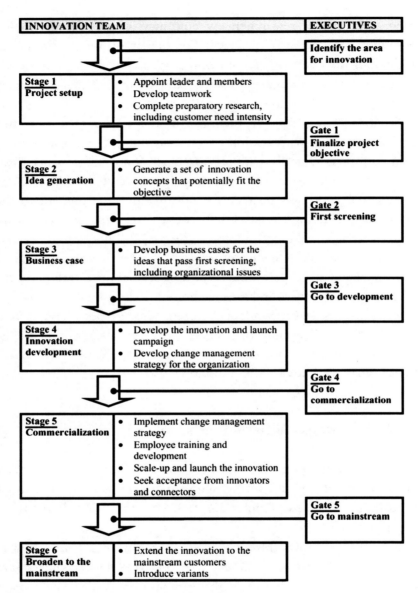

Exhibit 3.4 Towards better stage–gate methods.

The other stages follow the Cooper model but idea generation becomes a separate stage. As other authors suggest, this helps recognize that idea generation should involve work with customers rather than simply team brainstorming. Exhibit 3.4 also drops the testing and validation stage. Again, in current thinking

Gate	Key Criteria
Gate 1. Finalize project objective	1. *Strategy:* project objective meets corporate objectives
Gate 2. First screening	2. *Customer:* likely innovator acceptance 3. *Market:* size of potential market opportunity 4. *Strategy:* degree of fit to the project objective
Gate 3. Go to development*	Better estimates of 2 through 4 above, plus: 5. *Development:* technical feasibility 6. *Market:* feasibility of launch campaign 7. *Organization:* feasibility of organizational change 8. *Strategy:* level of competition expected, ability to capture profits and entry strategy
Gate 4. Go to commercialization	Better estimates of 2 through 8 above, plus: 9. *Customer:* likely acceptance by the mainstream 10. *Organization*: likely commitment of external partners 11. *Financial:* investment and return projections
Gate 5. Go to mass-market	12. *Momentum:* multiple measures of customer acceptance and market, financial and organizational performance during the initial launch

* For incremental innovations targeting markets that the firm understands, the Gate Committee can look at detailed financial projections (criterion 11) at Gate 2. For breakthrough innovations, they should do this later, as it is difficult, and potentially misleading, to make such projections until the innovation takes clearer shape.

Exhibit 3.5 12 key gate criteria.

testing and validation occurs throughout development, particularly within the framework of discovery-driven planning (see later). Pilot tests and test markets are also now a part of scale-up and launch, rather than a distinct stage, mainly so firms can achieve quicker time-to-market. As importantly, Stages 3, 4 and 5 acknowledge the need for organizational change, a key feature of current innovation.

Exhibit 3.5 shows the twelve key gate criteria that complement the stages and gates in Exhibit 3.4. These add to the standard criteria in the areas of organizational change and competition, while redefining the customer acceptance criteria to follow the ideas in Chapter 2.

The Governance Section of the Innovation Charter

Good firms reflect on and develop their stage–gate method so they can be as effective as possible with their innovation investments. Part of being effective is not only having a good method but also communicating to their people how this method should work and the criteria executives will use for decisions. Firms can achieve this transparency through the second, governance, section of the Innovation Charter. The first, strategic, section sets outs firm purpose, its growth targets and the role of innovation in meeting those targets. The governance section then complements this by setting out the stage–gate model and gate criteria that will apply to innovation projects. Taken together the two sections of the Charter make it clear where the firm seeks to innovate and how it will develop these innovations successfully. The Charter, and the active engagement of the leadership team, then helps everyone else understand both targets and the rules of the game.

Exhibit 3.6 lists the possible content of an Innovation Charter, divided between the roadmap and governance sections. The roadmap section partly builds on the work of Bart.[26] His research shows that while many firms have some formal policies towards innovation, most do not have a fully articulated charter. His research also shows that charters have positive impacts on innovation, both in the behaviour of employees and impact on the market. The governance section builds on the stage–gate discussion above and best practice in organizational transparency and fair process.

SETTING UP THE PROJECT AND DEFINING ITS OBJECTIVE

The Innovation Charter outlines general and specific objectives for innovation and governance procedures. The firm then meets these overall objectives through specific innovation projects. In turn, each of these projects needs setting up and its own objective defining. One important aspect of setting up a project is selecting the right team leader and team members to carry it through successfully. Chapter 4 will look at how firms select, prepare and support their innovation teams. Here we will assume the firm identifies a project that makes sense, chooses an executive sponsor for this project and appoints the project team leader and members. At which point it is also important the firm defines the project's objective well, and to do so the team should complete some preparatory research.

1. **The Strategic Roadmap for Innovation**
   a. *What is the purpose of the firm?*
      i. How the firm defines its purpose
      ii. The areas of business that fit this definition
   b. *What are the overall goals and strategy of the firm?*
      i. Brief link to current strategic plans
   c. *Where does innovation fit into the business and strategic plan?*
      i. The types of new products, services or business models that fit with the business and plan
      ii. The new markets or end-user activities that fit with the business and plan
      iii. The new technologies that the firm needs to fulfil its purpose
      iv. Any areas the firm wishes to exclude or avoid
   d. *What are the goals and objectives for innovation?*
      i. One compelling overall qualitative goal for innovation
      ii. Supporting general and specific qualitative objectives
      iii. Financial objectives, including:
         1. the gap innovation must fill to meet firm growth objectives, and
         2. the desired risk/return profile on projects
      iv. Non-financial quantitative objectives such as competitive position, market penetration, public image, et cetera.
   e. *What does the firm seek to leverage or develop?*
      i. Distinctive competences or competitive advantages
      ii. Fit with the firm's competitive strategy
      iii. Fit with the firm's values
2. **The Governance of Innovation**
   a. *Who is responsible for innovation?*
      i. The role of the CEO and CIO in innovation
      ii. The role of other members of the leadership team in innovation
      iii. The role and membership of the Gate Committee
         1. in particular how the committee judges projects and allocates funds across the portfolio of projects
      iv. The role of project teams in innovation
      v. The role of all employees in innovation
   b. *What are the procedures for innovation?*
      i. How projects start
      ii. Who selects sponsors, team leaders and team members and how does the firm do this
      iii. The firm's particular version of the Stage–Gate
      iv. The gate criteria the firm applies at each gate
      v. Budget procedures for projects
   c. *What is the mandate of project teams?*
      i. How the firm approves project objectives
      ii. How teams should work with the rest of the organization; including:
         1. how the team gets work done by other units, and
         2. seconding temporary team members
      iii. The responsibility and authority the firm gives to team leaders and members
      iv. Reward systems and career issues

Exhibit 3.6   The questions an innovation charter should answer.

Preparatory Research: Visualizing the End Point

Thorough preparation is necessary to translate the firm's overall goals for innovation into a specific objective for the project.[27] It is difficult to do this unless both sponsor and team have some depth of understanding of the market, and the likely challenges they will face. Setting a good objective requires information and thought. Informed managers with a clear objective in mind can then create ideas that have a good fit with firm strategy and customer needs. Uninformed managers, or managers with no clear objective in mind, create ideas with poor fit. Preparatory research also helps the team see the end-point they are aiming for with the innovation more clearly.

Preparatory research has several elements, loosely grouped into two phases. In the first phase, the team collects information on market trends, unmet customer needs, value chains and possible competition. All this information then forms the basis for the second phase of preparation. In this second phase, the team analyses and debates this information. They do so to (1) understand where it is possible to create new value for customers, (2) identify which alternative business futures are possible, and (3) develop a list of key assumptions that need corroborating.

For breakthrough innovation, the information collection phase may take some time. It should involve research on customer and non-customer needs using some of the techniques set out in Chapter 5 such as voice-of-the-customer or observation of customer experiences. For incremental innovation, the team also needs good customer insights and this may involve primary as well as desk research, especially if the firm has no recent market research on the target market. Understanding how value chains work also takes time and effort, as does looking at potential competition.

Note that all this is preparatory. The team does not put innovation ideas to customers or value chain partners or ask them for their ideas. It is far too early for that. A common mistake is to seize on an idea too early, before it has become clear what the other choices are, or indeed how to judge them. Innovation teams must avoid such mistakes. At this point, they are simply assembling a comprehensive picture of the existing and potential business, including any problems found in existing solutions or opportunities to create new value. The first stage at which to create ideas for potential innovations is Stage 2, not Stage 1. And the first time to decide which innovation will best fix customer problems or release new value is Gate 2.

The team uses this comprehensive picture in the second phase to produce a range of analyses, to clarify the objective of their project and to agree this objective with their sponsor. Three tools are useful in this phase, the strategy canvas, scenario generation and discovery-driven planning. This section briefly mentions these tools and the Toolkit at the end of this chapter outlines their application to innovation.

The Strategy Canvas

This idea comes from Kim and Mauborgne's *Blue Ocean Strategy*.[28] The strategy canvas is a simple representation of the value to the customer of all the potential features or benefits in a target market, both for current products and services and for potential innovations. Exhibit 3.7 shows the classic Blue Ocean example of *Cirque du Soleil*. The 'as-is' value curves (dotted lines) represent offers from traditional circuses before *Cirque du Soleil* came along. The 'to-be' curve (solid line) represents what could be, and was, done by *Cirque du Soleil* through innovation.

The strategy canvas and its value curves are a useful tool for considering which features of the innovation create real value for the target customer. This helps the team to focus on the features that add value and de-emphasize or

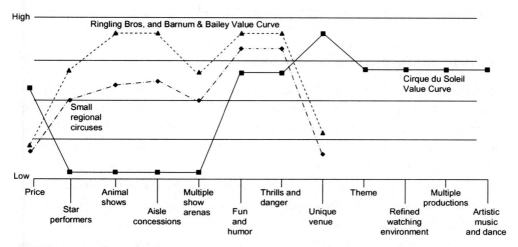

Exhibit 3.7 The strategy canvas of *Cirque du Soleil*.

Source: C. Kim and R. Mauborgne, *Blue Ocean Strategy*, Boston, Mass: Harvard Business School Publishing Corporatin, 2005, p. 40.

Reprinted by permission of Harvard Business School Publishing Corporation.

remove those that do not. This is a key contribution of Blue Ocean thinking. If the team creates new features, or increases performance on some existing features, while leaving others at current levels, this may simply add unnecessary costs and reduce profitability. For *Cirque du Soleil* some features of the traditional circus were removed (e.g. animals) and some de-emphasized (e.g. danger), to free innovation in other areas (e.g. artistic music and dance), while successfully improving profitability.

The strategy canvas is a planning and discussion tool that summarizes what the team understands about the target customer. Who are these customers? Chapter 2 suggests the first focus should be on the innovators, although an early view on the mainstream can also be helpful. At this early stage, the purpose of the strategy canvas is simply to guide the team in directions that add value to various customers and, in doing so, help finalize their project objective.

Scenario Generation

The other useful guide to objective setting is to generate scenarios using procedures from the scenario planning discipline.[29] For innovation development, scenarios are logical and believable stories about what the future market might look like. They are not predictions, they are simply sketches of what might be, but sketches in which the pieces fit together and the assumptions are clear. The vignette *Siemens paints pictures of the future* illustrates this idea.

Siemens paints pictures of the future[36]

Siemens is one of the world's largest electrical engineering and electronics firms and holds leading market positions in all of its businesses. Innovation is one of Siemens' traditional strengths, and the company classifies itself as a trendsetter. In the words of former Chief Executive Officer Dr Heinrich von Pierer: 'Predicting the future works best when you create and shape it yourself.'

To ensure it keeps ahead of the competition, Siemens has developed a method to choose the technologies on which to focus, which it calls 'Pictures of the future'. To paint these 'Pictures of the future', Siemens looks at developments of today's technologies in combination with systematically developing scenarios of the future. This method gives the company a clear idea of the best way to move forward by identifying promising trends, future consumer wishes and new business possibilities.

Siemens' vision of the future predicts driving forces and trends for the coming years in various areas. The main areas include information and communications, energy, automatic and control, transport, health, services and materials. In transport, for example, Siemens predicts the car will remain the dominant form of personal transport, with road and ship transport providing for the worldwide growth in freight. Governments and private firms will meet traffic demands by major investments in traffic telematics and highway construction.

The firm predicts that electronics will provide more help to drivers, including the in-car delivery of traffic reports, road signs and warnings of dangers ahead. As a result the number of electrical devices within cars will increase, and higher voltage power supplies will be necessary to improve reliability and reduce costs. New methods of fuelling cars will become more dominant in the market, as will environmentally friendly, lightweight materials and recycled parts.

For rail vehicles, magnetic levitation technology and automated freight transport will become more important. Recording of traffic flow in road and rail networks, electronic fare management and dynamic passenger information will improve the passenger experience. Systems for operations management, safety and computer-aided decision-making will improve central control of fleets. They will also allow automated, demand-driven rail operation and prediction of unforeseen events. Systems within vehicles used for public transport and freight will report problems to the head office to allow remote diagnostics and maintenance. Novel technologies will allow drive-through payment of tolls, and enforcement of emission controls will be easier through real-time monitoring.

Siemens updates these 'Pictures of the future' constantly to decide the technologies on which Siemens will eventually focus. The firm believes this method makes it easier to identify technologies with high growth potential and broad scope, and to anticipate future business opportunities.

Scenario generation complements the strategy canvas in useful ways. The strategy canvas addresses customer needs but these needs exist in a social or business context that is changing. The market into which the innovation launches may not be the market of today. Besides, the innovation itself may influence and change this market. Given the wide variety of social and business trends, and possible innovations, the team will be uncertain about the future. This is especially true for breakthrough innovations but even incremental innovations are uncertain because of the possible moves of competitors, increasing power of distributors, regulatory changes and so forth. Scenario generation helps to clarify which of the many possibilities are more likely. The other useful aspect of scenario generation is that it forces the team to debate their assumptions and in doing so differences of opinion about these assumptions become clear. That can then lead to further information collection or market research to test the assumptions. Such testing and refinement of assumptions is the central theme of the third tool here, discovery-driven planning, and so scenario generation can also provide some of the first inputs to that tool.

Discovery-driven Planning

The third tool in this section is one that can help the team throughout innovation development as well as with the preparatory stage. This is discovery-driven planning (also called assumption-based planning), a recent approach to planning that is gaining wide acceptance.

Discovery-driven planning has its origins in corporate ventures and suits innovation development well. However, as proponents of this method, particularly McGrath and MacMillan, note, it is different from traditional management planning.[30] In traditional planning, managers extrapolate in areas that they understand well and where the future is predictable. So they treat assumptions as 'facts' and are usually not caught out by this. However, this is the wrong approach to innovation plans. Breakthrough innovations may change buying patterns and may take several years to take off. Even incremental innovations may have areas of uncertainty such as competitor reaction, production efficiency or channel uptake. Treating assumptions as if they are 'facts' can be dangerous, especially in the early stages of development when the project team is often ignorant of all the implications of the direction they are taking. Discovery-driven planning is a systematic way to test assumptions and identify the dangerous ones. These can then receive more attention as the team seeks to validate or refine them.

The strategy canvas, scenario generation and discovery-driven planning all complement each other and help the team understand better the potential for innovation in the target market. All three also help the team visualize the end they are trying to achieve more clearly. Once the team has this understanding, they can move to the final step in preparation, finalizing their project objective.

Finalizing the Project Objective

At the end of preparatory research, the team can set the final objective for their project. Setting up this objective needs care. It should not be too narrow, thus stifling creativity or leading to the loss of major opportunities by the team. Nor should it be too broad, risking dilution of the team's efforts or making it difficult to identify suitable customers to involve in development. Thus, this objective needs broad discussion and a good degree of consensus before the next stage, as well as agreement from the leadership. The sponsoring executive can also play an important role in getting the objective right, especially if they have previous experience with innovation.

One classic example of such an objective is 'to significantly improve infection control in the hospitals of today and tomorrow at significantly reduced cost'. This example is from 3M.[31] It came about from 3M's wish to increase growth rates in their medical–surgical division through innovations that were more radical than in that division's recent history. The objective is not too broad, because it clearly identifies the customers (the hospitals of today and tomorrow), the area of innovation (infection control) and the requirements for value creation (improve infection control at reduced cost). Nor is it too narrow, because it leaves the question of how to improve infection control open to a wide range of possible innovations. Indeed, during Stage 2 the 3M team in question created several distinct and novel solutions that met this objective, including new products, services and business models.

ACTION STEPS: CLARITY OF DIRECTION, FLEXIBILITY OF ORGANIZATION

The action steps for the firm that follow from this chapter fall under the two headings of strategy and organization. *Strategy* consists of the critical task of developing the Innovation Charter and making sure everyone in the organization understands it. This charter follows from the firm's strategic plan and defines the portfolio of innovation projects the organization seeks. It also sets out the stage–gate method and decision-making criteria so all involved understand these. *Organization* includes key steps for the leadership such as forming gate committees, and selecting executive sponsors, team leaders and members for specific projects. Finally, each team needs to prepare for its project thoroughly so the final objective they agree with the leadership both fits the goals of the firm and encourages innovative solutions.

Firms should keep all this as simple and flexible as possible but pay careful attention to each task. Successful innovation does not need detailed policy documents, extensive bureaucracy or close and heavy-handed supervision. It does need a clear direction, transparent rules and attention to people. The ideas here apply to most companies and do not differ much by market or industry. Clear strategic direction, systematic decision-making procedures and careful project team selection are fundamental to well-run businesses in any industry. Stronger differences between firms may arise from their culture. Some firms have organizational cultures that support innovation, but many do not. Thus, when deciding who should be the project sponsor, gate committee or project team member, the firm's leadership needs to consider the surrounding culture carefully.

The main area that needs flexibility is in handling breakthrough versus incremental innovation. In essence, incremental innovation fits normal business methods whereas breakthrough innovation needs different rules, different people and a degree of protection from the mainstream business. Many organizations find it hard to allow this, but some flourish by allowing just such a diversity of approaches within the one organization. This diversity of approach should also reflect the nature of the challenge the breakthrough innovation represents. Breakthroughs on each of the three dimensions of customer, development and appropriation have different implications for leadership, personnel and procedures.

Different Types of Innovation Require Different Leadership

Firms should apply stage–gate methods differently for breakthrough versus incremental innovations. The stages and gate criteria remain essentially the same, but the firm needs to deploy its attention and resources differently for the two types of innovation.

First, at Stage 1, forming the right team is more critical to the success of breakthrough innovation projects than incremental ones. Developing breakthroughs often needs firm-wide cooperation and change – cooperation and change the right team members can make easy. This is especially true for innovations that provide a major development challenge around reorganization or need to draw on diverse sets of expertise. Similarly, innovations that pose an appropriation challenge will need some team members familiar with industry structures and competition, possibly with skills in understanding the mind-set of other players and negotiating with them. Finally, customer breakthroughs need customer-oriented team members familiar with techniques for understanding latent needs and the ideas of Chapter 2. Leaders need to consider the nature of the innovation carefully before selecting team members.

Second, the stages and gates critical to eventual success also depend on the nature of the innovation. For example, effective idea generation (Stage 2) and first screening (Gate 2) are more critical to breakthrough innovations than they are to incremental ones. This should not come as a surprise. The company has better knowledge of incremental than breakthrough innovation. It is therefore easier to create the next logical follow-on innovation and to evaluate its potential. Breakthrough innovation takes managers beyond their existing knowledge and therefore they need to pay more attention to creating enough ideas and to screening them carefully. There can be a tendency not to devote enough resources to this. This then results in too few ideas which, coupled with poor screening, allows weak ideas to pass through to the next stage. Overall, leaders need to ensure enough attention and resources are available for the early stages of breakthrough projects.

In contrast, the business case (Stage 3 and Gate 3) and commercialization (Stage 5 and Gate 5) are on some dimensions more critical for incremental than breakthrough innovations. This is chiefly because of the competition they face. Incremental innovations face incumbent competitors who are able to compete in similar ways to the innovating firm. Competitive analysis therefore needs to be thorough and the company needs to be sure it has an advantage over competitors before the innovation advances to development. At the commercialization stage, everything has to come together in marketing, sales and support to ensure the advantage translates into the competitive market.

Breakthrough innovations face less of a problem with competition, at least at the start of the new market. However, the circumstances they face depend on the nature of the challenge. For example, take the customer challenge of meeting the needs of non-customers. Here there may be no competition for some time. Given that the firm opts to pioneer, there may be breathing space to develop customer loyalty and improve cost structures ahead of competitive entry. Similarly, for an innovation with a low-cost business model, the incumbents are often unable to respond or match this model quickly. However, if this business model needs the distribution channel to cooperate, or indeed any other third party with complementary assets, the firm may face an appropriation challenge instead. It is not that the firm should ignore competition in either case, but that other factors are more critical to development decisions.

Finally, for launching breakthrough innovations, especially those involving new services or business models, the firm often needs to put significant resources into employee training. Training is necessary so employees understand why the breakthrough is important to the firm's success, and their role in delivering it. Training may also be necessary so they have the right skills, follow the right procedures and educate customers effectively. The exact content of the training may also depend on whether the main challenge of the innovation lies along the customer, development or appropriation dimension. Nevertheless, trained employees are better able to sell, deliver and support breakthrough innovations. This is less the case for incremental innovations. Both employees and customers are better able to understand these and the organization already has in place ways of delivering them. Training may still be necessary but not to the same scale as for a breakthrough innovation.

LINKS TO OTHER TASKS

The content of this chapter has three important links to ideas in other chapters.

Links to Chapter 4 – *Selecting, Preparing and Supporting the Right Team*. Chapter 4 looks more deeply into the issues first seen here, including which people the leadership should select as members of the team, and how they can encourage effective teamwork. The chapter also looks at how the team works with the rest of the firm. Chapter 4 mainly deals with the front end of development (Stages 1 and 2).

Link to Chapter 6 – *Changing the Organization to Deliver the Innovation*. Chapter 6 mainly looks at later stages of development (from Stage 3 onwards). Here the team may have to manage organizational change, either using the existing organization to deliver their innovation, or by creating a new business unit. Chapter 6 sets out the principles by which they can make these and other decisions.

Link to Chapter 5 – *Co-Creating Innovations with Customers*. The third link lies in a different area: customer needs. Teams need to explore these needs to finalize their project objective. By doing so, the team also identifies which customers to involve later in idea creation and solution development. Chapter 6 examines how best to involve customers, both during preparation and later, and the various methods available for doing so.

TOOLKIT FOR CHAPTER 3

The three tools for this chapter are the strategy canvas, scenario generation and discovery-driven planning. All three are important in helping the innovation team picture what they want to achieve with the innovation, and set up the right objective for their project.

Tool One: the Strategy Canvas

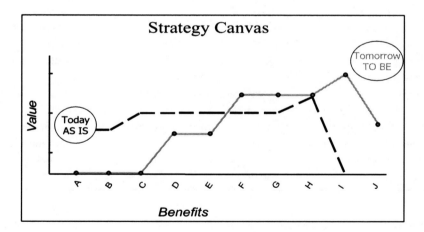

The six steps to draw a strategy canvas are as follows:

1. Define the target customer

The team should draw their strategy canvases for broad classes of customers. For innovation, the two obvious targets are the *innovators* and the *mainstream*, implying the team needs at least two canvases. The output from this step is a brief description of each target customer, which the team uses to guide the next steps.

2. Collect information on the market

The team should not draw their canvases in a vacuum. There has to be some preparatory research on the market and customers. This can come from discussions with experienced managers, previous market research or interviews with customers and experts.

3. Select the benefits to draw value against

The team should aim for a maximum of 10 benefits. If there are more than 10, the team should decide which 10 are best to include. The canvas should also allow space for creating and adding new benefits at Step 5. Note price is always one of the 10, although better restated as the benefit 'value for money'. The table below lists some examples of benefits.

Example benefits of products and services		
• Peace of mind • Quality of service • Breadth of service offering • Speed of delivery/ response • Efficiency/productivity • One-stop shopping/ single point of contact • Guarantees/service contracts	• Ease of use • Friendly staff • Provision of advice • Customer service for queries • Tailored services • Professionalism/knowledge of staff • Easy to comprehend during purchase • Transparency of fee structure	• Value for money • Environmentally friendly • Match to native language • Ease of access • Flexibility • Aesthetics • Geographical coverage

4. Draw the As Is curve

Team members then rate the value the current solution provides on each benefit using a simple scale from very low to very high. The reference point – average – represents market expectations. The current solution can be the firm's current offering, but for picturing innovations it is better to show the best product or service on the market.

The benefits go on the horizontal axis. They should be in order left to right, according to the value they currently provide. Thus at the left are benefits that currently provide little value to customers and on the right those that provide significant value to customers.

5. Eliminate, reduce, raise and create, and draw the To Be curve
The key debate the team should have is around how to change the value curve. Which benefits provide little value to the customer and can be eliminated or reduced? This can improve the profitability of the innovation. In contrast, where should the innovation provide more value to customers? Should this be by raising the value on current benefits, or by creating new benefits? This allows the team to draw the To Be curve – their vision of the value a significantly better product or service could provide.

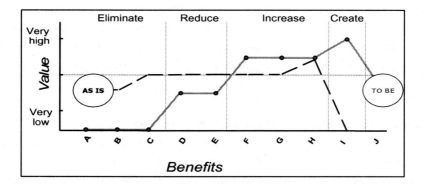

6. Verify the canvas
It is useful to verify the canvas with people outside the team. Mistakes are always possible, but more importantly this enriches the discussion around the canvas.

Key Source for Further Reference: C. Kim and R. Mauborgne, *Blue Ocean Strategy*, Boston, Harvard Business School Publishing Corporation, 2005.

Tool Two: Generating Scenarios of the Future Market

A scenario is essentially a credible story about a possible future. For innovation projects there are two reasons for creating several scenarios. First, these will widen the team's perspective on what the innovation might be. Second, they will allow the team to test how robust their innovation strategy is to future events. Each scenario therefore describes the possible future of the new market.

There are seven simple steps to building such scenarios.

1. Agree a timescale

The team needs to agree a common timescale for the scenarios. Normally this should include the time it takes to develop and introduce the innovation, and the time it takes to get sales take-off to the mainstream.

2. List all the driving forces

The team should produce a list of all the possible external forces that might impact on how the new market develops. These include regulatory changes, technological developments, social trends and competitors (within and outside the industry). Often this also involves some discussion of who might be the stakeholders in the new market, and drawing some broad boundaries around the exercise.

3. Identify the critical drivers and key events

The list of external forces is usually lengthy. The team should therefore work through these, asking two questions. Does the driving force have high impact on how the new market will develop? Is it difficult to predict the direction in which this force will evolve? The team should only keep forces that have high impact *and* high uncertainty.

The goal of this step is to identify two or three dimensions on which scenarios should differ. Either this comes about because two or three forces stand out, or sometimes the team sees that several forces correlate with one another and they can summarize them into one global dimension.

4. List all possible scenarios

The team then looks at all combinations of the dimensions to develop a list of all possible scenarios. For example, with two dimensions, where the force of each can be (unpredictably) either high or low, there would be four possible scenarios. With three dimensions, there would be eight.

5. Reject implausible or uninteresting scenarios

However, some of the possible scenarios would be implausible, uninteresting or go against important assumptions the team may have. So the team carefully reviews each scenario and rejects any like this. The goal here is to end with a few believable and interesting scenarios.

6. Develop the interesting scenarios in depth

The team then writes each of the remaining scenarios up in more depth. Each scenario needs a provocative title, an interesting theme and a lively writing style. The goal now is to make the team (and other people) think and that requires the story to grab their attention.

7. Draw conclusions

The final step is to go back to the reasons for doing the exercise, and ask two questions. What do the scenarios suggest about the design of the innovation? How robust is the strategy the team is proposing to future events? The team should debate this widely amongst themselves and with other people before writing up their conclusions.

Key Source for Further Reference: P. Schoemaker, *Profiting from Uncertainty*, New York, Free Press, 2002.

Tool Three: Discovery-driven Planning

Many innovations fail because of planning assumptions drawn from the experience of their managers, or analogies to other markets, which are wrong. Innovation is an inherently risky business, but firms can reduce their risk by adopting discovery-driven planning. Discovery-driven planning works backwards from a quantifiable target of success and tests assumptions continually.

Traditional management planning often does not check assumptions until the product or service has already gone on the market. In contrast, discovery-driven planning builds in checkpoints that enable gate committees to cancel or reconfigure projects before the firm commits to major investments. Discovery-driven planning revolves around four 'living' documents: the reverse income statement, the operations specification, the key assumptions checklist and the milestone-planning chart.

Reverse Income Statement

The starting point for any innovation project should be the reverse income statement. This sets a minimum target for the profit of the venture and planners work back from this to calculate the necessary sales figures, production and development costs to meet it. A simple reverse income statement might look something like this:

1. To meet firm objectives the innovation needs to deliver a 10% increase in the firm's total profits = €100 million
2. Assuming a 10% profit margin on sales this implies:
   a. Revenues of €1 billion
   b. Allowable costs to deliver a 10% margin = €900 million
3. Required unit sales at €100 per unit = 10 million
4. Which implies:
   a. 30% of the estimated potential market will adopt
   b. Unit costs no greater than €90

As the project advances and the innovation team gains more information, it will be possible to see at any point whether they can meet these conditions or whether the project needs rethinking.

Operations Specification

The reverse income statement drives a more detailed specification of all the activities the firm needs to make this innovation work. For example, and from the statement above, sales of 10 million units drive further assumptions about manufacturing (production capacity, employees), sales force (average order, calls by day) and so on. The operations specification lists separately all the resources the innovation requires and the targets the firm must achieve in each area of the business.

Key Assumptions Checklist

The core of discovery-driven planning is a checklist of all the assumptions about the project. One team member is responsible for keeping this checklist and for ensuring the team tests and retests each assumption as the project advances. Teams can test some assumptions with reasonable accuracy based on easily accessible and reliable data. For example, can we keep the unit manufacturing cost of a key part below a certain cost? Others are much more difficult, especially for innovations for which close comparisons do not exist. For example, what will the market demand for this innovation be in the first year? However, keeping and revisiting the checklist focuses the team's mind on getting the best estimates possible.

Each time the team modifies an assumption they recalculate the reverse income statement to see the implications.

Milestone Planning Chart

The team should also map out their milestones for the entire development of the innovation, from Stage 1 to Stage 4. This is essentially developing a more detailed project plan for each stage, identifying the important milestones within each. For example, receiving the results of market research in Stage 3 would be one milestone.

By mapping the key assumptions checklist against these milestones, the team can pinpoint major flaws in their thinking immediately. For example, they should test quality and materials cost assumptions at the prototyping stage. Some assumptions, such as market demand or profit margin, they will test repeatedly at several milestones.

Key Sources for Further Reference: R. Gunther McGrath and I. MacMillan, 'Discovery-Driven Planning', *Harvard Business Review*, July–August 1995. J. Dewar, *Assumption-Based Planning*, Cambridge UK, Cambridge Press, 2002.

CHAPTER 4

SELECTING, PREPARING AND SUPPORTING THE RIGHT TEAM

INTRODUCTION

The key to successful innovation is an effective project team. An effective team gains deep understanding of customer needs, creates and develops novel solutions to meet them and devises campaigns for successful organizational change and market adoption. Yet many firms pay inadequate attention to setting up and supporting their innovation teams. The consultants Katzenbach and Smith note that experienced executives often fail to act as though they value the work of their teams. Either they do not know how to get good performance from a team or, if they do know, they fail to do so.[1] As a result they often ignore basic principles such as setting a clear and distinct team goal, getting the size and the skills of the team right, or ensuring the team reports to the right executive. Others also point to the failure to provide enough resources for innovation teams, in people, time and money.[2]

Firms can address some of these failings through the Innovation Charter and the Stage 1 project setup. Innovation teams should be clear on their area of focus, the firm's goals for innovation in that area, and report to an innovation-oriented executive. So the key issues for this chapter more concern the size and skills of the team, and the type of team most suited to the nature of the innovation the firm envisages. Should the firm go for a *multifunctional* or *autonomous* team? Both these types of team have their proponents in the literature and among leading firms. Or, to raise another important debate, should the firm set up a separate business unit to develop the innovation? There are also experts for and against this course of action.[3]

Choosing the type of team is a critical decision, especially in a world where service and business model innovation is increasingly important. Several authors note that this places more of a premium on collaboration between the team and other parts of the organization, since the team alone will not be able to deliver the innovation.[4] Ancona and Bresman take this argument further by suggesting it is now necessary to rethink what we know about team performance.[5] The body of knowledge on team performance developed in a business environment where inwardly focused teams could flourish. Hence the emphasis the literature puts on the internal workings of the team, including building commitment and trust, using all the skills in the team, and so on. But is this knowledge still useful in a world where the team must work to overcome resistance and secure commitment from the rest of the organization? Changes in how firms innovate also require changes in our ideas about how to get the best from teams.

This chapter is organized as follows. The first section examines the various types of team that firms use in innovation. These include multifunctional, autonomous, x-teams and separate business units. The section looks at their strengths and weaknesses and what we know about their performance. It also looks at the fit of these team organizations to the new world of service and business model innovation. From this examination, the second section sets out a set of principles for selecting, preparing and supporting innovation teams. This section focuses on the role of the core team in the front-end of development (Stages 1 through 3). It addresses selecting the project sponsor, team leader and team, including criteria for selection such as diversity of viewpoint, collaboration skills and experience. The third section looks at how the firm can prepare a fully functioning team, by investing in their development and understanding the problems that may emerge. The fourth section includes a discussion of the key actions that follow from this chapter, including how these might vary according to the circumstances of the project. In particular, how radical an innovation the firm is developing, the primary dimension on which it is developing it (customer, development or appropriation) and the scale and scope of the project. The fifth and final section looks at the links between teamwork and other chapters. The Toolkit for this chapter provides a team selection guide, an agenda for their first meeting and a method for diagnosing the climate in the team.

HOW TO ORGANIZE TEAMS FOR MAJOR INNOVATION

Discussion here focuses on major innovation. This includes some significant incremental innovations but mostly concerns breakthrough innovations. The conclusion from best practice and research is that firms can handle more minor changes within their existing organization or through functional teams. The latter are temporary teams set up and working within R&D, marketing or production. They lead the change and only need minor support from other parts of the firm.

Instead, the real challenges arise when the innovation project represents a major change from the past and spans several areas of the firm. For the project to be successful, these areas need to cooperate and coordinate their activities. This will be the case when the firm cannot manage the project within the existing organizational structure, or needs to work more quickly than it can within this structure. And it will also be the case when success requires parts of the organization that do not normally do so to work together. In the 1990s, the idea of a multifunctional team became popular as a way of handling innovation projects like these. Indeed, by the late 1990s four out of five firms were using them for product innovation.[6]

Multifunctional Teams

A multifunctional team draws its members from all the functions or business units involved in the project. (This section uses the word 'function' for the sake of brevity, recognizing that this can include business units as well.) A team for a major product innovation might have members from R&D, marketing, production and finance. The role of these members is not to represent their functions in a formal sense but to bring the necessary expertise to the project. Their role is also to use their relationships with their home function to draw on functional resources. Multifunctional teams came into prominence for several reasons, but chiefly to achieve the necessary involvement and coordination between functions.[7] Imagine Marketing fails to do its homework on customers and does not spot the need for a feature in advance. Later, the team discovers that their prototype needs an extensive rework to incorporate this feature. Or imagine that R&D works by itself without consulting Production. Later Production finds it cannot make the product to specification or that it will cost more than it should.

In theory, the multifunctional team should solve these problems. R&D should push Marketing to do its homework thoroughly, and Production should tell R&D about the practicalities of manufacturing. By working closely together, each will challenge the other, bring its functional knowledge to the table, and use it to identify and correct problems in a timely manner.

Unfortunately, while most experts agree the multifunctional team is an improvement, it has not been a universal success. Some firms have received great benefit from it, but many have not. Here we should set aside evidence from firms that only paid lip-service to the idea, of which there were many.[8] For firms that tried to put this idea into practice, there are two main reasons for the mixed results.

First, it is not easy for a project leader to manage a multifunctional team. Leenders and his colleagues point to two difficult tasks: achieving the necessary cooperation between team members and integrating the various professional perspectives effectively.[9] Cooperation means the team feels they are working together well and can trust one another for advice and support. In general this comes about through interaction between team members and a clear common goal. However, cooperation has a dual nature that makes leading innovation teams difficult (and different from teams for other purposes). High cooperation results in good relationships, speedy decision-making and lessens conflict. Unfortunately, high cooperation can also result in compromise or groupthink. This is not what an innovation project needs in the early stages of development. In Stages 1 and 2 the team needs to keep an open mind and progress several alternative solutions in parallel. This can even extend to Stage 3 if the gate committee sanctions the team to develop more than one business case. So the team leader has to ensure the team keeps productive disagreement alive in the early stages, and prevent premature compromise or convergence.

The leader also has to ensure team members integrate and communicate with one another, rather than remaining too bound to their function, or communicating only with those they have most in common with. An effective team needs satisfactory communication between people with different perspectives, not people with the same perspective reinforcing one another. That sounds easy when the project team has five members but innovation teams often have many more, making it hard to avoid fragmentation into sub-groups. In reality many large teams reverted to something that looked just like the existing organization structure. And their leader became an increasingly powerless coordinator between team members answering only to their functional bosses.

This leads naturally to the second reason some multifunctional teams failed. It is not just the team leader's leadership skills that matter; the authority the firm invests in the leadership position is equally important. Many firms appointed relatively junior managers as team leaders, equal in status to their team members, but often lower in status than the functional bosses those team members worked for. If the bosses were behind the project this was not a problem; the project went well. However, if those bosses thought the project was a distraction or threat to their business, the team member became torn between the person controlling his or her career and the team leader. The boss often won in such circumstances, undermining the project.

A team with a junior leader is called a *lightweight* multifunctional team. The leader is a design engineer or product marketing manager, mostly working on coordination issues, and need not work full-time on the project. Team members, as well as bringing their expertise to the project, also act as liaison people for their functions, and do their normal job most of the time. This lightweight team can work well where the functional heads are behind the project or where the project does not demand much change in the way these functions think or work. However, if the demands of the project are higher or resistance is likely, another solution is necessary. This solution is Wheelwright and Clark's *heavyweight* multifunctional team.[10] Here firms replace the junior team leader with one drawn from the ranks of senior management and given equal or greater authority than the functional heads. The firm temporarily assigns some core team members to the project full-time and co-locates them with the leader. Thus, while their career development may still depend on their functional head, the team leader becomes the primary influence on their day-to-day activities. And these team members become much more than liaison people with their function. They become ambassadors for the project and responsible for getting what the project needs from the rest of the organization.

A more extreme version of the heavyweight team is the *autonomous* team. Here the core team members receive a formal assignment to the team and the team leader becomes their boss during the project. Their career development thus depends on the team leader's evaluation rather than an evaluation from their previous boss. The firm's leadership also gives the team leader formal control over the resources the project needs from other functions or business units. Finally, the autonomous team is often given permission to be different, that is, to create new organizational procedures and practices, including norms and incentives. Pushed to the limit the autonomous team could become a *greenfield* team, charged with building a new, separate business unit.

It is easy to see that, where the nature of the project demands it, the heavyweight or autonomous version of the multifunctional team offers many advantages. It can exert more influence on the rest of the organization and can use existing processes and resources effectively.[11] The autonomous team is free of the existing organization and so can be more enterprising. But both heavyweight and autonomous teams also have disadvantages, in that they need significant investment and a leader with the right skills and experience. What is more, the ties between the heavyweight team and the existing organization may preclude breakthrough innovation. The priorities and prejudices of the organization may prevent it, or influence the team towards an incremental solution. Equally, the independence of the autonomous team may lead to an innovation so radical that it will challenge the firm's capacity for change. Such an innovation may be difficult or impossible to bring back into the existing organization. This contrast between the risks of too little or too much innovation raises a major debate in organization design. Is it possible to develop breakthrough innovations alongside existing business or must the firm set up a separate unit to develop and commercialize them?

Breakthrough Innovation and Existing Business: Can Organizations Juggle with Both Hands?

Christensen argues that this decision hinges on values. By values he means the criteria employees use to set priorities.[12] If the existing business and the innovation team have (or need) different criteria, the firm should opt for the autonomous solution. In particular, Christensen argues that breakthrough innovations often dictate an *autonomous business unit*. For example, Compaq found it difficult to move into Internet retailing because their existing organization based its priorities on the needs of their bricks-and-mortar channel partners. Christensen argues that they may have done better to set up an autonomous Internet unit with a new brand. Other authors take this stance further. For example, Govindarajan and Trimble argue that strategic innovation always benefits from being organized as a separate business unit.[13] They call this separate unit NewCo to distinguish it from the original CoreCo. NewCo can borrow assets and resources from CoreCo but to be successful it must forget old assumptions, business models, and operational mind-sets. NewCo must also be free to learn about the new business.

Tushman and O'Reilly and colleagues take a different stance. They show that some organizations have ambidextrous organizational designs, managing both existing business and breakthrough innovation within the same business unit.[14] In their mind the key to success with these designs is the ability of an executive to handle relationships between different projects and the organization as a whole.

For example, one team might be focusing on incremental innovation, located within the main business and working under normal policies and reward systems. Team members would spend most of their time in their normal managerial roles and only work part-time for the innovation project. In contrast, another team might focus on breakthrough innovation. Here, the firm assigns some team members to the project full-time. The breakthrough team may also work from a separate location and under different policies and reward systems. But both teams, incremental and breakthrough, report to the same ambidextrous executive.

The advantage of this arrangement is the executive can shield the breakthrough team from the rest of the organization, giving them freedom and rewards to encourage creative thinking. Equally, the executive can help ensure that tensions do not grow up between the breakthrough team and others. This they do by communicating the reasons the firm needs the team to succeed, and by using their relationships with the rest of the organization.

By being responsible for more than one team the executive can also ensure that ideas flow between teams and that each team's objectives are clear to all. When the innovation is finally integrated into the main organization, the process will run more smoothly because everyone will be aware of the team's work. This focus on the ambidextrous executive in no way lessens the requirement for a heavyweight team leader for major innovations. The team leader still takes the central role in developing the innovation, while the executive provides support and counsel.

Tushman and O'Reilly's research shows that not only do ambidextrous organizational designs work, but for breakthrough innovations they often out-perform other solutions.[15] Interestingly, firms that successfully set up ambidextrous designs also show better performance in their existing business. This supports the conclusions of other researchers. For example, analyses of survey data show how firms that both exploit their existing knowledge base and experiment to develop new knowledge outperform those that do only one or the other.[16] As Tushman and O'Reilly note, making the two modes distinct – but connecting them through the firm's leadership – can reinvigorate the existing business as well as liberate the new. In their view, the innovation should only be spun off into Govindarajan and Trimble's NewCo when the team and its innovation can gain no leverage from the existing business. This is uncommon. In Tushman and O'Reilly's data, a breakthrough innovation needed to be spun off into a separate business in only one case out of 36.

Another point to make here concerns the timing of any spin-off. This is discussed further in Chapter 6. The conclusion there is that organizations are unlikely to spin out an innovation before the Gate 4 decision. Before Gate 4 the firm does not fully understand the challenges of commercializing the innovation. Also, any assessment of how much the innovation needs to draw on the existing organization, or how difficult this might be, is likely to be premature. Thus, for breakthrough innovation, an autonomous team reporting to an ambidextrous executive is a good solution for Stages 1 through 4. At Gate 4 the firm can then consider whether to set up a separate business unit to commercialize the innovation. The vignette *When the left eye knows what the right eye is doing* shows an example of how one firm innovates ambidextrously.

When the left eye knows what the right eye is doing ...[44]

When studying how successful firms with different organizational designs are with innovation, Tushman and colleagues found that 'ambidextrous' designs were more effective. CIBA Vision's development of a daily disposable contact lens provides an example of such a project.

The concept of a daily disposable lens was first raised at a meeting of the top management of CIBA Vision in 1992. Alan Fisher, head of central marketing, said that he believed such a 'breakthrough' process technology was needed for CIBA Vision to compete with its main rival Johnson & Johnson. The proposed project needed a major commitment in R&D and capital. Other members of the senior team wanted more extensive market research to be conducted before the company undertook such a financially demanding project. Some also feared that this type of lens would eat into CIBA Vision's own contact lens franchise. Further, a technical breakthrough in manufacturing would be needed to produce a daily disposable lens that was competitively priced.

To achieve the breakthroughs needed, Fisher recommended a different approach to the project from previous practice. He suggested creating an autonomous project team with a project leader who had full control over the entire project. And this leader was to report to the Operating Management Committee rather than R&D as before. The proposed team was to be responsible for all project and process development and would be unrestricted technically. Moreover, they would have an incentive package tied directly to commercial goals. Fisher also wanted to locate the team in Germany to take advantage of excellence in automation and optical engineering and to avoid the potentially restrictive influence of the current business.

The project leader was given dedicated resources and staff and the freedom to design the research unit with distinct competencies, cultures and processes. This manager reported to and met regularly with the ambidextrous general manager, Glen Bradley. Bradley was a senior leader of CIBA Vision, charged with directing both exploratory and exploitative subunits. Indeed, Bradley put forward the idea 'Healthy Eyes for Life' that provided an umbrella for both the innovative and conventional products. The research unit leveraged specific resources from the existing organization. For example, cross-product teams met to share material science expertise from their conventional products to speed up progress in the new daily disposable products.

Because of this novel approach, CIBA Vision launched its first one-day disposable contact lenses in 1996, setting new performance and price standards in the market. Between 1992 and 2000, the ambidextrous organizational design allowed CIBA Vision to develop several other successful innovations. These include a pharmaceutical product to stop progression of age-related macular degeneration (launched in 2000) and extended wear lenses (launched in 2001), besides producing incremental innovations in its conventional lenses.

Up till now, our discussion has implicitly assumed a team physically working together in one place and focusing mainly on product innovation. Indeed, until recently, these were the assumptions that underpinned the recommendations of both academics and practitioners. However, innovation has changed in at least two important respects. First, firms have become global and members of innovation teams are often separated from one another by distance and time zone. Developments in communication technology also now allow teams to work virtually rather than face-to-face. Second, service and business model innovations have become much more important. Prescriptions for team organization from a world of product innovation may no longer hold for these. Both of these changes have important implications for how firms set up and manage their innovation teams.

Globalization and Technology: The World of Teams Has Changed

The business press is full of stories about the attractions of developing markets or the pros and cons of outsourcing activities to various localities. Most major firms now work in many countries and have offshore centres of excellence, for example, centres for engineering in Germany or software development in India. These centres play an important role in innovation, raising the issue of collaboration and coordination across continents rather than within one country or building. Most firms make use of third parties to provide some part of their development activities, like design, prototype manufacturing or marketing support. These third parties are also spread around the globe. Innovation development now takes place on a global scale, placing even more demands on the core innovation team.

While the difficulties of coordinating global projects are obvious, there are many benefits. These include lower costs, the advantages of specialization or unique resources. But beyond these, Doz and his colleagues document how clever firms are taking advantage of new global knowledge,[17] mobilizing it to out-innovate their competitors. From this perspective a global project is far from a coordination problem: it is a distinct opportunity to do better. How does this innovative advantage work? First, a team might identify in one location an emerging customer need or new technology that has global application. Second, the integration of knowledge and skills from various localities contributes to better solutions. And third, the firm can use its global scale to commercialize the innovation to its full potential. Exhibit 4.1 shows how one firm's unique knowledge and skills are spread around the world.

In the new global world the core innovation team has to be globally aware; which has implications for team member choice and the team's work during Stages 1 and 2. The global capabilities of the firm and third parties come more

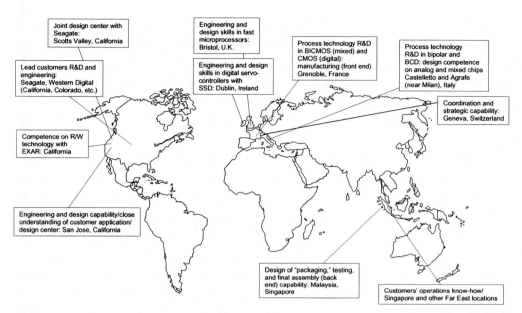

Exhibit 4.1   Knowledge dispersion profile for STMicroelectronics in HDD Electronics.
Source: Y. Doz, J. Santos and P. Williamson, *From Global to Metanational*, Boston, Mass: Harvard Business School Publishing Corporation, 2001, p. 16.
Reprinted by permission of Harvard Business School Publishing Corporation.

into play for Stages 3 through 6. What are the issues in doing all this well? Consultants identify two obvious and one less obvious risk in global innovation projects.[18] All three are risks that exist for non-global projects, but which global dispersion aggravates. The first obvious risk is that development times may slow unless the core team proactively maintains communication with and between the various localities. If this is not done, problems and inconsistencies only emerge at formal checkpoints, often calling for referral, rework and loss of time. The second risk is that, without frequent communication, various localities may follow their own goals without considering how these interact with the goals of others.

The third and perhaps less obvious risk concerns competitive advantage and intellectual property. If the team allows the pressures of global coordination to overwhelm its priorities, intellectual property or competitive capabilities can pass to third parties. This can also happen if the team gives too much licence to other decision-makers within the firm. The core team needs to decide what knowledge it should protect and what can be open to third parties. The team should take this decision during Stage 3 and seek approval for their intellectual property guidelines at Gate 3. This timing is apt because the team cannot specify the knowledge and skills required to develop the innovation until the idea takes shape. Only then can it decide what internal skills and knowledge the project will develop or use, or which third parties it will need to plug gaps or to gain specialized expertise. Once the gate committee approves them, the team needs to communicate its guidelines to all those it hopes to involve in developing the innovation.

Communication leads naturally to the topic of virtual teams. Can new communication technologies, such as the Internet and videoconferencing, overcome the barriers of distance and time? Researchers point out that, just as there is no such thing as a team that is always working together in physical proximity, there is also no such thing as a virtual team.[19] For most global firms, reality lies somewhere between the two extremes. Indeed, running an effective global project centres more on choosing a combination of face-to-face and virtual communication that makes sense for the particular project. How much time should the team spend together and how much apart? What technologies can they use when they are apart, or when they need to communicate with others? The main criterion in finding good answers to these questions is whether they improve the team's creativity.

Studies show that team creativity comes more from interaction between people, and less from the individual creativity of each member.[20] But as noted before, interaction can be a double-edged sword, as it can also bring about groupthink. Physical proximity thus increases the tendency towards groupthink, even if the individuals in proximity have different backgrounds. So the key to managing global projects is to balance physical proximity and global dispersion in a flexible way. Indeed research shows that high performing teams discuss face-to-face when they take complex multifunctional decisions, but use e-mail to resolve simple or single-issue decisions. Videoconferencing can also be a substitute for face-to-face meetings for complex decisions. With firms such as Cisco and HP working to advance holographic telepresence, videoconferencing may well play a greater role in the future.

Task structure also comes into this picture through the interdependencies between the various subprojects that are running across the world. If these interdependencies are strong, the core team will need to communicate more than they would on stand-alone subprojects. Equally, links will have to be set up between subprojects to ensure they communicate with one another effectively. The core team needs to understand the nature of the task structure and to develop a suitable strategy for meetings, delegations and links between sub-projects. The conclusion here is that, just as for intellectual property, the Gate 4 business case also needs to outline the team's project management and communication strategy.

Innovation is also changing, with greater emphasis on services and business models. These innovations often entail collaboration across the organization and with many third parties. Just what does this mean for the skills of the core innovation team?

Implications of the Change to Service and Business Model Innovation: Collaboration and the New Perspective on Teams

Ancona and Bresman believe various changes in the business environment, including those to do with innovation, have marked implications for teamwork.[21] They form these views from recent research on teamwork, as well as case histories of successful and unsuccessful teams. It is not that the prescriptions from an earlier age of teamwork are wrong; it is just that they are now only half right. Teams still need to focus on their goal, build trust among their members and assign responsibilities intelligently. But the *x-teams* that these authors recommend now focus as much on *external collaboration* as they do on these inward-looking activities. The evidence they provide shows that these x-teams outperform traditional teams in several dimensions.

External collaboration includes scouting for information, acting as ambassadors for the project to top management and coordinating the work of others. Scouting is synonymous with the Stage 1 setup and the Stage 2 generation of ideas. Coordination is synonymous with project and change management, especially during Stages 4 through 6. In these areas much of what Ancona and Bresman say is consistent with conclusions drawn before, as well as those to come in Chapter 6. However, they do add two important topics to the debate on effective innovation teams. These are (1) the role of ambassador and (2) the pressures of adding external collaboration to the team's demands.

Ancona and Bresman argue that marketing the project to top management and lobbying for resources is important for the success of the project. They also see upholding the team's internal reputation and keeping track of allies and opponents within the organization as equally important. Essentially, the team needs to nurture and defend its political capital within the firm's leadership.

Ancona and Bresman document instances where failure to do this leads to a downward spiral. Others within the firm interpret lack of information as lack of progress and opponents move into the gap with negative comments. The team begins to see the rest of the organization as the enemy, becomes even more inward-looking and progress does indeed slow because of internal debates. Finally, top management cancels the project because cancellation is the easiest route for them to take. These ideas are consistent with those of the change management literature in Chapter 6. Ancona and Bresman are therefore right to point out that teams should take the ambassador role seriously.

On the surface, the demands of adding external collaboration to the team's work might potentially cause overloads. This is Ancona and Bresman's view: they say the team must compensate through 'extreme execution' inside the team. That is, the team must do all its internal work more efficiently to leave time for external collaboration. But surely this depends on the scope of the project, the resources behind it and the sequence of events? For example, incremental innovations may need less effort on collaboration than breakthrough innovations. Or some project task structures may need more collaboration than others. Equally, if the firm wants major innovation it needs to put the necessary people and funds behind the project. Finally, for the core team, the traditional team-building phase logically occurs during Stage 1, leaving more scope for other tasks later. Thus the message to take from Ancona and Bresman's work is the team should explicitly add external collaboration to its project planning.

Another and different aspect of the new view of teams is creativity. Creativity can be defined as the ability to recombine existing ideas into novel combinations. The different perspectives and backgrounds of team members provide the raw ideas for innovation projects. And the team itself is the vehicle for recombining these ideas into valuable innovations. Thus teamwork experts stress the need for creative interplay between team members and underline the role of the team leader in promoting this. There are also many methods and tools the team can use to aid their creativity. These include group methods ranging from the venerable technique of brainstorming to more recent ideas like the slingshot.[22] They also include many analytical tools ranging from simply recombining existing product and service features to the complexities of the Theory of Inventive Problem Solving (TRIZ).[23]

None of this is new. However, more recently some experts have suggested an extra consideration. Just as cognitive psychology changes our views on decision-making and choice (Chapter 2), it also changes our views on creativity.

In particular, each of us sees the world through our own mental models built from experience, education and imagination. These models can help or hinder the progress of an innovation project. So people working on innovation projects need to re-evaluate, experiment with and if necessary reinvent their models. If the team leader encourages members with different models to challenge one another positively, a more powerful model can emerge. There is also the suggestion that teams should learn to value the views of radicals and extremists, rather than reject them, as commonly happens.[24] Extreme views help others re-evaluate and reinvent their mental models. Some experts go further, recommending that teams collaborate with creative thinkers drawn from the rest of the organization or from outside, including customers.[25] However, it is important to recognize that diversity and challenge are only valuable in certain areas, like understanding customer benefits or developing technological solutions. The team needs common mental models for their overall task and the ways in which they work together.[26]

ORGANIZATIONAL PRINCIPLES FOR INNOVATION TEAMS

The Core Team and the Front-End

In the mind of most, a team is a small group of people who work together until they achieve some common goal. The analogy of a sports team trying to win their league often comes to mind. However, while this is not a bad analogy for innovation teams, it breaks down in two respects. First, innovation projects can sometimes involve hundreds, if not thousands, of people. For example, take developing a new automobile or retail financial service. Such projects clearly involve many teams of differing types and durations, working to a common goal, but focusing on their particular assignments. So when we say innovation team we usually mean the *core* team leading the project and coordinating the activities of all the others. It is nevertheless important to remember that these others may form the majority. An innovation team is therefore both a team in the usual sense but also a project management organization. Second, even for the core team there is a distinct difference between their activities during the front-end (Stages 1 through 3) and those after (Stages 4 through 6). While the overall goal remains the same, the team's focus during the front-end is on creating a winning idea for the innovation. Subsequently their focus changes to turning this idea into reality in the market place. The front-end is therefore much more about two tasks, managing creativity and securing top-level support. The later stages are much more about project management, and are, of course, where the project begins to involve all those other people. For service and business model innovations the development stages are also often about managing change within the organization. Because of this difference in activities the rest of this section concentrates on the role of the *core team* during Stages 1 through 3. Chapter 6 looks at the later stages.

Since the focus here is on major innovation the assumption is the firm will dedicate a core team to be responsible for the project. Some of the team's members will work full-time on the project and some will stay with the project for its duration. Continuity is important in complex projects, both for keeping direction and remembering what the team learns. Several experts point to the stupidity of human resource policies that rotate or promote key team members on a faster cycle than the project itself.[27] This does not mean that all members will stay for the duration or that other people may not join the team temporarily – simply that a few key individuals are always members. These individuals keep the project on course.

Core Team Size

How big should the core team be? Research on teamwork in general (not specifically for innovation teams) suggest between five and 12 members. This is also the range consultants and team developers recommend,[28] although some would extend the maximum to 25.[29] And the ideal size that gets the vote of most experts is five or six members. Their argument is that with more than five or six members, social loafing or free-riding can happen; team discussion also becomes harder to manage. However, it is clear the ideal team size depends on both the nature and scale of the task and, as recent research suggests, the ability of team members to support one another.[30] Teams can be larger if they do not need to coordinate their work. Equally, teams can be larger if they develop strong relationships between members. There is less solid evidence for the specific case of innovation teams but what does exist is consistent with these views.

To express this another way, if the firm wants to set up a core team with more than five or six members, then it needs to invest more time and funds to developing good teamwork at the start of Stage 1.

There are two main issues in setting up the core innovation team. These are (1) embedding the project at the top of the firm and (2) selecting an effective team. Examining each leads to the basic principles for team organization.

Embedding the Project at the Top Level

Earlier discussion shows having top-level support for the project is as important to its success as good customer insight or effective teamwork. General support comes through the firm's Innovation Charter. However, support for specific projects hinges on a few people, in particular the executive who sponsors the team, the team leader and the gate committee.

Selecting the Project Sponsor: Ambidexterity and Political Capital

The project sponsor is the senior executive to whom the team will report. The sponsor will also mentor the team and help its relationships with the rest of the organization. Selecting the sponsor needs some care, but in most organizations the candidates for this role are obvious and follow the organization's hierarchy. Since these individuals are senior executives, they typically have the political astuteness to help the team and the competence to place the project in a larger strategic picture that others can grasp. The main question is whether the sponsor has the incentive and time to do a good job, which is an issue for the CEO, rather than this book. Occasionally organizations do strange things, like appointing a sponsor whose only incentive is to kill the project, or one already supervising 20 projects, but usually they avoid these mistakes. It is also important to have the right incentives in place to motivate senior executives to support innovation. These include common fate incentives determined, in part, by successful innovation. So assuming there are candidates with time and motivation, what are the characteristics of an effective sponsor?

Ambidextrous organizational designs have clear advantages for the front-end of innovation, if not beyond. Thus the sponsor's characteristics should include: (1) the mental flexibility to sponsor projects with different goals; (2) the ability to explain to others why each project deserves support; and (3) enough political capital within the firm to protect and nurture each project. Tushman and colleagues point out that in large firms it is also important they have a strong relationship with one of the top leaders.[31] That relationship can be important in providing added support for the project.

Selecting the Leader of the Core Innovation Team: Mental Flexibility

The right sponsoring executive is critical to top-level support but the team leader is the person who will bring the project to a successful conclusion. The first requirement for a major project is a heavyweight leader, that is, a manager with enough authority to carry out the project without frequent recourse to the authority of the sponsoring executive. Beyond authority, the temptation is to make a long list of characteristics for the job description – possibly so long that only a few outstanding individuals would qualify for the job. Indeed, some experts go down that road, looking at the many characteristics and knowledge areas the team leader should have.[32] While these lists deepen our understanding of innovation leadership, it is important to realize that all members of a core innovation team will need to display leadership in some shape or form. Indeed, when Stage 4 involves large numbers of people or changing the organization in some significant way, the team needs leadership from all of its members.[33] In these circumstances, firms are unlikely to appoint individuals with weak leadership skills to the core team, unless they have some valuable compensating skill or knowledge. In this context, the team leader does not have to do everything. So the real question is; what special competences, if any, does the team leader need besides the normal requirements for being a team member?

One way to identify these special competences is to look at the front-end tasks – and then ask what is uniquely the role of the team leader in these. From a previous discussion the team has to complete six tasks: (1) understand the area for innovation; (2) create a solution that meets the firm's goal; (3) preserve top-level support; (4) gain cooperation from the rest of the firm; (5) develop a business case, and (6) meet the project deadlines. Looking at these tasks it is clear they all need joint teamwork but more than one team member could potentially take the lead on each. For example, if a team member has a track record of putting good business cases together, why not delegate leadership on that to him or her? The same might apply to preparatory research or project management, in the sense of planning and coordination. To take another example, the leader will obviously play an important role in keeping top management support or gaining cooperation from other areas. However, other team members can also help here, and may take the lead in some circumstances.

So the unique role of the team leader lies less in the specific tasks and more in how they handle the different and conflicting nature of these tasks, and the way tasks change from Stage 1 to Stage 6. To do this well, the team leader needs to adopt different leadership styles as circumstances demand them. These include the leadership styles of:

1. *An ambassador:* ensuring the project gain supports from the organization, especially at the top levels of the firm, but also from other areas of the business.
2. *A business strategist:* helping the team complete structured, logical processes – such as the market analysis or business planning – thoroughly and accurately.
3. *A coach:* developing good dynamics among team members, from team formation to performing together on the project and all the steps in between.
4. *A creativity facilitator:* ensuring the team is creative, by managing divergent and convergent thinking and the differing personalities of team members, perhaps using unfamiliar analogies and tools.
5. *An explorer:* driving the team to complete its voyage of discovery, from receiving an unclear assignment – as it must be by definition – to building sales in the market through a concrete product or service.
6. *A project manager:* ensuring that a complex development project runs to time and budget, by making sure that many subteams and perhaps thousands of people coordinate their efforts to good result.
7. *A change agent:* where necessary, implementing an organizational change effort, requiring a parallel series of activities that fall under the rubric of change management.

Taken alone each of these seven leadership styles is familiar to most managers; taken together they suggest the leader should have some special competences. Buijs is not the first to point this out, but in using the analogy of innovation leaders as controlled schizophrenics he makes it most graphically.[34] Schizophrenics have multiple personalities. The team leader of an innovation project needs all of these styles. And he or she also needs to know when to use each style and how to mix them when necessary. That sounds a tall order but essentially it boils down to *mental flexibility*. The leader needs the mental flexibility to use

Stages \ Styles	Ambassador	Business strategist	Team coach	Creativity facilitator	Explorer	Project manager	Change agent
Analogy	*Diplomacy*	*Logical thinking*	*Coaching*	*Divergent thinking*	*Navigation*	*Coordination*	*Politics*
1. Project setup							
2. Idea generation							
3. Business Case							
4. Development							
5. Commercialization							
6. Mainstream market							

Exhibit 4.2 The seven styles of the core team leader (and when to use them).

these seven styles well. If the leader lacks the skills or tools in one of these areas, these can be learnt when preparing to lead the project. There is nothing in any of these areas that an able and educated manager cannot grasp easily. And in every one of these areas the leader should have back-up from one or more members of the team. But if the leader is too mentally rigid or one-dimensional in leadership style, he or she will not be able to meet the demands of a major innovation project. Exhibit 4.2 shows how the demands for each style might vary across the stages of the project.

Selecting Gate Committee Members: Objectivity and Balance

The role of the gate committee is different from that of the project sponsor or leader. While its members may change, the committee itself is a permanent body and plays a critical role in the firm's innovation strategy. The gate committee is the group of executives and senior managers responsible for vetting innovation projects and deciding what resources to devote to which projects. They do this at each project gate, carefully balancing the investment necessary to go to the next stage against the likely returns of the final innovation. They are also responsible for the big picture, that is, for deciding which projects make best strategic and financial sense for the organization, given its purpose and strategy. This committee draws its members from the existing hierarchy of the organization, particularly senior management and executive levels.

Firms need to select gate committees with care, especially when encouraging breakthrough innovation. For example, if the members of the committee are executives solely rewarded for existing business performance, then they may unduly favour incremental projects. There is a case for making the leader of this committee the CEO or the chief innovation officer (CIO). The committee leader then has enough authority to manage conflicting interests and ensure the right balance of different types of innovation. And it is the CEO, in consultation with the CIO, who should choose the members of this committee. Following from Chapter 3, and the goals of the stage–gate method, the CEO and CIO should choose members who can be thorough and objective. They also have to be flexible enough to assess a mix of projects, using different approaches for incremental versus breakthrough innovations. Having the right gatekeepers is clearly critical to achieving the firm's goals.

Selecting an Effective Team: Compromise Intelligently, in Stages

There are many considerations in selecting the right team members for an innovation team. These include diversity, external collaboration, the three challenges inherent in innovation (customer, development and appropriation) and team member experience. Balancing all these considerations is not easy, reinforcing the conclusion that firms should invest in setting up projects correctly. The sponsoring executive, the team leader and the gate committee should put enough time and effort into this.

Selecting for Diversity of Viewpoint

Diversity helps creativity by bringing different experiences, perspectives and mental models to team discussions. Individuals have different types of intelligence and talent, all of which can contribute to the team's efforts. If the goal of the project is breakthrough innovation, include in the team some people – perhaps outside consultants or managers known for their creative thinking – with unusual or extreme (business) views. Combining people from different areas of the business also helps to provide the broad expertise necessary for such projects. And it helps to keep links with the rest of the business, which will prove important as the innovation goes into development. If the firm is global in scope, some team members should know about the firm's centres of excellence around the globe.

Selecting for External Collaboration

Another important consideration concerns the relationship skills and social capital of team members. Relationship skills allow the team to work together effectively and increase its likelihood of gaining the support of the rest of the organization to complete its task. Social capital means team members have credibility within their area of expertise and perhaps across the firm. Both skills and capital help with external collaboration. For example, suppose the support of the information technology (IT) department is going to be critical to an innovation, as it will often be for service and business model innovations. In that case, the team should include an IT manager who has not only technical competence but also good relationship skills. This individual will be the *ambassador to IT* and can seek out and involve other members of IT as necessary.

While not all team members need to be ambassadors, some do. Some also need to be spokespeople. This is the internal marketing job. The team must make sure the rest of the organization is aware of its project, recognize its importance and understand that their involvement and contribution to the project's success is welcome.

Selecting for Customer, Development or Appropriation Expertise

Some members of the team need to have experience of potential customers and insight into their needs. Understanding the innovation from the customer's view is an important part of creating value. So, an innovation team should include at least one customer-facing member, preferably more if team size and other selection considerations will allow. These individuals will often come from a marketing role. However, their empathy and experience with the target market are more important than their job title or function. They need to be open-minded and willing to listen to customers and colleagues. They also need to be persuasive and to make sure the organization understands the view of the customer.

If the innovation includes services, the team might usefully include a front-line manager or employee, especially if good service will result from interactions between front-line employees and customers. In this case, choosing the right employee will bring the relevant customer insight into the development process from the start.

While customer focus is a necessity, selection should also address the other two dimensions of innovation. These are development (technology and organization) and appropriation (business model). If the innovation is likely to require significant technological developments for the firm, major organizational changes or new business models, the team should have some members with the relevant expertise. While it is not always easy to identify this expertise at the start, the general area of innovation itself should provide enough guidance to select the core team.

Selecting for Experience with Innovation

Some companies select team members who have a track record of previous experience with innovation, possibly those who have graduated from smaller to bigger projects over their career. This experience is useful to the team because it takes time for a person to become effective at innovation development. For example, experts on the various innovation tools, such as the strategy canvas (Chapter 3) or voice-of-the-customer (Chapter 5), say it takes most managers two or three applications of the technique to grasp and use it effectively. It therefore makes sense to select some team members with previous experience of these and other techniques.

But there are three qualifications to this argument. First, if the firm applies the criterion of experience too strictly it risks creating two classes of manager – those who have fun with innovation projects and those who grind away at normal business.[35] This might create resistance to the innovations the team develops. Firms should strive for balance by including some people who have experience of innovation and others who, while they have something else to contribute to the team, have little or none. Second, managers gain experience through failure as well as success. Everyone knows that innovation is risky and that projects will fail despite the best efforts of talented managers. There is a strong argument for considering talented people whose previous projects failed for reasons beyond their control. After all, they may help to identify and resolve a fatal flaw in the next innovation. Third, the membership of the core team can change by adding temporary members as the project advances. For example, if the team wants to use voice-of-the-customer, but lacks experience, they can add a temporary member for Stage 1. They can do this either by finding a manager who has the necessary experience or using a consultant as instructor. Similarly, organizational change does not become an issue until Stage 4. If the team lacks experience in doing this, it can add a temporary member in Stage 4, most likely a consultant. Later, as launch approaches, the team may consider adding other members. For example, a learning development manager to design and manage training programmes for a new service.

Selection Is Always a Compromise

Clearly balancing all the various considerations in team selection is not easy, especially within a team of five to 12 members. The list of possible considerations includes diversity of perspective, social capital, global knowledge and previous experience with innovation. It also includes expertise in the customer, development and appropriation challenges of innovation. While some members may have more than one of these desirable qualities, selection is always likely to be a compromise between the ideal team and the talent available. An added difficulty is the project sponsor and team leader may not be sure of the ideal skills and background for the team at the start of the project. The full requirements will become clearer only as the team defines the innovation more sharply.

This suggests the project sponsor and team leader should take two steps *before* selecting the team. First, define the essential skills the team will need to start work. At the minimum, this definition should include the customer insight and external collaboration skills that are relevant to the area of innovation. It should also include a statement of the different mental models whose interplay might spark the creativity of the team. Second, undertake a full scan of the people who could be potential team members. In firms with high-level human resource (HR) managers, who are familiar with the pool of talent, they can do this in partnership with HR. In firms without these HR managers, more homework will be necessary by the sponsor and leader. Once the sponsor and leader identify potential team members who fit their definition, selection of the initial team can begin.

Who should not be a team member? Well, there are obvious candidates; managers who are too conservative, have too many incentives to keep the status quo, or who are neurotic and likely to impede teamwork. But as well, innova-

1. Internal teamwork is undoubtedly important. But core teams for major innovations should give equal emphasis to collaborating with the organization at large and managing their project through external subteams and partners.
2. Core teams normally have five or six members. If necessary they can have more, but in that case the firm should put extra investment into team building during Stage 1.
3. There should be a strong connection between the core team and the firm's leadership. The executive sponsor and the team leader provide the main links, but there should also be a professional relationship with the gate committee.
4. As well as leadership skills, and strong competences in one or more disciplines relevant to the innovation, the core team leader should have the mental flexibility to use the seven styles well – that is, ambassador, business strategist, team coach, creativity facilitator, explorer, project manager, change agent.
5. The sponsor and leader should select team members to balance three criteria, namely: different viewpoints on customers and solutions, skills for external collaboration and experience with innovation. In addition, while innovation teams should always have members with a customer focus, team composition may also need to reflect the relative emphasis on the other dimensions of innovation (technology or organization).

Exhibit 4.3   Five organizational principles for core teams.

tion teams should not include senior executives. Senior executives lack the time to be effective team members and often confuse the purpose of the organization with the purpose of the team.[36] They can also dominate other team members through their position of authority.

All in all, team selection requires a large investment by the firm, especially the time spent on it by the sponsor and leader, and other executives and managers. This is correct: after clarity on the firm's strategic goals for innovation, selecting effective teams is the next most important step toward success. Exhibit 4.3 summarizes the five organizational principles firms should follow in setting up core teams. The first tool in the toolkit for this chapter also turns these principles into a selection guide.

SEVEN PRACTICAL STEPS TO DEVELOP TEAMWORK

Investment should not stop at team selection. The sponsor and leader should launch the project correctly. This includes the normal steps, such as effective briefing from the sponsor about why the project is important to the firm and what the team's goals might be. But it also includes early attention to team building. If a team of people with different perspectives and talents is to move beyond existing business and create something new, then it must work together effectively. If it cannot, the pressures of dealing with an innovation that is important to the firm will aggravate common team failings. Lencioni lists these failings as lack of trust, fear of confrontation, absence of commitment, absence of accountability and failure to focus on goals.[37] For innovation projects, three items need adding to his list: failure to be creative, failure to gain top-level support and failure to listen to the customer. Which leads to seven practical steps firms and teams can take to avoid these failings. These steps draw on the work of Lencioni[38] and other teamwork experts but adapt this to building innovation teams.

Step 1: The First Meeting

Firms should devote at least two days to a first off-site meeting of the team. This is a significant but necessary investment. The purpose of this meeting is to introduce team members to one another in depth, review the assignment and begin to build trust within the team. Since the goal here is innovation, a major part of the time should be spent discussing three key topics. These topics concern how the team can: encourage the creativity of its members; gain the support of the rest of the organization; and go about conducting the preparatory research outlined in Chapter 3. This first meeting can be led by a professional trainer, the core team leader or together. The leaders can also use various team-building techniques within the context of these three topics above.

Typically, team members prepare for this meeting by completing diagnostic questionnaires about their individual or group styles and behaviour. They then share the findings at the meeting as an aid to assigning team roles, at least initially. Many managers are familiar with standard organizational consulting approaches using the Myers–Briggs Indicator or Belbin Team Role Inventory. However, the validity of these has been questioned by academic research, and some experts argue the Big Five personality inventories mentioned in Chapter 2 are more valid and useful than these standard approaches.[39] The vignette *The project will kick off at 9am* describes how a firm might approach the first meeting. The toolkit for the chapter also provides a template for the agenda.

The project will kick-off at 9am[45]

SportTech Ltd (a subsidiary of MobyCorp) has decided to create a techno-logical solution to the problem of deciding when the ball has crossed the goal line in football. The CEO identifies a sponsor for the project, and both executives then identify and appoint a Team Leader (TL). They give this

TL authority to pick and lead an innovation team to realize SportTech's objective.

For the project kick-off meeting the TL is joined by the key players she selects from R&D, production, marketing, finance and IT, both in person and by videoconference from other MobyCorp offices. Although this is the first time the team is to meet to discuss the innovation, the project started several weeks ago. Already the TL and others have put in many hours of preparation work to ensure the kick-off meeting launches the project on the right foot.

Since being briefed by the sponsor, the TL has thought about the goals of the project, identified team members, compiled a list of assumptions about the project, and worked up a preliminary plan. She has subsequently met again with the project sponsor and together they have defined in specific terms the key success factors relevant to each team member.

In scheduling the kick-off meeting, the TL took care to find a date and time when all the core team members could attend, not allowing anyone to catch up later. She also took time to impress on everyone how important their commitment to the project is and to ask them to complete their diagnostic questionnaires. In advance, everyone receives a pack of materials, including agenda, team contact details, background information and draft project plan. There are clear instructions to everyone to review their part in it and to reflect on the results from their questionnaires. The day before the TL conducts a final review herself, rehearsing how she will present the agenda and noting the most important points she needs to make.

All the preparation pays off when kick-off arrives. The TL is on top of the project and drives the meeting with authority. She takes the team step-by-step through the overarching business goal of SportTech and the draft project plan, fixing the timeline and highlighting the key factors for success. Team members introduce themselves to one another thoroughly, building in part on their questionnaires. The team then decides the roles and responsibilities of each member in a way that empowers rather than directs.

With the confidence and good humour born of thorough preparation, the TL is able to keep the meeting flowing. She anticipates tricky questions and prevents proceedings becoming bogged down in unnecessary detail that can be dealt with later. The agenda closes with a team-building exercise that demonstrates some of the principles of effective collaboration, pairing off particular team members who will need to cooperate closely.

By the end of the meeting no one is in any doubt that they are embarking on an important and well-planned project that has a good leader at its head. This impression is reinforced when a thorough but concise set of minutes appears in their inboxes the next day. These itemize each team member's actions and provide the schedule of future meetings. Game on.

Step 2: Develop a Schedule for Building the Team as Well as Project Work

Set up a schedule of meetings where the team devotes time not just to their project but also to reflecting on and assessing how their team is working as a whole. For example, a two-day quarterly review meeting might take place off site. On the first day the team reviews its progress on the project, and on the second day it reviews its progress as a team. There are now approaches specifically designed for monitoring progress and diagnosing problems in *innovation* teams. These include the Team Spotter's Guide[40] and Team Climate Inventory (TCI).[41] Both can provide useful material for the team progress review and the toolkit outlines the TCI in more depth. The need to monitor and improve teamwork never disappears, but after two or three such reviews this should not require as much time in the schedule.

The difference in the team's activities between the front-end and later stages suggests it is useful to hold another off-site meeting after Gate 3. This meeting would be to reinvigorate and refocus the team, include any extra members the team needs for the later stages, and say farewell to any members whose work is done. The meeting should also celebrate the team's success in getting the Gate 3 approval for developing the innovation. This is a major milestone in its project.

Step 3: Make Sure Each Member Gives Adequate Time to the Project

Experts raise time commitment as a major issue for most firms. There seems almost a universal tendency to over-commit among individuals and organizations. For major innovation projects, the assumption is that some members of the team will work full-time. Their time commitment is not an issue. However, other members are likely to work on the project part-time and have other responsibilities for the rest of their time. For part-time members, time commitment is a major issue the core team should address early on.

The project sponsor and team leader should make sure these part-time team members have enough time for the project and that their superiors fully support them. If the project is going to take one or two days of an individual's time each week, the organization has to ensure that other tasks do not distract them during those days. While innovation projects often become so interesting that people choose to work on them at night or on weekends, this way of working is not sustainable. Most of the project work should be done in normal working hours.

Step 4: Ensure Adequate Face-to-face Contact in the Early Stages

The firm should locate the core team together in the same workspace or, if this is not possible, ensure there is the time and budget for them to meet face-to-face regularly. This is not just for scheduled meetings, but also for working sessions and chance encounters. Videoconferencing can be successful but some aspects of both team building and innovation need physical proximity. In particular, building trust and encouraging creativity need face-to-face meetings. Both can result from team meetings but are also sustained by less formal exchanges between individual members. Preparatory research may also require team members to be able to work closely together; to understand ambiguous data, interview customers jointly, seek assistance, and so on.

The need for face-to-face contact is greatest during the early stages of the project. In later stages the team can use videoconferencing, telephone, e-mail and project websites. Indeed as the core team may increase in size, and will work with many other individuals and subteams, efficiency dictates this.

Step 5: Agree the Project Dashboard

The team should agree from the start on a simple set of performance metrics. They can build these into a project dashboard and use them to track their progress over the project. The dashboard provides a visual tool to see what stage they have reached and helps to identify the areas that need more or less effort in the next phase of the project.

Discovery-driven planning (Chapter 3) can form the basis for this dashboard. One part would summarize the team's current reverse income statement, including questions and actions necessary to improve their estimates. Another part would list the key assumptions relevant to each stage of the project and the team's progress in checking them. As the project advances the team can add a third part that begins to lay out the pro forma operations specification, and a fourth that begins to list organizational change issues. As noted before, these are all living documents and a team member should take responsibility for maintaining them.

Step 6: Making Sure the Team Focuses on the Customer

An innovation team will always include one or more individuals with customer expertise. However, it is important that *all* members of the team have exposure to target customers and develop a good understanding of them. Innovation teams create advantage when they combine their firm's strengths with a thorough understanding of the customer, and so develop a compelling innovation for that customer. It is difficult to see how the team can delegate all of that responsibility to the sole marketing manager on the team. Instead it needs to be a team effort. So, the sooner the project team gets out into the market and starts to develop the necessary understanding, the better.

What may be less simple is to make sure the non-marketing members of the team understand how customers adopt breakthrough innovations. In particular, how adoption works for their target market. Without a common language it is difficult to see how technologists and marketing people, for example, can work together effectively. Besides, unless this common language reflects the realities of adoption in the specific market, it is unlikely that a useful innovation will result. The team should therefore develop their own model of adoption by adding market-specific details to the general framework in Chapter 2. For example, they should decide what the important gains and losses are to various customers, and what customers will compare innovations to.

Step 7: Ensure Thorough Preparation

The nature of preparatory research is discussed more extensively in Chapter 3. To summarize, preparation entails gathering internal and external background material and discussing the project with experts and other useful sources of advice. It also involves gaining the necessary customer understanding. However, the main point to make here is that preparation is important to good team decisions and creativity in Stage 2. Contrary to popular myth, creativity does not spring from a vacuum; it comes from deep immersion in the subject matter.[42] Here that subject matter includes all that is relevant to the particular area of innovation, as well as a general understanding of development and research methods.

ACTION STEPS: INVEST IN THE TEAM

The key conclusion of this chapter is the firm needs to select, prepare and support the team carefully. Only in that way can the team become an effective engine for the desired innovation. None of this can be done quickly or casually. It requires consultation, debate and deliberation within the leadership of the firm, and strong guidance from the CEO and CIO to ensure alignment with the innovation goals of the firm. Stage 1 – *Project Setup* – is so critical to success that it is worth this investment, especially of executive time.

The main principles for setting up the team should be to:

1. Choose an executive sponsor who can gain support for the project among his peers. Preferably one who can guide both breakthrough and incremental projects, and who can capture and share lessons across the firm.
2. Assign the team leader role with enough authority to get the project done. Then choose a leader who also has enough talent and credibility with the rest of the organization to use this authority effectively. The core team leader also needs the mental flexibility to use the seven styles of innovation leadership well.
3. Choose the remaining members so the team has a good balance of diversity of thought, external links, expertise and experience.
4. Develop teamwork properly during Stage 1 by taking the team through the seven steps. This should preferably be done with support from executives with experience of innovation, as well as professional trainers.
5. Gate 3 approval marks an important point at which to reassess and change team membership and mode of operation.

However, the precise implementation of these steps will differ according to circumstances, depending on three factors: how radical the innovation is; which of the three innovation challenges is the main focus and the size and scope of the project.

Breakthrough Innovations Need Autonomous Teams

Innovations the existing organization may resist, fail to understand or fail to prioritize enough, require an organizational solution outside normal ways of doing business. This is most likely for breakthrough innovations; including new-to-the-customer, major technological or organizational change, and architectural disruptions. Here an *autonomous* multifunctional team is likely to be the best way forward. Autonomous teams have members who report to the team leader rather than the function or business unit they came from. So the strongest influence on the career progress of individual members is the team's performance and their part in it. These teams still need to collaborate with the rest of the organization but are more able to focus on their priorities rather than those of others. Further, firms can authorize teams to obtain resources from the rest of the organization. Here the executive sponsor protects and nurtures the project, while working at the top level to ensure the necessary cooperation is forthcoming.

In contrast, the firm can achieve major incremental innovations through a standard (*heavyweight*) multifunctional team. Here people in the existing business will understand the innovation and readily see that it builds on current ways of doing business. In a standard team, the functions or business units of each member still have the strongest influence on their career and most still formally report to their functional boss. However, there will be fewer conflicts because the innovation extends existing business, and people in that business will see working on the project as a legitimate task.

The firm's leadership should decide between the two forms of multifunctional team once they identify the area for innovation and their objective for that innovation. For one example, creating a new market with the goal of building large revenues in five years would suggest an autonomous team. For another, substantially upgrading product benefits in an existing market would suggest a standard team. This early decision is necessary because the choice of one form of team or another influences the leadership's selection of both executive sponsor and team leader. Once they make these selections it is difficult to undo them.

Thus the leadership needs to exercise careful judgement about the degree to which the eventual innovation will or will not fit into the values, procedures and priorities of the existing business.

Customer, Development or Appropriation: Team Membership Should Reflect Focus

Innovations can focus on one or more of the three challenges, or on some mixture of these. And the specific challenges an innovation faces will determine in part team membership. Innovation teams whose primary focus is on the customer will have more customer-facing members. Innovation teams whose primary focus is on technological breakthroughs will have more members with technological expertise. Some experts call these variously 'market attack' and 'technology attack' teams.[43] Equally, teams whose focus is to deliver a new service or new business model may place more emphasis on organizational change than the market or technology. An 'organizational attack' team perhaps?

The difficulty here is the team may not know the relative focus between the three challenges at the start of the project. Indeed, solutions with different focuses may well emerge from idea generation, or the weight of each challenge may change in the team's mind between gates. This argues for keeping flexibility in team membership, while preserving continuity and consistency of purpose through core members. For example, suppose a team with a customer focus finds later the organization will need to change to deliver this innovation? If so, their business case to the gate committee at Gate 3 should recommend that change experts or consultants join the team for Stage 4.

Scale and Scope Dictate the Need for Skills in Managing Complex Projects

Many of the writings and recommendations on innovation assume the core team does most of the intellectual development of the innovation. Others outside the team may contribute but this is a minor part of the overall work. A partner from a market research agency might present some customer data, or a manager in another part of the business might contribute some ideas. But the team itself does most of the work in developing the innovation from idea to full specification. This is true for many innovation projects.

However, the reality is that many other projects involve hundreds or even thousands of people from the firm and partner organizations. Some of these people also develop the innovation, often working in subteams around the globe. For projects like these, the core team's role becomes as much project management as development per se.

Where the project is large in scale and scope the core team needs skills in managing complex projects, especially from Stage 4 onwards. But arguably the team also needs these skills at earlier stages. In particular, their Stage 3 business case should accurately reflect the size of the challenge so the gate committee understands the commitment it is making. People lacking experience and expertise in managing large, complex and global projects cannot do this well. So, in these cases the team should include people with this expertise from the start.

LINKS TO OTHER TASKS

In an important sense the ideas in this chapter underpin all those that follow. Core team members are those who will create the innovation and lead and manage its development and launch. Their selection and preparation is therefore critical to success, as is the support they receive from their sponsor and other leaders. The Innovation Charter in Chapter 3 is part of that support, while the stage–gate and the gate committee provide an organizational framework within which to pursue the goal the firm gives them. However, beyond this, the content of this chapter has one other link that is worth special mention.

This is to Chapter 6 – *Changing the Organization to Deliver the Innovation* – a chapter that concerns mobilizing the organization as a whole behind the innovation. Here the sponsoring executive and the project team may have to manage organizational change, especially if the innovation involves new services or business models. Chapter 6 looks at how to assess the degree of organizational change necessary and how to develop an effective strategy for achieving that change. It also looks at how to carry out this strategy as the firm scales up the innovation, especially for complex projects involving many others beyond the core team.

TOOLKIT FOR CHAPTER 4

The first two tools for this chapter are straightforward and easy to apply. They consist of a team selection guide and a possible agenda for the first meeting of the team. Their purpose is chiefly to remind managers of the key steps in selecting and preparing teams properly for the front-end of the project. Readers should take these as simple templates, which they may need to adapt or expand to their own circumstances. The third tool provides diagnostics for checking the work climate in the team. This allows the team leader to assess and intervene if necessary to make sure the team remains productive and creative throughout the early stages of the project. Here only a short introduction is given, readers need to get the questionnaire instrument and the accompanying manual from the original authors. The benefit of this tool is that it is designed for innovation teams.

Tool One: Team Member Selection Guide

Step 1: Decide the Focus of the Project

Is the main challenge the customer, development or appropriation? What is the likely need for major changes to the organization? If there is more than one challenge, what is the balance between them?

Step 2: Identify a Pool of Potential Team Members

With the focus of the project in mind, identify a pool of potential team members. This should be significantly larger than the size the firm envisages for the core team. It might also include people outside the division or business unit, consultants or facilitators. Make sure the pool includes some managers known for creative thinking or unusual views on the business. Make sure the pool contains not only those with previous experience of innovation, but also some managers who would benefit from learning more about innovation.

Step 3: Give Each Potential Member a Score out of 10 on the Following Attributes

1. A set of perspectives or mental models thought useful to the project. For example, marketing, finance and IT. Or customer, employee and partner.
2. Potential to be an ambassador or spokesperson for the project.
3. Their fit with the primary focus of the project (and if necessary secondary focuses).
4. Experience with innovation projects or important tools the team may use.
5. Motivation to succeed and potential to learn.
6. Ability to work in teams.
7. Any other attribute the firm thinks important.

Step 4: Remove Weak Candidates and Choose the Best Combination of the Rest

This is the difficult step. The scores on the various attributes should not be used mechanistically. Rather they provide summary profiles of the potential members to help discussion. These can be presented as 'snake-plots'. The leader and sponsor should then use these profiles to look at possible teams.

To make this task manageable they may first remove any weak candidates. In doing this, they should take care not to remove unusual views or people without experience. A weak candidate is someone who scores moderately or low on all the attributes. Someone with a clear strength on one attribute but weak on others may still be a candidate for the team.

They can then assemble the remaining candidates into several hypothetical teams for debate, winnowing this down to the two or three teams they prefer. They can then discuss these teams with other executives and senior managers to make the final choice.

Step 5: Revisit at Gate 3

At the minimum, the firm should revisit team membership after Gate 3 approval. The nature of the project changes once the innovation goes into development and so the team's composition may also need to change. The leader and sponsor can apply a similar procedure for adding new members or replacing existing members.

Tool Two: First Meeting Agenda

1. Before the meeting
    a. Drafting of the preliminary objective (project sponsor + team leader)
    b. Preparation of pack of materials for the meeting (team leader)
        i. Agenda, contact details, preliminary objective, assumptions and project plan, and supporting background
    c. Completion and reflection on diagnostic questionnaires (team as individuals)
2. At the off-site meeting
    a. Short presentation on what the firm hopes to achieve from the project and why this team is selected (team leader)
    b. Team member introductions and an ice-breaking exercise (team + facilitator)
    c. Presentation and discussion of more detailed background on the project, preliminary objective, assumptions and project plan (team leader + others)
    d. Short exercise building a list of the major opportunities (team + facilitator)
    e. Extensive discussion of how the team can be creative, gain the support of the organization, and start go about the preparatory research
    f. Short exercise building a list of the risks to be overcome (team + facilitator)
    g. Discussion of possible metrics for the project dashboard (team)
    h. Assignment of team roles, including the owner of the dashboard (team)
    i. Team building exercise (team + facilitator)
    j. Final discussion of next steps and future schedule (team leader)

Tool Three: Team Climate Inventory[46]

The Team Climate Inventory (TCI) is a way of measuring the 'climate' within a team specifically tasked with innovation. Research shows that innovation thrives in teams with the following four characteristics:

- *Participative Safety* – the team climate is safe and encourages members' participation;
- *Support for Innovation* – the team encourages innovative thinking, either verbally or through practical means;
- *Team Vision* – the team's objectives are clear and shared by everyone;
- *Task Orientation* – the team strives for excellence and reviews its performance.

Team leaders compile the inventory by questionnaires that all team members complete anonymously. Their responses produce a score against 13 subscales that group under the four characteristics above. A fifth heading – *Social Desirability* – acts as a check on the others, highlighting insincere responses from team members saying only what they think management wants to hear.

The resulting scores between 1 and 10 show where the team climate for innovation is weak and where it is strong. For example, take the subscale 'perceived value' under *Team Vision*. A score of 2 on this subscale will signal the team is not convinced of the value of the project's objectives.

By plotting the scores for each subscale, leaders can see whether a team is strong overall, or where there is a weakness they need to address. In the example above, the team leader should consider if the project's objectives align with those of the firm. It may be helpful for them to hold extra team building sessions to further explore and develop the project objectives and ensure everyone's buy-in.

Far from being a one-off exercise, leaders should use the TCI regularly as a check to see if the first round of team building interventions built an effective team. They can compile the TCI at team away days for example. This is especially useful at key milestones in the project where it is essential to confirm that everything is on track. TCI scores can highlight where a team may be backsliding against particular measures. For example, a team's commitments to offering practical help to one another, or to achieving the highest performance possible.

Repeating the TCI is also valuable where there has been some turnover in team membership – an unavoidable event over longer and more complex projects. It is important to make sure that changes in personnel have not had a harmful effect on team cohesion. Also, that new members know exactly what the team expects of them, as team members and individuals. Key source for further reference: N. Anderson and M. West, *The Team Climate Inventory*, Windsor, UK, Assessment Services for Employment, NFER–Nelson, 1994.

CHAPTER 5

CO-CREATING THE INNOVATION WITH CUSTOMERS

INTRODUCTION

Co-creating innovations with customers is a logical outcome of the lessons on innovation adoption set out in Chapter 2. Customers face challenges in deciding to adopt innovations, especially breakthrough innovations. To minimize these challenges firms should thoroughly understand the needs and decision-making of their target customers. The most natural way to do this is to seek customer views while developing the innovation. Indeed, all intelligent firms seek such views in one way or another before they launch the innovation. But to gain a *thorough* understanding of customers we need greater clarity on several questions. When should we seek their views? From which customers should we seek them? How closely should we involve customers in development? Which method should we use to get their views? Since there are many alternative opinions on these questions, each with vocal supporters, we need also to consult best practice.

This chapter is built around these questions. The first section addresses the question of when to seek customer views. The next section examines which customers to involve, building on the adoption model of Chapter 2. The third section looks at how to involve customers in co-creation, relating this to each stage of the innovation's development. This section mainly focuses on the various methods for gaining accurate and useful views from customers. The fourth section provides the action steps that follow from this chapter, both in general and according to the circumstances of the innovation. These include not only the three challenges of innovation, but also the nature of the product or service. The latter has an important influence on which research methods are best to use for specific innovations. The fifth and final section looks at the links between this chapter and the other tasks. The Toolkit for this chapter includes voice-of-the-customer, choice experiments and criteria for choosing which customers to involve in co-creation.

WHEN YOU SHOULD SEEK CUSTOMER INVOLVEMENT

Best practice firms are moving to involve customers in co-creation, often from early in development, or even before as preparation for innovation initiatives. A recent workshop of the Marketing Science Institute provides examples of this trend from firms such as Diageo and GE Healthcare.[1] There are five reasons for this.

Using the Eyes of the Customer

First, the adoption model outlined in Chapter 2 suggests the innovation requires at least two things to have any chance of success in the market. It must have an advantage in the eyes of the customer and the firm needs to frame this advantage in the right way. Understanding both needs customer insight. What better way to get this insight than to involve customers from the beginning in discussions about the firm's objective and the potential innovations that might meet this objective?

Benefiting from Early Customer Involvement

Second, the costs and risks of developing innovations, especially breakthrough ones, are high. Weeding out poor ideas early saves money and reduces the overall risk of the innovation to the firm. If customers can help the firm in choosing between competing ideas, will this improve the firm's chances of eventual profit? Yes, it will. There is strong evidence that successful firms listen to the customer effectively, while innovation failures often stem from deficiencies in market research.[2] Often this occurs through organizational overconfidence ('we know what is right for the customer') or the egos of managers ('obviously the project I've been working on for a year will be a success').[3] The vignette *Sometimes the next isn't always the best* graphically shows the dire results of managerial overconfidence and ego. However, the firm can counterbalance both these biases by involving customers effectively and early on.

Sometimes the next isn't always the best[22]

Third-generation (3G) mobile phone networks allow users to transfer larger amounts of data faster than the second generation. 3G networks make video calling and messaging services possible for the first time on a mobile phone. A trial 3G service was first launched in Japan in June 2001 and a commercial service followed in October that year. In 2003, Hutchison launched its 3G network in the UK – representing its first foray into the British mobile phone market. Vodafone, an already successful mobile phone provider, followed suit in November 2004, in time to take advantage of the Christmas market. Vodafone was quickly followed by three further companies. The UK public had already developed a seemingly insatiable need for phones with new features and gadgets, and so 3G seemed destined for glory. It has become increasingly clear, however, that it may never be the great success initially expected.

Several reasons underlie the failure of 3G to meet expectations. In the UK, the British government chose to auction 3G licences to the highest bidder. Believing in their own hyperbole, operators in the UK paid a combined total of £22.5 billion for their licences. This has made it difficult for them both to break even and provide high-quality and high-coverage services for 3G phone users. In 2004, for example, Vodafone's 3G services could be accessed by only 60% of the population.

Early promotion of multimedia applications also led operators, especially in Europe, to overestimate the expected average revenue per user. But the consumer market showed much less interest than operators expected. Indeed, first reviews by the consumer magazine *Which* discouraged consumers from buying on the basis the coverage was poor, handsets were bulky and the applications did not represent value for money. As the lack of consumer interest in multimedia applications became clear, the 3G providers had to refocus on low-margin services that consumers wanted. Meanwhile, they were also forced to upgrade networks more rapidly than expected to provide services that did appeal to customers.

The problems were compounded by competition from technologies not anticipated when the expensive licences were bought. These include flat-rate wireless voice over Internet protocol (VoIP), Wi-Fi, mobile services provided by non-mobile operators and mobile broadband. And while the 3G providers were struggling to recoup their investment, Ofcom – the UK's phone regulator – was considering whether to fine them for failing to meet licence targets. Targets that now seem largely unattainable unless the 3G firms take further losses on their operations.

3G managers misread customer needs, overestimated demand and underestimated competition, with an overconfidence that hurt their shareholders badly. The result is that while other mobile phone platforms continue their rise, five years after launch the future of 3G is still in doubt.

Achieving an Early Understanding of Customers

Third, for innovation objectives that target non-customers or seek to build on emerging social trends, it is necessary to develop an understanding of the customer ahead of any development. Proponents of approaches for such innovations argue there are several steps *before* the team starts to create ideas. These steps include identifying the deficiencies in existing products and services; paying close attention to customer behaviour, especially on their barriers to consumption, and using solutions in other industries as points of reference. They may also include calibrating the intensity of any latent customer need. Only when all these steps are complete should the firm move on to looking at potential innovations.

Making Use of Customers' Ideas

Fourth, studies, notably by von Hippel, have identified major innovations that were first created by customers and later picked up by suppliers.[4] Von Hippel's 'lead user' customers had a high need to solve a problem and were thinking ahead of both their peers and the suppliers to the market. These examples are more prevalent in B2B than B2C markets, but they exist in both sectors. Well-known examples include certain developments in electron spectroscopy, open-source software and mountain bikes but many more exist. A recent example is robot lawnmowers. This was first invented through spouse pressure on a lazy partner, who later commercialized the invention as Robomow. Now major manufacturers such as Electrolux are entering this market and some commentators are even claiming that lawnmowers may be the killer application for household robotics. The vignette *Wife's cutting remark triggers worldwide product success* gives more detail on Robomow.

Wife's cutting remark triggers worldwide product success[23]

In 1995, Udi Peless, a former F-16 pilot with the Israeli air force, was a successful entrepreneur. He was also one of the few Israelis with a lawn, which his wife wanted him to keep in check with a weekly cut. As Peless hated mowing the lawn, his wife challenged him to make a machine to do the job for him.

Peless joined forces with his friend and former army colleague Shai Abramson to create the company Friendly Machines, which later evolved into Friendly Robotics. His bachelor's degree in electrical engineering came in handy during development of the first automated lawnmower – the Lawn-keeper. Although bulky and unattractive, it cut around 200 square feet of grass without help.

The company's current mower is the Robomow. It works by using a sensor to recognize a wire the owner lays around the outer edges of the lawn to ensure the mower stays within the designated area. The wire connects to a base station which is typically covered by grass and becomes unnoticeable in a few weeks. Robomow mows the grass several times from side to side, ensuring it covers the entire lawn and cuts the grass from different angles.

The Silver Classic, made in 1998–9, was the first generation of Robomow. It sold mostly in Europe, with just a few hundred models in the United States. This large, bulky and heavy mower with slick wheels provided a great quality of cut with just a single large blade. Disadvantages included the fact only a dealer could replace the batteries and blade, the product had some water-resistance issues and it did not cope well with shipping.

Since 1999 Friendly Robotics has improved their design for Robomow several times. The second-generation Robomow, launched in 2000, had three blades and a mulching chamber. The chamber removes the need to collect and remove clippings and saves up to 25% on irrigation and fertilizing costs. Owners can also replace the blades and battery pack easily with no need for any tools. Later models improve traction and water-resistance, and incorporate heat sensors to improve reliability and prevent overheating because of unexpected resistance. Better software now provides a more efficient mowing pattern and edge mode.

The design continues to evolve and current models include the choice of a docking station that allows automatic mowing for the whole season. The customer simply sets the days of the week, hours and mowing duration. The mower docks at the docking station for recharging, starts mowing at the set time and returns for charging without intervention.

Five models of Robomow are available and distributed in most markets. With more than 50000 models sold, it seems that it sometimes pays for a man to listen to his nagging wife!

More generally, if it is the case that some customers create successful innovations, why not involve such lead users in the development process? These customers' understanding of their latent needs and their creativity can help the project team in developing better solutions. Indeed, several leading firms have done this with success, most notably 3M.[5]

Achieving Success Using This Technique

Lastly, and most importantly, leading firms in different industries are achieving success by involving customers early. Examples include Cisco Systems, who use design tools to collaborate with key customers; Procter & Gamble, who share market analysis with retailers; and Goldman Sachs, who provide simulation tools to certain customers. All have gained from sharing information and promoting a discussion around potential innovations.[6]

In conclusion, the case for the early involvement of customers in development is compelling. The more important questions are located around which customers to involve and how to involve them and these will be the focus of the next sections. However, before moving to these questions it is necessary to make two points of clarification.

Forget Old Ways of Market Research

Involving customers in the early stages of innovation development does not mean using traditional methods of market research, such as focus groups and surveys. These have their place in the later stages of development but are now discredited for the front-end of innovation. Traditional market research assumes that customers understand what they are talking about and they can predict their future behaviour. These assumptions largely hold true for existing products and services as well as for incremental innovations that build on the customer's previous experience. However, they do not hold good for breakthrough innovations. Most customers will not understand the ideas behind the breakthrough easily and only a minority will be able to give useful advice. Besides, they cannot predict their future behaviour because the idea is not yet realized, nor have social and other local influences come into play. Traditional market research also gives equal weight to each customer in the sample or group, yet Chapter 2 shows this is wrong. Different customers play greater or lesser roles in building new markets. So whenever the objective involves breakthroughs the firm needs different methods to create and evaluate early ideas. Exactly which method to choose depends on the target market and the objective the firm has for the innovation. Later sections of the chapter examine this choice in more detail.

Customers Are Not the Only Source of Ideas

Involving customers early also does not mean that customers are the only source of innovation ideas. They can potentially be the most valuable source, but firms should be open to all sources of good ideas. Indeed, they need to source them effectively and efficiently from all the external and internal sources that are relevant to the objective.

Where customer involvement is critical is in evaluating these ideas. Advantage lies in the mind of the customer and so the customer is in the best place to guide the firm to those ideas worthy of development. But you do not need to involve every customer. The biggest lesson from theory and practice is that the firm needs to involve the right customers at the right time for the right purpose.

WHICH CUSTOMERS SHOULD BE INVOLVED IN CO-CREATION?

This question has two aspects, first defining the identity of the target customer and then deciding which of these customers are open to innovation and can contribute to it.

Who Will Use the Innovation and Who Will Adopt it?

At the start innovation teams need to define the identity of their customer more tightly so they can involve the right people. Chapter 2 makes it clear the customer of primary interest should be someone who uses and benefits from the innovation and someone who makes the adoption decision. The former can help in developing the innovation while the latter can help in assessing the likelihood of its success. In many markets these are one and the same person. For example, in most B2C markets a single person both makes the adoption decision and uses the innovation. In these markets identifying the right customer to involve is straightforward.

However, in some B2C and most B2B markets more than one person may take part in and influence the adoption decision. For example, for an innovation in manufacturing technology what the production managers of the customer organization think and say about the innovation is decisive. They will be the ones who will use the technology and who will be responsible for making it benefit their organization. However, many others will also take part in the decision and influence its outcome. These include, for example, the customer's chief finance officer, who will need convincing there will be a return on the investment. Also, the chief marketing officer, who will need convincing of the quality of the products made with this new technology. Even production workers may play a role, as well-managed organizations will involve them in assessing the practicalities of using the innovation. Decisions of this importance thus involve many people and will be subject to influences from their differing perspectives.

For such markets the innovation team needs to be clear about whether the purpose of involving customers is for idea generation or for evaluation. Customers involved in idea generation should always be the users, or potential users, of the product. Only they have the necessary depth of knowledge about the underlying need for the innovation and the potential benefits of the innovative solution under consideration. For evaluation, the customers to involve should be the decision-makers. That way the team gets an accurate view of the innovation's chance of success and the challenges they will have marketing it. These decision-makers will include users but may also include others whom the team identifies as likely to play a role in adoption decisions in the target market.

Who Is Open to Innovation and Who Can Contribute to It?

The other lesson from Chapter 2 concerns individual differences. Most customers, whether they are users or decision-makers, are not open to innovation until it is available in the market and local influences start to work. Asking mainstream customers to co-create an innovation before a concrete product or service exists puts them in an artificial situation. Most buy an existing product or service and are happy to do so. Status quo biases are strong, as is risk aversion to anything new. It is difficult for the typical customer to grasp the need for change or that new benefits might be possible through innovation. Besides, common knowledge supporting the innovation does not exist, so any opinion they voice about it is necessarily incomplete. Involving such customers in innovation development is not the right approach. This is also one reason traditional market research, with its emphasis on representing the whole market, is less useful in innovation.

Involve Lead Users in Idea Generation

This is most clearly to be seen in idea generation. The best lead users to involve in creating possible innovations are unlikely to be typical customers. These lead users should have a high existing need for a better solution and already be thinking ahead of most customers about what that solution might be. They should also be creative and have expert knowledge of the area of application, or some analogous area. Lead users like this can contribute to ideas for major incremental innovations and architectural disruptions in established markets as well as for breakthrough innovations. Lead users may be a subset of Chapter 2's innovators; they are similar on several characteristics. But they also bring expertise and creativity to co-creation. So lead users are not typical customers, they are unusual people.

Involve Innovators in Early Evaluations

Evaluating alternative innovations for gate decisions presents a different picture. Here both users and decision-makers can contribute, but core teams must distinguish between customers by their openness to innovation, especially between the innovators and the rest. Innovators can evaluate these alternatives ahead of the launch and provide some guidance on their chance of success. They have less status quo bias and are more open to risk. There is also some evidence that they can evaluate abstract ideas better than the typical customer.[7] Further, the opinion of innovators is critical to the success of the innovation that eventually appears on the market. So involving innovators in the early evaluations of possible ideas makes sense. The Toolkit for this chapter includes criteria for selecting both innovators and lead users.

Involve Typical Customers Later

All the same, the opinions of the connectors and mainstream customers are also important. In particular, the team needs to be confident the innovation can cross the chasm from innovators to the mass market. The gate committee also needs an estimate of market demand beyond the innovator segment before they can commit to full investment. However, this is difficult to do without ideas that are more concrete, that is, fully developed concepts or even prototypes. The typical customer finds it easier to evaluate something closer to the final product or service. To be able to give a useful opinion these individuals also need to have the information that they will receive in the real market, including the local influences from Chapter 2. That is why involving typical customers is more effective in the later stages of development. Also, why approaches such as information acceleration (providing simulated advertising and word-of-mouth) are important to successful development. More on these approaches later.

The Catch-22

The catch-22 here is plain. There are many earlier decisions in which it would be useful to have a forecast of total demand or the views of the typical customer to choose and develop the final product. But unfortunately these would be inaccurate. So this book devotes no space to sophisticated demand forecasting models. While several such models exist, the material in Chapter 2 suggests they are not likely to work well in the early phases of development, especially for more radical innovations. They may work in the later stages. However, by then the project team has made most of the key decisions and the firm has put much of the total investment in the innovation. Indeed, one reason for the low use of these forecasting models by firms is that by the time they become useful their forecast is no longer needed or, indeed, relevant. This is not to say that demand forecasts themselves are unnecessary: the core team and senior executives do need them for gate decisions. But the conclusion here is that the simpler methods and rough estimates of discovery-driven planning will satisfy.

So in the early stages the project team has to rely on guidance from less typical customers, and their own judgement. As their work progresses they will be able to check whether the typical customers will follow their more innovative peers.

What is the Incentive for Customers to Help Firms?

It is important the team also considers the incentives customers need to help with innovation, especially for lead users and others who will put significant effort into co-creation. Often such customers will help because they need a better solution, through intellectual curiosity or goodwill toward the firm. However, sometimes they need modest compensation or recognition for their time and effort.

Sometimes firms see competitive secrecy as a barrier to early customer involvement, either because customers may pass ideas to a competitor or because they see their customers as potential competitors. However, creative firms have found solutions to these problems through agreements of one sort or another. And, as is clear from above, the potential benefits of co-creation usually outweigh the risks.

HOW TO INVOLVE CUSTOMERS IN CO-CREATION

A vast array of approaches exists for involving customers in innovation development. These range from simple methods to complex ones and from using small numbers of customers to using large representative samples. Most use some form of verbal dialogue with the customer but some use indirect or observational methods. Lastly, some approaches seek simple global evaluations of the innovation, whereas others seek detailed knowledge of the preferred specification. Key questions are which of these approaches makes sense, given the lessons of Chapter 2, and how to apply them to the stages of development set out in Chapter 3? In answering these questions this section will focus first on the early stages of project setup and idea generation, and then on using customers to help in evaluating innovations during the later stages.

Improving the Team's Knowledge at Stage 1: Project Setup

In the setup stage teams should largely involve customers to help improve their knowledge. The team should understand customer needs and their market in greater depth than might be available from existing sources (such as standard market research, internal analyses and consultant reports). The voice-of-the-customer is the main approach to eliciting customer needs but there are also newer extensions to this approach that suit certain purposes better. The voice-of-the-customer is also not the complete solution, as other methods are necessary to link customer needs to the potential characteristics of the innovation. It is also important the team understands how intense the need is for the customer. To stand any chance of success with the innovation customers should have a strong need for a good solution.

Principles of Voice-of-the-Customer

Voice-of-the-customer originates from the total quality movement and is one of the first systematic approaches to discovering customer needs. Put simply, the core team interviews selected customers and develops a list of their needs. However, it is the principles behind how to elicit these needs that provides important lessons for conducting market research in project setup stage. There are three key principles to note.[8]

Team members must do the first interviews. The team members themselves, and not market researchers or consultants, must do the first interviews with the customers. This is critical. While third parties can help with setting up the interviews, there should be no unnecessary barriers between the customers and the managers responsible for developing the innovation. That way team members gain customer knowledge first-hand and can also connect this to their areas of expertise as well as possible innovations. This is hard for a consultant or market researcher to do. Typically the team completes interviews with 30 customers, with two members of the team present at each interview.

Team members must use depth interviewing techniques. The voice-of-the-customer uses depth interviewing techniques with an emphasis on probing for deep rather than superficial expressions of need and the interview tries to focus mostly on the customer's experiences and outcomes, rather than asking about their needs directly. Experience has shown that asking direct questions biases the discussion to current rather than future needs. Overall this interviewing approach ensures that a comprehensive list of the real needs emerges.

Teams should confirm their understanding with new data. The final steps entail organizing the hundreds or thousands of customer comments first into specific needs and then grouping similar needs into categories. These categories or *higher-level needs* help the team's understanding; sharpen their analyses and provide the base for subsequent confirmation. To get this confirmation, teams then collect additional data from a new and often much larger sample of customers. The main goal of this research is to understand how important their target customers think each need is.

Exhibit 5.1 shows an example from the field of assistive technology for physically disabled individuals, specifically battery chargers for powered wheelchairs and scooters. Here the team used a series of qualitative research studies to identify 159 specific needs. These needs group into 11 categories of higher-level needs such as *effectiveness*, *reliability* or *safety*. The team then confirmed how important these needs were through a survey of 100 experienced users. Exhibit 5.1 shows the top 25 of these 159 needs, with the higher-level need they belong to. Given the customers are physically disabled it is not surprising the most intensely felt higher-level need is for *reliability*. If the charger fails the customer is immobile. However, what is interesting is that many of the specific needs in this category concern services rather than the product itself. Here useful innovations may lie more in the area of services.

Best practice suggests external agencies are better for conducting such confirmatory surveys than the team itself. This is because customers often view needs differently from managers. Managers place too much weight on what their company does well and rate their main competitors too highly. So having the

	Battery charger characteristic	Weight	Criterion
1.	The vendor should provide a loaner charger immediately.	0.99	Reliability
2.	The charger should be returned to the vendor for repair or replacement.	0.99	Reliability
3.	It is important to know specific hazards associated with the charger.	0.97	Reliability
4.	The manual should detail the conditions under which the chargers should be operated.	0.93	Reliability
5.	A guarantee should allow for immediate replacement if the charger is not working.	0.91	Reliability
6.	Manuals should detail how to operate the charger for different batteries.	0.89	Reliability
7.	The charger should be time-efficient when charging.	0.87	Reliability
8.	The user should be able to check the charger independently.	0.77	Reliability
9.	The manual should tell you what the gauges mean.	0.73	Effectiveness
10.	The manual should tell you the proper way to set up the charger before charging.	0.73	Effectiveness
11.	Charger warranties should be for the life of the wheelchair.	0.71	Reliability
12.	The charger needs to display the same info as the power meter on the chair.	0.71	Reliability
13.	Chargers should reduce voltage or shut off when too hot.	0.71	Phys. sec./safety
14.	The chargers should have a safety warning directly on the case.	0.71	Effectiveness
15.	Chargers should have surge suppressors.	0.69	Reliability
16.	The charger should have a gauge to show if it is operating.	0.69	Phys. sec./safety
17.	Chargers should have overload protectors.	0.69	Phys. sec./safety
18.	The battery connector should be in an easily accessible location on the chair.	0.69	Phys. sec./safety
19.	A charger should not have to be assembled.	0.69	Effectiveness
20.	The charger should be included in the price of the chair.	0.68	Effectiveness
21.	A charger should have a signal when it's not working properly.	0.67	Phys. sec./safety
22.	Manuals should detail how to operate the charger.	0.67	Phys. sec./safety
23.	The user should be able to independently check the charger for safety.	0.67	Phys. sec./safety
24.	Owner manuals should come with each charger.	0.66	Phys. sec./safety
25.	The manual should tell you when the charger needs maintenance.	0.66	Effectiveness

Exhibit 5.1 Voice-of-the-customer. Top 25 needs and their weighted scores for battery chargers for powered wheelchairs. A higher score indicates greater importance.

Source: J. Lane, D. Usiak, V. Stone and M. Scherer, The Voice of the Customer: Consumers Define the Ideal Battery Charger, *Assistive Technology*, Volume 9, Number 2, 1997, pp. 130–139. Table 5. Top 25 Characteristics and their weighted score for battery chargers, p. 136. Reprinted by permission of RESNA, the Rehabilitation Engineering and Assistive Technology Society of North America.

confirmation done through a third-party agency avoids misperceptions of the market. Sometimes the agency also collects data on how well existing products or services meet needs. These allow the team to identify any gaps in the market.

A detailed picture of needs is a sound basis for the team to start thinking about possible innovations, but it is not the complete solution. This is because needs themselves can be abstract and not linked to technical features of the product or service. However, before dealing with this issue it is necessary to first look at how some limitations of the voice-of-the customer can be overcome.

Limitations of Voice-of-the-Customer

There are two main limitations of this method, both of which stem from its engineering origins. These limitations are that the method does not incorporate understanding of market dynamics and uses verbal reports from customers. They are not so much limitations if the project is an incremental innovation but they can be if the goal is a breakthrough on the customer dimension. Fortunately, methods exist to overcome both.

Failure to incorporate market dynamics. The technique was developed by engineers with little understanding of the market dynamics outlined in Chapter 2. Further, the original focus was chiefly on incremental innovation. Thus standard approaches to the voice-of-the-customer assume that customers fully understand their needs, which may not be true for breakthrough innovations. Fortunately, this limitation is easy to put right. Usually teams using the voice-of-the-customer collect a broad sample of customer types, including existing customers, dissatisfied customers and non-customers. This is an extra strength of the method.

However, in selecting customers to interview, the core team also needs to recognize that some customers are better at thinking ahead than others. For example, failing to include lead users and potential innovators may result in overlooking some unmet needs that mainstream customers might value in the future. Provided the team considers customer selection carefully they can easily extend the voice-of-the-customer to breakthrough innovations. Some experts also recommend discussing one or two possible innovations in the first interviews, not so much for feedback on these innovations, but instead to stimulate and broaden the dialogue around what the future could be.[9] Customer selection and interview questions also need tailoring if the objective is an architectural (low-end) disruption of an existing market. Here the team needs to select sufficient numbers of the target segment and focus some questions on cost–benefit issues.

Use of verbal reports. Another limitation of the voice-of-the-customer is its emphasis on voice as the means of eliciting needs. Again the standard voice-of-the-customer works well with B2B customers when they are focusing on important and well-understood technical applications. In this case discussions between professionals stand a good chance of discovering all the relevant needs. Especially if the team's interviewers are good at probing beyond superficial answers and can get at deeper reasoning or less conscious motivations. However, there are customer needs that are hard to discover through words, typically because they are subconscious or latent needs. Therefore, other approaches to eliciting needs have been developed that rely less on voice. One is observation and another is using images and metaphors.

Methods for Eliciting Latent Needs

Using observation. A recent example of the power of observation is in infection control. Infection in hospitals is a major issue, as microbes develop immunity to existing antibiotics. Many medical researchers and innovative firms are working on this problem, trying to improve antibiotics or create more sterile environments. In contrast, two medical students saw doctors and nurses reusing the same rubber tourniquet when taking blood samples or inserting drips. They quickly proved that this practice is an important source of infection, and went on to develop a cheap disposable tourniquet. Strikingly the need for a disposable tourniquet remained latent until the two students made their observation, despite the attention and money pouring into infection control. The vignette *Tightening the strip on MRSA infections* gives more detail on this breakthrough.

Tightening the strip on MRSA infections[24]

Staphylococcus aureus (*S. aureus*) is a bacterium that often colonizes human skin and mucosa. The bacteria usually pass between people by a person touching another person or transferring them to objects that others then touch. Most people carry the bacterium for anything from hours to months without any symptoms. However, if the bacterium has the opportunity to enter the body, it can cause diseases ranging from superficial local infections, like pimples, to life-threatening wounds, chest and bloodstream infections. The so-called hospital superbug, methicillin-resistant *S. aureus* (MRSA), is a variety that is resistant to methicillin and other antibiotics used to treat infections. It is a particular problem in hospitals, because sick people are more vulnerable to infections and because complicated medical treatments, including operations and drips, provide opportunities for the bacteria to enter the body.

MRSA was first identified in the 1960s after the widespread use of antibiotics led to the problem of antibiotic resistant bacteria. A few more cases of MRSA were then seen in the 1980s, but the problem exploded in the mid-1990s. Indeed, data show the number of infections and deaths directly related to MRSA increased year on year until 2005. Falls in rates have been seen since this time, but the degree of improvement has been small, and rates of surgical site infections have worsened in some hospitals.

Number of infections with (1990–2004) and deaths related to (1993–2005) *S. aureus* **in England and Wales**

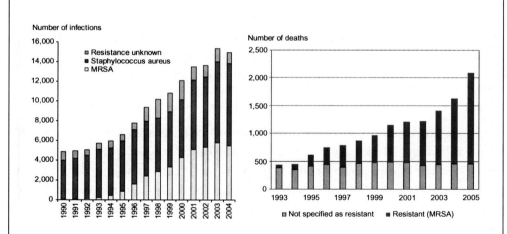

Junior doctors Christian Fellowes and Ryan Kerstein became aware of the emphasis placed on good infection control measures during their undergraduate placements. Critically, their close observation of practising doctors and nurses gave them the insight that tight hospital budgets lead to compromises in infection control. For example, rubber tourniquets – which doctors and nurses use to widen veins to take blood samples or insert drips – are used again and again. With tourniquets involved in about 40 million procedures every year, the two junior doctors saw these as a potential source of bacterial transfer.

Fellowes and Kerstein then studied the risk of infection from tourniquets and found a real risk of transferring bacteria to vulnerable patients. In fact, they discovered the superbug MRSA on three of 52 tourniquets taken without notice from doctors, phlebotomists and nurses and non-resistant *S. aureus* on 30. The staff confirmed the tourniquets had been used for anything from two to 104 weeks and an average of 11 times a day!

Further research proved there was no commercially available alternative to the rubber tourniquet. So these resourceful doctors in training decided to use their knowledge of the existing device, alternative materials and similar products outside the medical market to design a suitable replacement. They also approached business consultants and medical personnel before they produced the final version. The end product – the Tournistrip – is a long strip of plasticized paper similar in size to a watch strap. Health practitioners fasten it using a quick-seal, quick-release sticking mechanism similar to that used for security at large events such as concerts.

Fellowes and Kerstein won the Imperial College Innovation Competition in 2004 and were finalists in the 2005 Imperial Business Plan Competition. Hospitals in the UK are already placing orders for Tournistrips, seeing them as a welcome addition to the fight against infection.

Some firms apply observation more systematically, relying not on serendipity as above, but by deliberately using anthropological techniques. The most notable example is the design agency IDEO. IDEO is on record as saying their anthropologists are their single biggest source of innovation. By 'anthropologist' IDEO means highly educated observers with backgrounds in the relevant social sciences. IDEO's general manager, Kelley, puts this success down to the six principles of scientific anthropology:

- having an open mind;
- observing, not judging;
- using intuition as well as analysis, especially when dealing with emotional motivations;

- seeing what others have not seen;
- regularly recording unresolved questions and good ideas so they are not forgotten;
- looking for insights everywhere they can be found, including the garbage bin.[10]

Using principles like this, anthropologists can watch customers buy, use and discard products and services, including interactions they may have with other customers or service employees.

Using images and metaphor. An example of approaches using images is the Zaltman metaphorical elicitation technique.[11] This allows customers to use images and metaphors to describe their relationship with the product or service. Typically 15 to 30 customers each spend several hours preparing for a two-hour interview. They prepare by selecting the images that describe this relationship. A professional interviewer then helps them put these images into a digital collage that is faithful to the underlying metaphor for this relationship. An example of such a metaphor is *transformation*, that is, 'through using this product I can become somebody else'. The collage would then show what person the customer might become.

Core teams working in certain areas need to consider using observation or metaphor. These areas include innovations where it is difficult for users to explain their needs (for example, toys for infants), or where verbal explanations are biased or misleading (for example, in contraception). They also include less tangible innovations, like services, or products whose purchase is driven by image and emotion. Observation and metaphor can be an extension of the voice-of-the-customer approach or even, in certain cases, the primary method of approach. However, it is often necessary to link these methods with verbal explanations to gain a full understanding of the customers' thinking. For example, anthropologists often supplement observation with depth interviews to clarify what they see or understand motivations better.

Linking Customer Needs to Product and Service Features

A major challenge in innovation development is linking customer needs to the characteristics or features of possible product or service solutions. Customer needs can be expressed at many levels of abstraction but typically the clusters emerging from the voice-of-the customer are at the product or service category level. For example, a need cluster might be for a product that is 'easy and intuitive to apply on the production line'. Or for a service where the 'call centre agent knows the history of the current problem'. These clusters can also be at higher levels. For example, the service 'protects my family when I am away'. Such needs do not provide the specifics of a solution, nor are they something the typical R&D scientist, production engineer or business process analyst can work with to develop an innovation. So various approaches exist to link customer needs with the features that engineers, scientists and service designers can work with. These approaches complement the voice-of-the customer and can also suggest ideas for innovations. There are two main approaches here: means–end analysis from psychology and marketing; and quality function deployment from the total quality movement.

Using means–end analysis to link customer needs and innovation features. Means–end analysis seeks to build a hierarchical map or chain of these links. First, from the product or service characteristics to the customer benefits the product or service provides. Second from these benefits to the higher-level needs that customers might have. This is done at the individual customer level, as shown in Exhibit 5.2. The method does not need large samples of customers as in this stage of innovation development the goal is insight and ideas, not certainty. Differences between customers are also often of greater interest than commonalities because they suggest alternative solutions.

Teams build means–end chains by a technique known as laddering. This uses probing questions to build from the features of the product or service to the higher levels of need shown in the exhibit. Done well, laddering also brings subconscious thinking and motivations to the surface as well as the obvious reasons for valuing the product. In Exhibit 5.2 there are both obvious utilitarian reasons for valuing the benefits of orange juice (health) and less obvious social ones (romance). Good laddering also aims to judge the relative importance of the various influences on purchase and consumption. In the example given here, health might be a stronger driver of consumption than romance, just as avoiding colds may be a more immediate influence than not missing classes.

Understanding the full chain produces ideas for innovations. In particular, it moves the team's focus from the current features of the product or service to other possibilities that may exist for solving the customer's problem. In the example, the chain suggests one possibility might be to add natural ingredients to the juice that conquer bad breath or improve oral health.

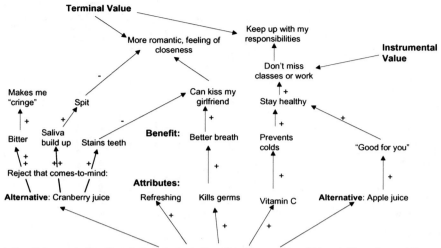

Exhibit 5.2 Laddering from product features to customer needs.

Source: A. Woodside, Advancing Means-End Chains by Incorporating Heider's Balance Theory and Fournier's Consumer Brand Relationship Typology, *Psychology & Marketing*, vol. 21, No. 4 (April), 2004, pp. 279–294. Figure 4. Means-end chain laddering findings for Peter's first beverage on Monday morning, 2–10 February 2003.
Reprinted by permission of John Wiley & Sons, Inc.

Means–end analysis is customer-based. So, as before, the team should carefully select the sample to fit the objective of the project. If the objective is breakthrough innovation, examples of possible innovations may stimulate discussion. It is also possible to view means–end analysis as an extension of the standard voice-of-the-customer. As well as listing the customers and understanding the hierarchy of needs, the team can get a deeper and complementary picture of what drives them.

Quality function deployment. Quality function deployment is also an extension of the voice-of-the-customer. The goal here is to link the voice of the customer with the voice of the designer (products) or the voice of the business (services). The link is through a house of quality, which is a diagram that links customer needs to the features of the product or service. Exhibit 5.3 shows one such house of quality for an e-bank. However, quality function deployment also covers a wide range of techniques and three more houses

Exhibit 5.3 House of quality for an Internet bank.

Source: M. Gonzales, R. Muleller and R. Mack. 'An Alternative Approach in Service Quality: An e-Banking Case Study,' *Quality Management Journal*, Vol. 15, No. 1 (January), 2008, pp. 41–58, Exhibit Four: An Alternative Approach in Service Quality: An e-Banking Case Study p. 53.

Reprinted by permission of American Society for Quality.

beyond this house of quality. These techniques range from simple ratings to stimulate discussion to complex algorithms to calculate development priorities and schedules. Some experts look only at the first house whereas others go on to consider the second house (solutions), the third house (process operations) and the fourth house (detailed technical and production requirements). But all of this is far too complex for the early stages of development.

So here we focus on the first house of quality. This can add value to the early stages of development, chiefly by stimulating debate around priorities and potential solutions. The house of quality can also handle some market situations that means–end analysis cannot, namely those where customers cannot provide or do not understand the links between their needs and the technical features of the product or service. This is because data linking features to customer needs can come either from the customers themselves or, if this is not possible, from experts in the core team.

In the exhibit the symbols in the cells represent the strength of the link between customer needs and technical features. For example, the need for a *user-friendly interface* strongly depends on *web accessibility* (•) but only weakly depends on *talking ATMs* (∇). Technical features may also be linked to more than one need, as is the case for several in this example. Thus, to some degree *talking ATMs* link to six customer needs, and *auto speak tool tips* to five. Both of these might be reasonable candidates for innovative solutions.

However, to help decide on innovation priorities the house of quality incorporates other information. The first is the relative importance of the customers' needs. In the example, *safety* is important, but *standardization* is much less so. Secondly, the house shows the current market, including both the firm's product as well as those of its leading competitor. The planning matrix (the rightmost room of the house) shows ratings for the ability of existing products to meet customer needs. Thirdly, the roof matrix shows the interrelationship between the technical features. For example, to meet customer needs better through both talking ATMs and personalizing accounts may involve compromise as technically they relate to each other negatively. In contrast, talking ATMs increase the ability of the firm to provide auto speak tool tips.

Combining customer, technical and competitive information together allows the team to set the target values shown in the bottom room. In this example, they represent major improvements to the e-bank through talking ATMs, auto speak tool tips and other helpful aids. In this way, the house of quality links the voice of the customer to the voice of the innovation designer.

Most experts agree the value of the house of quality comes from the discussion it produces, rather than the specific ratings and calculations.[12] In particular, it promotes understanding between customer-facing members of the team and their technical colleagues and through them builds links between R&D, marketing and operations that are important to eventual success. Most important of all, it focuses discussion on the technical developments that are relevant to the needs of customers.

However, while the house of quality has strengths, it is an approach that firms apply chiefly to incremental innovation. Where both customer needs and technical features are well understood it works well. But if the innovation is more radical, the house requires applying carefully. The team must assess the relative importance of latent rather than expressed needs, as well as incorporate technical features that they may not fully understand at this early stage. Neither of these tasks is easy to do. The comparisons in the planning matrix also need changing. Following Chapter 2 the benchmark should be the best example of an existing solution to customer needs. Most importantly, the team needs to focus more on the single key advantage that will build the new market, rather than improving all features incrementally. With such adjustments the house of quality can also work for breakthrough innovations.

Involving the right customers is critical. The voice-of-the-customer and its extensions to means–end analysis and the house of quality help the team to prepare for the idea generation stage. At this point they should have a thorough understanding of the customer. They should also be beginning to have ideas on how to change the market and what the possibilities for innovation might be. All of this helps them finalize their project objective (as discussed in Chapter 3) and shapes their plans for the next stage. However, one important qualification from earlier in this chapter merits repeating here. The usefulness of voice-of-the-customer depends on involving the *right* customers. Provided the team does this correctly, their plans for the next stage will be on solid ground.

The output from this stage is threefold. Firstly, the final objective for the project: an objective the team can seek approval for at Gate 1. This objective identifies the possible areas for innovation and the goal of this innovation. Secondly, a better understanding of customer needs in this area, including latent needs, both utilitarian and emotional. Thirdly, a better understanding of the links between customers' needs, the potential benefits of the product or service, and the technical features or characteristics of this product or service.

Customer Involvement During Stage 2: Idea Generation

The goal of Stage 2 is to create ideas for possible innovations that meet the agreed goal and reflect what the team learns about customers during Stage 1. These ideas are essentially the beginnings of a design specification, although it is not yet a detailed one. Often the team can record them as diagrams or pictures with an accompanying short written description. This description should include a discussion of how the benefits of the proposed innovation meet the identified customer needs better than current products or services. If the innovation idea includes more than one benefit, the description should also point out which one the team sees as the main lever to change the market. The goal is to have several such ideas so the team is well placed to select the best one or two to write a business case around. It is not easy to evaluate embryonic ideas like these by themselves, especially as it is hard to get a useful market forecast at this stage. The ability to compare and contrast several innovations is important to progress.

There are three ways of involving customers in creating this range of potential innovations: through lead-user workshops, user toolkits and rapid prototyping. It is best to do all of these with atypical users who can think ahead of the market but also have the necessary creativity and expertise to co-create useful innovations. Because of this, the lead-user profile mentioned before is the best for idea generation.

Lead-user Workshops

Lead-user workshops are two or three-day workshops involving lead users in idea generation. These follow small-group creativity approaches that will be familiar to many readers, and so are not mentioned here. They need satisfactory preparation and good facilitation to be successful, as well as the full involvement of the core team working as partners with the lead users. All participants need a thorough briefing at the start of the workshop. This briefing should cover the objective of the innovation project, as well as what the team has learned about the market and customers to this point. This is all easy to do. The challenge is to get the right lead users at the workshop to start with.

User Toolkits

User toolkits extend the idea of customer involvement by inviting lead users to do part of the idea generation and design on their own.[13] The firm achieves this by giving them a toolkit, which is simply a device allowing them to translate their needs into product features. The best example of this is the product category where this approach became the industry standard: application-specific integrated circuits. These are microchips built for specific purposes (such as regulating refrigerator temperatures or selecting gears in automobiles). In this category the user needs are so varied and the costs of understanding them so high that it make sense to delegate design to the user. Suppliers do this by writing software that allows users to describe their application in their own engineering language. The software then turns this description into a design specification that a chip designer can produce in a fabrication plant. The professional financial services, statistical software, online games and food industries also use toolkits

The users in these examples highly customize the product or service to their own needs and presumably they are the ones who best understand these needs. However, unlike lead-user workshops, they do this on their own and may not get the creative stimulation that comes from being part of a diverse group. However, proponents of this approach argue that toolkits can provide one source of good ideas. If a particular user design might be applicable to other customers, or has an interesting and innovative feature, then the project team can add this to their list of ideas for evaluation. That said, user toolkits are not applicable to every circumstance. In many markets they would require significant investment to develop and it is not clear the benefits to the innovating firm would justify this. So while some firms consider user toolkits an important approach, they have limited general applicability.

Rapid Prototyping

In contrast, rapid prototyping has broader applicability and is a natural step to take after or during the lead user workshop. There are three main principles behind rapid prototyping.[14]

First, turn an innovation idea into a rough prototype as quickly as possible. Perfection is not necessary at this stage of development and the competitive clock is ticking. The emphasis is on the term, 'rough'. Often this is a simple mock-up that provides a three-dimensional picture of the innovation but cannot do anything. That does not matter; in product innovation form often suggests function. Indeed, several technologies now exist for taking three-dimensional computer-aided designs and turning them into solid models. For example one of these technologies is the three-dimensional ink-jet printer.[15] While solid models are sometimes useful, a cardboard and sticky tape mock-up will often do just as well.

Second, use discussions with a group of lead users and developers to stimulate further ideas and improvements. Rough prototypes can make brainstorming much more effective, especially where several alternatives for innovation exist. In this case, new and useful combinations of these innovations may emerge as well as novel concepts that build on earlier ideas. The best way to take this second principle forward is through a rapid cycle of learning. A lead-user workshop produces several ideas for innovations that could potentially meet the firm's objective. The core team has these rapidly turned into rough prototypes. A further workshop then refines and builds on these prototypes or produces new ideas. If it is easy for the lead users and developers to produce rough prototypes themselves, say with cardboard or modelling clay or using workshop support personnel, then one workshop might be enough. Highlighting the benefits of rapidity some authors call this an 'Innovation Blitz'.[16]

The third principle of rapid prototyping is to get immediate feedback from the lead users and experts on the prototypes. However, best practice suggests evaluation should occur after and be distinct from idea creation sessions. Prototypes help evaluation by giving potential customers something tangible to discuss, and a rough prototype will avoid costly investments into finished prototypes that prove unsatisfactory. It is desirable that such evaluations include multiple innovations and, where possible, alternative variants of each. Customers are good at choosing the best and worst from sets of innovations and poor at evaluating single innovations, as discussed later in this chapter. These choices help the team focus on the best of their potential innovations and the real prototypes the team develops as a result are likely to be better investments.

People often associate rapid prototyping with products but it works for service innovation just as well. Many service firms use rapid prototyping. These include building miniature store prototypes in a warehouse, using mock-ups of computer screens for online services, experimenting with staff location and duties in hospitals and developing video prototypes of new services.[17] With the rapid advances in computer animation, video prototypes are a cost-effective means to get the benefits of rapid prototyping into service innovation. Videos can also simulate customer interactions with personnel or systems. As the benefits to the customer often come from these interactions this provides the team with further insight.

Evaluating Ideas and Prototypes during Stage 3: Business Case

The best customers to involve during Stage 3 are the potential innovators. The innovators can understand rough prototypes and will eventually lead the market through their response to the finished innovation. They can form an opinion from the limited information available at this early stage, just as they would do in reality, and this opinion is important to the eventual development of the market. An important tool for getting and understanding these opinions is a *choice experiment*.

Using Choice Experiments to Obtain Evaluations from Potential Innovators

The most accurate and useful market research tool for evaluating innovations is a *choice experiment*.[18] Indeed, a major lesson from the past two decades is that choice experiments are far superior to any market research using traditional methods. It is, in fact, so superior that it is remarkable that people still use the older methods. Choice experiments build on ideas from experimental design and the study of human choices. Experimental design originates from agricultural field trials but is now a highly developed science applied in many areas. The study of human choices draws from economics and psychology and concerns the best ways to represent and analyse choice decisions.

In a choice experiment, customers evaluate several hypothetical variants of the product or service innovation and point out which variants they prefer. In stating these preferences they make comparisons between the variants, and this is where the power of the choice experiment lies. Namely, the researcher is asking the customer to do a task similar to what they do in real life. For an illustrative example, the customer might be making a choice between various power drills, where each tool has different features. They may be shown 16 such possible drills, often in pairs, and asked to make a choice of which drill in each pair is better for them. Here, unlike older market research methods, the comparisons between the different drills force the customer to think carefully about the trade-offs between them. Which feature do they care about? Does it matter that drill A has 25% more power than drill B? Or does the fact that drill B has variable speeds provide an acceptable compensation for its lower power?

Because the overall set of drills follows an experimental design, statistical methods can then extract the relative importance of the various features. These methods also show what amount of each feature the customer would prefer. For example, they can show that drill shape is the most important feature but that customers prefer a smooth, curved shape to a boxy drill with projections. Or that power is the second most important feature and customers prefer 500 watts to either 300 or 700 watts. Choice experiments can handle both qualitative and quantitative features and both linear and nonlinear relationships between the levels of these features and customer preferences. *Price* and *brand* can also be included in these designs adding insight into the price point and positioning for the innovation. Further, if the innovation is within an existing market, the experiment can include competitors' products and services. Or, for a totally new market, it can include the status quo or possible substitutes for comparisons.

Most critically, these experiments allow the team to understand the *ideal specification* for the innovation. That is, the specification that will maximize the chance innovators gain benefit from the innovation, adopt it rapidly and influence the rest of the market to follow.

Recently *best–worst scaling* has improved choice experiments significantly. Best–worst scaling overcomes some technical issues in analysis, provides more accurate results and makes the task simpler for customers. Exhibit 5.4 shows this method applied to space tourism. Here researchers gave customers choices between specifications for possible trips including high altitude, zero-g and suborbital flights. In the exhibit these various specifications are called *options*. From the experimental design customers made 16 choices, each involving three options. The exhibit shows *one* of the 16 choices. For each choice the customer had to state which of the three options they thought best for them, which worst, as well as which they might buy. The toolkit for this chapter uses the space tourism example to show how choice experiments aid innovation design.

Choice experiments with best–worst scaling suit the challenge the core team faces *after* idea generation. The rough prototype for the innovation may exist but the team still needs to decide many details, particularly how much of each

SPACE TOURISM

Choice Task

Scroll down to read all the features, and answer the questions below.
You can click on a feature name to view its description in a pop-up window.

ZERO-G		SUB-ORBITAL		ORBITAL	
Price of Zero-G flight experience	US$4,000	**Price of sub-orbital flight experience**	US$10,000	**Price of orbital flight**	US$21.5 million
Total time in Zero-G	8 mins.	**Total duration of sub-orbital flight**	60 mins.	**Total duration of orbital flight**	7 days
Stringency of physical requirements	moderate	**Stringency of physical requirements**	moderate	**Stringency of physical requirements**	high
National identity and location of operation	UK	**National identity of operator**	Germany	**Anticipated wait before commercial services become available**	available in 10 years
*Assume any of the package features that aren't listed, but that you'd like to know about, are at least minimally acceptable to you.		**Anticipated wait before commercial sub-orbital services become available**	available now	*Assume any of the package features that aren't listed, but that you'd like to know about, are at least minimally acceptable to you.	
		Sub-orbital experience of operator (in years) and safety history of this venture	10 years experience & no harmful incidents		
		Safety history of other sub-orbital ventures	1 fatal accident		
		Safety standard of this venture as judged by independent experts	meets required standards		
		Duration of weightlessness (and maximum altitude)	10 mins. (150km.)		
		Launch craft/sub-orbital craft/return craft combination	VTO Rocket		
		Launch location type	commercial space port		
		Launch and return location geography	North America		
		Return location	5 miles downstream from launch location		
		Seating and viewing arrangements	small window shared with another passenger		
		Number of accompanying passengers	1		
		Zero-G floating	strapped to seat, no floating possible		
		Opportunity to conduct Zero-G activity/programme	no, insufficient time and space		
		Overall duration of the space experience training and flight package	2 weeks		
		Medical testing	level-4 testing		
		Parachute training required	wind tunnel & several free-falls		
		Launch vehicle training	limited training required		
		Further educational enhancements	presentation by little-known NASA astronaut		
		Licensed status of operator	has operating license from the launch site local authority		
		Insurance coverage	fully covered by operator's insurance policy		
		Terms for withdrawal by customer	inflexible payment and withdrawal terms and conditions with high financial penalties		

1. Which one of the options described above do you prefer MOST?
Check ONLY ONE:

◉ Zero-G   ○ Sub-Orbital   ○ Orbital

2. Which one of the options described above do you prefer LEAST?
Check ONLY ONE:

○ Zero-G   ○ Sub-Orbital   ◉ Orbital

3. Thinking realistically, if the three options described above were available in the next 12–24 months (rather than there being an 'anticipated wait' for any option) would you actually spend your time and money to choose any of them?
Check ONLY ONE:

○ I would choose Zero-G   ○ I would choose Sub-Orbital   ○ I would choose Orbital   ◉ I would choose any of them

To proceed to the next screen, please click the 'next' button:

[Next]

Exhibit 5.4 A choice experiment for space tourists.

Source: T. Devinney, G. Crouch and J. Louviere, *Going Where No Tourist Has Gone Before*, Sydney: Future Choice Initiative, 2006.
Reprinted by permission of T. Devinney, G. Crouch and J. Louviere.

feature the innovation should have. Often market research agencies present the results from choice experiments as a simulation tool. Such tools provide projections for the likely adoption of innovations with different specifications. These then allow the team to infer the ideal design for the innovation, at least to the degree that development of the innovation can proceed. Using data from innovators about their choices provides an important customer view on the design for the innovation. However, in getting an accurate view from these innovators the devil is in the detail.

Choice Experiments Need to Elicit Realistic Judgements

While a choice experiment is the best way to get the views of potential innovators it is useful only if the experimental design elicits realistic judgements from these innovators. To obtain such realism the team must explain the background to their innovation and the differences between the various alternative specifications well. A key consideration here is the link between the target customer's needs and the features of the innovation. An earlier means–ends analysis or house of quality can help with making these links clear, allowing the team to design the experiment correctly and brief the innovators accordingly. Another consideration is the degree to which adoption of the innovation involves emotion. All adoption decisions do involve emotion but if the emotional component is high the choice experiment will also need to evoke the right emotions. Video, images and sound can help here. Finally, showing and explaining the rough prototype can also help to make the exercise real.

While a choice experiment can be done with data from one individual the team will advance more confidently with data that comes from a larger sample. Typically this sample is in the range of 50 to 1000 innovators depending on the nature of the industry and market (for example, smaller numbers for B2B and larger for B2C). The experimental design and data analysis also needs expert and skilled support, most probably from a market research agency. For these reasons choice experiments are expensive and make most sense for Stage 3. The innovation ideas that reach Stage 3 warrant the expense of the experiment; also the results are useful for preparing the business case. This is because they allow more precise estimates of likely early market adoption on which the team can make some financial projections. But as noted in Chapter 3, how important financial projections are for the Gate 3 decision depends on the level of innovation. For incremental innovations gate committees can give them due weight. However, for breakthrough innovations gate committees need to be aware that they are imprecise and not give them the same weight, lest their insistence on precision kills a good idea. To allow breakthrough innovations to pass Gate 3 committees should look for three compelling results. First, innovators have a clear and intense need for innovation. Second, they support the solution the firm is developing. Third, they show a strong likelihood of adopting one or preferably more of the alternate specifications they see in the experiment. These results can support simple financial calculations but insisting on precise cash flow projections for breakthrough innovations is unrealistic.

Finally, the ideal specification that emerges from the choice experiment also provides insight into the scale of the technical and commercial challenges ahead in Stage 4. That provides a second useful input into the business case that goes to Gate 3.

Using Information Acceleration to Obtain Evaluations from Typical Customers during Stage 4

Choice experiments are also useful for market research later in development when a more complete prototype of the product or service is available. But the purpose and design of this market research need to change for Stage 4 *(Development)*. The purpose is now two-fold. First, to check the finished prototype does deliver the specification that innovators expect. Second, to check the idea and specification of the innovation also works for connectors and mainstream customers.

However, to achieve the second purpose requires two changes to the design of the experiment. First, the team should discover how the innovation needs adapting to meet the needs of mainstream segments. This is easy to do by incorporating possible variants into the design. Second, the team now needs to simulate the local information environment that would be available to typical customers during launch. The decisions of connectors and mainstream customers will rely on this information; including the views of innovators and other customers, as well as the range of advertising messages that might be available. Techniques that seek to simulate this local information environment are described as *information acceleration*.[19]

Information acceleration seeks to provide the evaluating customers with full information through briefings or the materials the researchers use in the experiments. For example, the customer might see advertisements or point-of-sale material from the firm or see a video of a salesperson making a pitch. To simulate all the local influences in real markets they may also see videos of 'customers' talking about the innovation (positively or negatively)[20] or receive third-party 'reviews' of the innovation. In the real market it might take weeks or months to receive such information, but here potential customers receive it in a short period of time, hence the description 'information acceleration'. However, without exposure to these local influences the evaluations of typical customers will not be good predictors of eventual demand. Getting the necessary realism in these experiments is not easy and it is often expensive. However, there is a silver lining here. By adding local influences to the experimental design the team can also learn about the marketing strategy necessary to launch the innovation. This includes learning the objections customers might raise and how to counter them, and the specific local influences that will have the most impact on this innovation.

A Stage 4 choice experiment like this can be of great value to the team. It helps to confirm their assumptions, provides projections of possible demand, allows them to refine the innovation specification and think about their launch marketing strategy and campaign. Since the marketing campaign may involve significant investment it is important to get a head start on this. All in all, if properly done, this research will put the assessment at Gate 4 (*Go to Commercialization*) on a sounder basis.

However, a note of caution should be injected here. Choice experiments are not the real market. For one thing the time and order in which a customer will experience the various local influences will be different in the real market. Therefore, while choice experiments are the best guide we have, the projections made from them are still imprecise, especially for more radical innovations. Gate committees still need to challenge the team's assumptions and judge the accuracy of their projections carefully. The Gate 4 projections will be more accurate than the Gate 3 ones but they will still have a margin of error.

Co-Creation in Stage 5 and Beyond: Scale-up Rather Than Big Bang

The innovation team can also involve customers in other activities later in developing the innovation, such as alpha and beta tests of the innovation as it goes from prototype to production model. For services, they can involve customers in a series of tests to get the operational details right. Indeed, services experiments and operational tests often merge into the launch of the innovation, because of the difficulties of going directly to full-scale operations with a service. So co-creation often merges into Stage 5 (*Commercialization*) where the firm introduces the innovation to the market. It should also continue into Stage 6 (*Mainstream*) as the firm brings variants and improvements of the innovation to market. These also need creating and testing with suitable customers. Indeed, the idea of a new product that is launched on a specific day is obsolete. In a world where services and business models are as important as products, development and customer involvement never stops.

ACTION STEPS: INVOLVING THE RIGHT CUSTOMERS AT THE RIGHT TIME AND WITH THE RIGHT METHOD

Exhibit 5.5 summarizes the typical sequence of steps a team might go through to co-create innovations with customers. Note that this sequence assumes the team did thorough preparation in Stage 1. Having a clear project objective with clarity on the customer needs that the innovation intends to meet is more than half the battle.

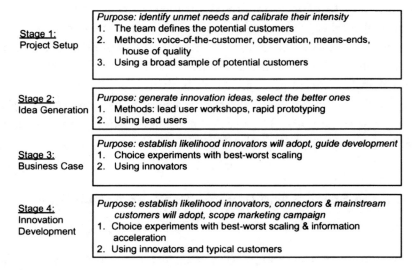

Exhibit 5.5 Steps to place customers at the centre of innovation.

The precise implementation of these steps will differ according to the nature of the innovation the team envisages, including which of the three challenges is the primary focus.

Stage 1: The Nature of the Innovation

If the team feels that talking to customers may not reveal the whole story, or may give a biased view, then their preparation should include observation or metaphorical elicitation as well. This could either complement or replace the standard voice-of-the-customer. Similarly they should consider means–end analysis as a complement or replacement for the customer portion of the house of quality. This will enable them to assess how important various needs are, and link these needs to possible features of the product or service. Normally they are more likely to take this route in B2C than B2B markets but there can be occasions where observation may be valuable for B2B markets as well. Irrespective of the market, those team members with good customer understanding have to think deeply and with an open mind about the nature of customer decision-making. Only then can they make an informed choice of method.

The team needs to keep an equally open mind in defining the sample of customers they observe or question. It is important that this sample includes all the potential customers for the innovation, not just the ones who first come to mind. Many important innovations have come from outside the firm's existing customer base, including from lost customers, competitors' customers and non-customers. Further, some firms have failed to see the full potential of their innovation by excessively focusing on the first area of application and the innovators for this area. In defining customer needs the team has also to build a vision of the future. A vision that includes all the possible applications of the innovation they can see and the customers for these, both innovators and mainstream. The firm may subsequently decide to focus on one area but it will do so fully aware of what might be the next steps in building business beyond this area. All of which suggests casting a broad net for 'customers' during Stage 1, but one influenced by the challenges the innovation poses. For example, customer challenges suggest more attention to latent needs and non-customers, development challenges to extending current markets, and appropriation challenges to price-sensitive, unhappy or competitors' customers. Depending on the precise mix the team can cast a broad and useful net.

Whatever the team decides in defining their target market they also need to incorporate the ideas of Chapter 2, especially into how they go about interpreting the voices of customers. Essentially teams should involve at least three types of customer in co-creation; lead users, innovators and the typical or mainstream customers. This typology cuts across any definition of the target market and helps put the different voices of customers into perspective. Naturally, given the model of adoption in Chapter 2, involving lead users, innovators and mainstream customers is useful for different purposes and at different times during development. Here we start with the lead users.

Stage 2: Which Lead Users for Which Type of Innovation

In Stage 2 the project team needs ideas for innovative solutions and can look to lead users as *one* source of these. Lead users bring expertise and creativity that can be an important ingredient of successful development. The principle of involving them is valid for most projects but the exact characteristics of the lead users to involve might vary by innovation. Examples of differences in these characteristics are that where the innovation represents a customer challenge lead users are more likely to come from analogous markets or areas of expertise. If the customer need is unmet or new it is not enough to simply involve existing customers. The team also needs people with different and challenging perspectives, and these can come from other fields. For example, although one of 3M's projects focused on infection prevention for people in hospitals, they also involved a veterinary surgeon for his expertise in difficult operating environments. This is the idea of a lead user from an 'analogous' market. Similarly they involved a theatrical make-up artist for expertise in attaching materials to human skin, since potential innovations might also be attached to skin.[21] This is the idea of analogous expertise. In contrast, lead users for incremental innovations and development or appropriation challenges are more likely to come from existing markets and customers. Note, however, this is a question of balance and not one type of lead user excluding others. Lead-user workshops need diversity, whatever the goals of the innovation.

The Strategy Canvas from Chapter 3, and the principle of eliminating, reducing, raising and creating value, can provide guidance for the team in suggesting where to look for lead users. Scenario generation can also help in this regard. Finally, reviewing the assumptions in the discovery-based plan and deciding which the team can test during Stage 2 may also suggest who to involve.

Stages 3 and 4: The Duty of Giving the Customer Adequate Information before Asking Their View

Stages 3 and *4* also involve co-creating with customers, not only lead users but also innovators and mainstream customers. For team and customers to work together effectively requires the team explain the nature, purpose and potential value of the innovation to these customers. Unless customers understand the innovation they are unlikely to give useful opinions or suggestions. Again the type of the innovation decides the depths of explanation the team must provide. For incremental innovations, and development or appropriation challenges, the team does not need to explain the innovation as deeply as they need for breakthrough innovations. These innovations build on the current experience of the customers, so they should be able to grasp the benefits (or not) of the innovation idea or prototype easily. Simple briefings building from the present to the proposed innovation should be enough. However, for breakthrough innovations the team has to give a much more thorough explanation to customers, especially when the innovation requires a change of thinking or behaviour from the customer. Much time and effort has to go into designing and giving a satisfactory briefing here. Setting up the buying context properly is critical to gaining useful guidance from customers.

This also includes providing innovators and typical customers with the *relevant* information when asking for their reaction. The team needs to provide the innovators with a rough prototype and discussion of possible benefits before seeking their views. Connectors and mainstream customers should view a more finished prototype and receive a clear explanation of final benefits before the team seeks their views. More typical customers also need examples of what they might see, hear and experience during the innovation launch.

Stages 3 and 4: Identifying Innovators and Mass Market Customers for Evaluating Innovation Ideas

Innovators, connectors and mainstream customers are necessary to evaluate ideas for innovations. You need innovators at Stage 3, and you need all three categories of customer in Stage 4 when a prototype is available. In defining these categories for their target market the core team should always include potential users of the innovation. In some settings the team also needs to involve other categories of customer, particularly decision-makers if these are different from users. And again there will be differences in definition according to the challenge the innovation poses. The innovator for a non-customer innovation does not have the same profile as one for an incremental innovation. Equally the mainstream customer for a business model innovation may be a subsegment of an existing market, rather than the typical customer of that market.

The point to make here is that defining the profiles of these customers and then finding individuals to involve in choice experiments and other market research is a vital and difficult task. Not so much for the mainstream customers perhaps, but especially for the innovators. The core team needs to make the necessary investment to achieve this. Unless they do, market research agencies may recruit the wrong individuals and thus undermine the validity of research that can make a major contribution to the success of their project. The Toolkit for this chapter discusses one way to identify customers in more detail.

LINKS TO OTHER TASKS

This chapter shows how to involve customers in co-creating the innovation. In doing so it builds on both Chapter 2 on creating advantage in the mind of the customer and Chapter 3 on chartering innovation within the organization.

This chapter makes extensive use of the ideas in Chapter 2, with two being important. First, the early stages of development should place more emphasis on lead users and innovators, who are more open to new ideas and thus easier to involve to good effect, than on typical customers. Second, the local information environment is just as important as the innovation itself to the typical customer. Bringing such local influences into the later stages of development through information acceleration methods can provide valuable insights. The material in Chapter 2 thus underpins the ways in which this chapter proposes to involve customers. In particular, by proposing a sequence and design for the various market research studies that support gate decisions in a way that follows the new model of adoption set out in Chapter 2.

The link to Chapter 3 concerns gate decisions. Choice experiments can provide the basis for projecting how well different variants of the innovation realize market potential. This can be done roughly for early gate decisions and more thoroughly (when a finished prototype is available) for scale-up and launch decisions. Also, it provides a unified method that allows comparisons between different innovations. When the project team is progressing two or three innovation ideas simultaneously, they can compare the best specifications of each against one another. This removes the problem of comparing generic innovations whose details are not yet clear. It is important, however, to recognize that market potential, while important, is not the only criterion for gate decisions.

The ideas in this chapter also link to the chapters and tasks that follow. Co-creating innovations with customers produces better products, services and business models. It also leads to good team insights into the information environment that best encourages customers to adopt these innovations. As a result the team can now begin to plan for how they will deliver both the innovation and the right information environment. This plan is the central focus of Chapter 7, which deals with building the new market. And delivering the innovation is part of Chapter 6, which looks at how the firm may need to change to do this well.

TOOLKIT FOR CHAPTER 5

The tools for this chapter are intellectually demanding and require significant effort to apply well. The three tools are the voice-of-the-customer, criteria for selecting innovators and lead users, and choice experiments. The voice-of-the-customer is vital to calibrating the intensity of customer needs during Stage 1. Selecting innovators and lead users is important for many tasks during Stages 2 through 4. And choice experiments are the best way to evaluate innovations and identify the ideal features for them to have. All three tools need the core team members to think about their design and carry out much of the work themselves. If they do not do this, interviewers will ask the wrong questions, or they will put unnecessary filters between themselves and their customers. Outside expertise can help, and indeed is highly desirable for choice experiments which need sophisticated expertise, but the core team should drive the agenda and stay in touch with the customer.

Tool One: First Steps in Getting the Voice-of-the-Customer (VOC)

What is Voice-of-the-Customer?

VOC is one method for discovering the nature and intensity of customer needs and shaping product and service innovation. In simple terms it is a way of conducting depth interviews with customers, which produces a depth of qualitative information that conventional market research techniques often do not.

Why is Conventional Research Not Enough?

Conventional market research typically provides quantitative information such as 'X% of people think that Y is better than Z'. Typically this involves much prompting, multiple-choice and closed questioning. This is fine for many purposes but not for the early stages of innovation where insight and understanding are necessary. Conventional research dictates the questions, rather than listening to the customer. Conventional research is also best at evaluating existing ideas, rather than probing into new areas where customers may not have consciously voiced a need or desire.

Core team members conduct the first steps in VOC, not third parties, and in direct contact with their target customers. With their in-depth knowledge of their own field these innovation developers can react to interesting statements in a way which market research interviewers or focus group moderators cannot. The questioning is much more open and allows more reflective and flexible responses, freeing developers to follow particular lines of thought thrown up in the questioning.

How to Conduct VOC Research

1. Choose the customers you will interview
Don't automatically go for existing key customers. Ex-customers, non-customers or even a competitor's customers could reveal more about their needs or about the deficiencies of your product or service than those who are already happy with it. Although there is no need to be rigorous about

representative population samples, it is important to select a good range of different kinds of customer. Be sure to interview the end–users and the people with most influence in the buying decision. Around 30 interview-ees will generate nearly 100% of all the needs, so larger samples are not necessary. Make it clear that this is not a sales pitch, nor an attempt to fix a problem with an existing product. Reassure respondents about confidentiality.

2. Interview customers individually, not in groups

Focus groups may save you time but they do not save you money and they will not identify more customer needs per hour than interviewing individu-ally. They are also difficult to arrange if your target customers are high-level executives whose time is precious. Group settings can encourage consensus thinking, and do not easily allow questioners (or interviewees) to go off on a tangent and explore one person's ideas. Interviews should involve teams of two questioners, for about 45 minutes per customer.

3. Choose your venue

Teams can conduct interviews on–site, at their premises or at a neutral venue. Visiting customers on–site is good for seeing first-hand how a product will work in its context, but not all products have a physical place of use (for example, financial services). Bringing customers to you saves time, and neutral venues can be useful for customers who are easily distracted in their normal workplace, or cannot be coaxed far from it. A combination of venues is fine, and even telephone interviews can achieve much with important customers the team cannot reach any other way.

4. Plan your questions

Questions that produce descriptions of personal experience yield more useful information than asking directly about needs. For example, ask them to describe how they use a product or carry out a process, not 'What would you like to see in this product?' Progress from unaided questions ('Describe how you use X') to aided questions where you focus on specific points ('Tell me about a time when the product broke down'). The latter kind of question will often be prompted by what the interviewee has brought up themselves. In probing, try and find out what they mean when they make vague evaluations. What do they mean by 'well made', – as compared to what? Questions need to be open, encouraging description and discouraging yes/no answers.

5. Record your customers' answers

Wherever possible make audio recordings of the interviews for transcription. This enables questioners to focus directly on probing and reacting to responses rather than writing down what the customer said and potentially missing an important comment. Teams can analyse the customer's exact words later (and should NOT filter or rephrase these). Several core team members should go through each transcript, highlighting key phrases and statements to pick up all the important points in the customer's own language.

6. Organize and analyse the responses

Edit the highlighted phrases (there may be more than a thousand) into groups, removing duplication, until you have a list of about 100 unique statements. Both the core team and a small group of customers can then organize these into 15–25 related bundles. They do this by moving statements about on cards or Post-Its under generic headings. The resultant list of customer-generated needs and desires can then be fed back to customers and analysed for priority using more conventional market research techniques.

Key Source for Further Reference: G. Katz, Chapter 7 in P. Belliveau, A. Griffin and S. Somermeyer (eds), *The PDMA Toolbook 2 for New Product Development*, Hoboken NJ, John Wiley & Sons, Inc., 2004.

Tool Two: Seven Criteria for Identifying Lead Users and Innovators

These fall into two categories: general criteria that might apply to both inno-vators and lead users, and added criteria necessary for customers to qualify as lead users. Teams can use this template as a prompt in designing scoring and selection systems for use during Stages 2 through 4. They will need to express these in a way relevant to their target market, as well as developing questions to go under each criterion. Exhibit 5.6 shows one such scoring system. This was used by an engineering firm to select a lead user company to work with in developing an innovative machine tool.[25]

Criteria	Evaluation of indicators: -1 no (bad) 0 may be, don't know 1 yes (good) 2 yes (very good) **Weighing of criteria:** Total: 100%	Weighting	Customer 1	Customer 2	...	Customer 28
1. Qualification as pilot customer						
a)	Right machine type	20%	2	2		2
b)	Right machine volume	20%	2	2		2
c)	Top-performer	20%	1	2		1
d)	Confidential cooperation	20%	1	2		0
e)	Independent, self-managed company	20%	1	1		2
	Result	*100%*	*1.4*	*1.8*		*1.4*
2. Motivation to cooperate						
a)	Actual need for new machine	20%	1	1		1
b)	Tangible benefit for customer	20%	1	1		1
c)	Good cooperation through cultural fit	20%	1	1		0
d)	Good cooperation through geographical fit	20%	1	1		1
e)	Good cooperation through strategic fit	20%	2	2		1
	Result	*100%*	*1.2*	*1.2*		*0.8*
3. Motivation to innovate						
a)	Innovative customer, early adaptor of new technologies	25%	1	1		1
b)	Dissatisfied with existing solutions	25%	1	1		1
c)	Engagement in improvements	25%	1	1		1
d)	Tangible benefit from new technology	25%	1	1		1
	Result	*100%*	*1.0*	*1.0*		*1.0*
4. Qualification to innovate						
a)	Professional know-how about operation	20%	2	2		1
b)	Professional know-how about function	20%	2	2		1
c)	Professional market know-how, trend-setter	20%	2	2		2
d)	Sufficiently skilled employees	20%	1	1		1
e)	Feasibility of quality control	20%	1	1		1
	Result	*100%*	*1.6*	*1.6*		*1.2*

Exhibit 5.6   Lead–user scoring and selection system for an engineering firm.

Source: E. Enkel, J. Perez-Freije and O. Gassman, Minimizing Market Risks through Customer Integration into New Product Development, *Creativity and Innovation Management*, Volume 14, Number 4, December 2005, pp. 331–442, Table 2. Matrix used to Evaluate Potential Customers to Co-develop 'Betty', p. 431.
Reprinted by permission of Blackwell Publishing.

General Criteria

1. Have needs in the target area
The customer should have explicit or latent needs relevant to the proposed innovation.

2. Ability to innovate

The customer should have the profile of an innovator for the target market, especially in attitude to risk and willingness to go before others. In many markets they also need the right knowledge or expertise to innovate.

3. Motivation to innovate

The customer should potentially be motivated to innovate, either through dissatisfaction with existing products or services, or through receiving a high benefit from likely new solutions.

4. Motivation to cooperate

The customer should be willing and able to cooperate in whatever tasks the core team envisages.

Additional Criteria for Lead Users

1. Ahead in their thinking

The customer should already express a need for better solutions and have ideas about what these might be.

2. High expertise

The customer should be able to contribute to co-creation through relevant expertise in this or an analogous industry or discipline.

3. Creativity

The customer should be able to contribute to creative development sessions.

Tool Three: Using Choice Experiments to Evaluate Innovation Designs. The Case of Space Tourism

The Opportunity

Most innovations are either new versions or new applications of products or services that exist. Usually they provide a solution to a known problem or customer demand. Sometimes, however, innovations have no precedents and no basis on which to judge demand or design the product.

With the advent of space tourism as a realistic possibility there were several problems to address because of the uniqueness of the service. How do you gauge the demand for leisure trips into space? How much will people pay for a trip? What form of transport and what kind of trip will attract people?

Earlier research in the 1990s into the idea of travelling into space had produced highly encouraging responses from surveys of ordinary consumers, but these were both hypothetical and unconstrained. It was easy for people to say they would spend $100 000 on a trip into space when there was no realistic prospect of them ever facing the genuine opportunity to do so. These positive responses were based more on fantasy than serious consideration.

By the middle of the following decade, however, the possibility of space travel for leisure was considerably more realistic, and the possible alternatives for doing so becoming much clearer. In 2004 the Zero-G Corporation began offering the experience of weightlessness to teachers and the public. This they did by flying a conventional plane in a so-called parabolic orbit. SpaceShipOne won the Ansari X Prize in 2004, adding sub-orbital flights to these alternatives. By 2005 three billionaires had also paid $20 million each to travel into orbit as passengers on flights to the International Space Station. In 2006 it was time to do some serious research into who would pay to travel into space and how.

Using Choice Experiments that Elicit Realistic Judgements

The *Future Choice Initiative* was a research project carried out in Australia in 2006 to answer these questions. However, most people had still not thought about taking a trip, never mind whether zero-g, sub-orbital or orbital flight made best sense for them. So it was necessary to take a different approach, both to look at these alternatives and avoid the unrealistic results of the surveys of 1990s. *Who might the innovators in space tourism be and what would be the features of the best experience for them?* The researchers used a technique known as information acceleration-based discrete choice modelling. This technique provides reliable responses based on realistic information about space travel, and comparison of different alternatives. It also allows assessment of the different features of possible innovations (such as price, risk, duration or comfort) and varies the degree of information presented to different respondents.

Using a web-based questionnaire, the researchers gave respondents as thorough a picture as possible of what various forms of space travel might look and feel like. Respondents could then make informed choices between zero-g flights, sub-orbital flights or orbital space travel.

The visually rich information gave respondents some realistic basis on which to make their choices. They could imagine themselves flying out of the Earth's atmosphere, seeing the curvature of the planet, and experiencing weightlessness. Exhibit 5.7 shows one example of this information, although it is not possible to reproduce the full website here.

In this study, it is thus possible for potential customers to express a thoughtful preference for a zero-gravity flight in an aeroplane, or for a trip in a still-to-be-built sub-orbital passenger vehicle, or even a fully orbital space trip. By manipulating features such as cost, risk and excitement of the experience across the study, it is also possible to analyse how these features influence people's preference for one type of flight over another.

The researchers also gathered demographic and lifestyle information to enable targeting and market segmentation. Men were more enthusiastic than women, especially men who use risky toys like jet-skis or hang-gliders. For some of them sub-orbital flying was just too boring, however cheap it was.

Who is the Likely Innovator and What do They Prefer?

The most likely customer for sub-orbital space travel is a younger male with high income or assets who already engages in risky activities and owns risky 'toys'. They prefer vertical takeoff rockets over other vehicles and react strongly to safety concerns. They are not hugely affected by price within the range of A$20 000 to A$250 000, although the relationship with price depends on the wealth structure of the potential customer. Although individuals with higher incomes have a greater preference for all modes of space tourism – from zero-g to orbital – those with higher net worth prefer the sub-orbital alternative more.

The Value of These Tools

What the *Future Choice Initiative* demonstrates is the necessity of thinking deeply about how you gauge demand for and design innovations that fall

SPACE TOURISM

Descriptions

High-Altitude Jet Fighter Flights

Several commercial operators today offer the general public the opportunity to experience the exhilaration of flying aboard a jet fighter. Such experiences are available in several countries including, for example, Australia (flying a British Aircraft Corporation Strikemaster jet fighter/bomber) and Russia (in a MiG-25 "Foxbat" jet fighter).

These flights can simulate air combat missions, and low-level strike attack missions. The experiences include a range of aerobatic manoeuvres or high-altitude flights at 3 times the height of Mt. Everest and 2.5 times the speed of sound. At an altitude of 80,000 feet, the daytime sky above is black and a translucent-blue hue hangs over the Earth's horizon which is distinctly curved.

Zero-G Flights

Astronauts and cosmonauts undergo part of their training on board zero-gravity flights. These flights, which use regular jet aircraft, simulate the experience of floating in zero gravity by flying a series of "parabolic" loops. Similar to the feeling on a roller coaster when one is at the point of lifting off the seat at the top of a hill, these flights enable a customer to actually float safely in the air inside an aircraft.

Such commercial operations are available to the general public today, for example in Russia using a modified Ilyushin 76 and the US in a modified Boeing 727.

Sub-Orbital Space Tourism

In October 2004, the first successful privately-developed sub-orbital spacecraft, SpaceShipOne, made two flights to an altitude of over 100 kilometres, which is the officially recognised boundary of space.

Sub-orbital spaceflight occurs when a spacecraft ascends to at least 100 km, floats in space for several minutes at the highest segment of the flight, and then descends to Earth. The speed and altitude involved is sufficient to reach space but is not sufficient for the spacecraft to circle the Earth in orbit continuously (as do the Space Shuttle and the International Space Station).

During a sub-orbital flight passengers experience a rocket-propelled ascent at several times the speed of sound. As the spacecraft ascends, the region of the Earth's surface that can be viewed from the spacecraft increases considerably. The sky turns a deep blue and eventually becomes black. The curvature of the Earth's surface is very clear and the thin atmosphere is readily apparent. Passengers view the Earth from space as astronauts see it.

When the rocket engines are switched off, several minutes of zero-gravity or weightlessness are experienced. Loose objects float within the spacecraft. The zero-gravity experience ends when the spacecraft begins its controlled return to Earth, but the experience of viewing the Earth from this very high altitude continues for some time longer.

Orbital Space Tourism

In April, 2001, Mr. Dennis Tito became the world's first space tourist. As a paying passenger onboard a Russian Soyuz rocket, he accompanied a crew to the International Space Station where he spent several days with the other astronauts and cosmonauts before returning to Earth in a Soyuz capsule. Prior to the flight he spent several months training at the Russian cosmonaut training centre. Mark Shuttleworth became the 2nd paying space tourist when he repeated much the same experience as Dennis Tito. The 3rd orbital space tourist has begun training for an April 2005 launch.

Orbital space tourism takes paying passengers a step further than sub-orbital flights. It uses powerful rockets that can reach the speeds and altitudes required to reach low-earth orbit.

Orbital tourists are currently limited to stays of several days at the International Space Station operated by NASA and the Russian Space Agency, however there are plans to design and build commercial space stations and "space hotels".

To proceed to the next screen, please click the 'next' button:

Next

Exhibit 5.7 Description of the basic alternatives.

Source: T. Devinney, G. Crouch and J. Louviere, *Going Where No Tourist Has Gone Before*, Sydney, Future Choice Initiative, 2006.
Reprinted by permission of T. Devinney, G. Crouch and J. Louviere.

outside customers' current experience or knowledge. By taking the time to present detailed visualizations of hypothetical scenarios it is possible to gather good data about the size and nature of the market. People make choices all the time between one product and another, and between doing something and not doing it at all. They do so using information. It is possible – and necessary – to give them the same opportunity in your market research, even when the innovation does not yet exist.

Key Source for Further Reference: G. Crouch, T. Devinney, J. Louviere and T. Islam, 'Modelling Consumer Choice Behaviour in Space Tourism', *Tourism Management*, forthcoming 2008. doi:10.1016/j.tourman.2008.07.003.

CHANGING THE ORGANIZATION TO DELIVER THE INNOVATION

INTRODUCTION

In a business environment increasingly typified by service and business model innovation it is natural that change management should be an important topic. Such innovations often require changes to working practices, employee skills, organizational charts and corporate cultures. Because achieving the necessary changes in an efficient, effective and fair manner is a key challenge, the core innovation team needs to understand the principles of change management. The team also needs to have the authority and resources to deliver the degree of change needed. Indeed, at the radical end of innovation, implementation may be firm-wide, actively involving the leadership, and have far-reaching outcomes. This is the scale of change that most people understand when we discuss the topic of change management. Indeed, people often see change as synonymous with a transformation of corporate culture. On the other hand, most managers know that such transformations are challenging and often fail to reach their goals.

Most innovations do not need change on this scale. They can involve much of the organization, require many employees to learn new ways and even create new business units. Yes, these are major changes but they do not encompass a transformation of the organization. Not all the principles of change management apply equally to innovation. Given the variety of innovations possible, we need to understand not only which principles are most relevant but also how to use them to support different types of innovation.

This chapter has four main sections. The first briefly justifies why organizational change is important for innovation and summarizes what experts say about change management as a set of nine principles. The second section contrasts these principles with the change demands of major innovations, and it identifies five key organizational decisions. The main body of the chapter discusses these decisions in detail. These decisions also fix what the organizational principles for managing innovation projects should be. The third section sets these principles out, along with general organizational preconditions for successful innovation and management guidance for specific innovation projects. This section also includes some comments on how firms and teams might apply these principles in different circumstances. The fourth section identifies the links to the other tasks the team must achieve. The Toolkit for this chapter offers two tools for assessing the scale of change.

PRINCIPLES OF CHANGE MANAGEMENT

The central idea of big scale, transformational change management is that old ways of working must first be unfrozen, then changed, then refrozen into the desired new institutional practices.[1] To unfreeze the organization you awaken managers and employees to the need for change and help them to understand the new direction. Next, the details of this new direction need working out, agreeing and carrying out. Finally, once it is clear the new ways are working they become refrozen as standard procedures for everyone to follow.

Experts agree on this three-step process. They also agree that empowered employees who accept the need for change should resolve the details. In other words, the leadership of the firm should direct but, on this scale, change needs many people supporting and working on it to make the transformation successful. There is less agreement among experts on exactly how to make all this happen.

The main school of thought on change management is because of Kotter.[2] Kotter argues for an eight-step process driven by the leadership of the firm. His steps are:

1. establishing a sense of urgency;
2. forming a powerful guiding coalition;
3. creating a vision;
4. communicating the vision;
5. empowering others to act on the vision;
6. planning for and creating short-term wins;
7. consolidating improvements and producing still more change;
8. institutionalizing the new approaches.

Leading consultants provide similar frameworks, noting that much of this comes from common sense and good organizational practice, and the collective experience of many corporate change programmes.[3] Frameworks like these underlie thinking about change management but the priorities given to the various steps differ significantly, both in the sequencing of goals and on the role of emotions. Some experts focus on the leadership and management of change and on changing corporate culture through direct interventions. Some focus on the role of process consultants in helping organizations to change.[4] Others focus on the psychology of change or on the use of communication to achieve change goals. For example, some see the transition as a psychological process of accepting and working through change[5] and others see it as changing minds through the content and rhetoric of messages.[6]

Notably, recent thinking suggests that change is more the outcome of individuals altering their behaviour than something which leaders can target directly. This is not surprising. Developments in our understanding of how the brain works also influence the thinking of change management theorists and consultants. Indeed, there are strong parallels between the change management literature and the ideas of Chapter 2. Customers, employees, managers and executives can all resist change, be moved by their emotions or swayed by the arguments of others. Attention is therefore now focused on how to overcome resistance by providing counter-arguments; or how to handle emotions through rituals. The overall eight-step framework remains useful but experts now stress the tactics of communicating change. Kotter himself now highlights the role of communication in conveying change messages in a way that allows people to both see and feel them.[7] In other words, he shows how to send out messages which engage emotions as well as rational thinking.

Of the communication school, Gardner, presents the most solid approach.[8] Building on findings from neuroscience and the theory of multiple intelligences he outlines the steps you need to take to change minds. Recognizing the circumstances of change can vary widely, he argues the content and method of communication should also suit each circumstance. Gardner's diagnostic check-list for organizational change includes:

1. Understand the current discussion in the organization, the new themes that you want people to discuss, and possible counter-arguments to change.
2. Tailor your story to the size of the audience. Large audiences need powerful stories given by individuals whose lives are consistent with these stories. In contrast, smaller audiences need contextualized stories that are relevant to their goals and lives.
3. Adapt to the audience you are addressing. Unschooled minds need simple stories, groups with greater shared knowledge need more sophisticated stories and theories. You should have replies ready for possible counter-arguments when addressing the second audience.

In general, change is most likely when leaders can employ multiple levers together. These levers include Gardner's seven Rs: good *reasons* for change, backed by *research* which *resonates* with audiences, *represented* in multiple forms, backed by *resources and rewards* for change, consistent with *real-world* events, preferably where *resistance* is weak.

In this check-list Gardner raises two other important issues the simple eight-step framework obscures. First, it is necessary to understand the present context thoroughly before deciding on change strategy and tactics. Second, resistance is common and can be severe. Each of these warrants some discussion.

Several experts point out that it is necessary to understand the present context, especially in large, complex organizations. Their recommendations usually stress extensive data gathering through various techniques before any change interventions. The techniques themselves range from in-depth, qualitative methods and group meetings[9] to sophisticated surveys.[10] Often these methods focus on the organization's culture. This focus includes surveys to understand the mix of cultures in the current organization and peoples' preferences for the future,[11] or whether the culture is healthy or unhealthy.[12] To assess how successful managers will be in a particular culture or what new skills they need to develop, 360-degree surveys are useful here.[13] Some experts have recently stressed the need to understand the range of emotions in the organization, at least in a qualitative way.[14] Whatever the method or focus, the point all these experts make is that leaders need a thorough understanding of the starting point.

This starting point should also include an assessment of the likely resistance to the change. Chapter 2 mentions status quo biases and negative influence as potential reasons for customers to reject an innovation. Bias and negativity also exist in organizations but there can be other, stronger forms of resistance in an organization. In Chapter 2 the focus is a simple purchase by a customer; here it may be a change in career, in ways of thinking or in group working procedures. The cognitive and emotional brain processes are similar, but the change demands much more of the individual. Cognitively they may need to change their world-view or to abandon a publicly and strongly held belief. Emotionally they may face a powerful threat to their career, their job or their life. Further, as the section on personality in Chapter 2 shows, many people have rigid temperaments. They may find some changes difficult or impossible.

It is not surprising, then, that major change initiatives often fail, sabotaged by those who argue persuasively against them, those who ignore them, and worse yet, those who say 'yes' but do nothing. I once interviewed the CEO of a major bank that had been through a difficult but necessary reorganization. I asked the standard question, 'what would you do differently the next time?' The CEO's answer was, 'not underestimate the forces of darkness'. Major change initiatives are like political campaigns. They need planning, they need involvement, they need momentum and they have an active opponent – the status quo. That opponent, in all its guises, also needs considering from the start.

However, it is important to realize the opponent is not the devil; it is at least partly basic human nature. The brain is an extraordinarily efficient instrument. After time behaviour and thought patterns become habitual and shift to the basal ganglia in the brain. There they do not need conscious thought and so use less energy. Do not be tempted to confuse this with simpler thinking. A good metaphor for habitual behaviour is the gear shifts of a sophisticated automatic transmission.[15] In some fields, for example, an expert can reach a highly complex decision with little conscious effort.

Thus when a major change comes along there are two hurdles to overcome. The first is emotional. Changes to habitual behaviour or deeply held thought trigger a powerful warning signal that can potentially overwhelm conscious thought. The warning comes from the clash between what the brain expects and the new external stimuli. It is not hard to see that this is a useful early warning system for an animal to have. The past behaviour worked: be careful about this new idea! But the signal overwhelms conscious thought because the early warning system takes energy away from the thought-processing modules in the brain. And these modules need energy if they are to grasp and accept the change. This has nothing to do with intention or rationality; it is simply the brain automatically transferring energy from one module to another.

One way to sidestep these hurdles is for the ideas and solutions for change to come from within the individual. If the person on their own achieves the insight that changes to the way they think or behave are necessary, then warning emotions are less likely and more conscious thought will occur. So resistance can be overcome by getting people to focus on the broad need and direction for change without being excessively directive about what the detailed changes might be. The details should come from the individuals themselves. Such advice is consistent with that of change experts, but offers more precise guidance on how to empower others. It also gives a solid scientific basis to empowerment as the central principle of change. As will be seen later, this advice has major implications for innovation management, especially for innovations with service or business model changes.

Leaders can also motivate individuals and groups to develop solutions by altering their work environment. This can be by giving incentives, changing job definitions or reporting relationships, or choosing new performance metrics. Indeed, empowerment and a new work environment often go together. For example, it is hard to expect solutions in direction B to emerge if existing incentives are rewarding direction A.[16]

Of course, in organizational change there are other sources of resistance above and beyond how the brain works. Perhaps the main one is individual interests. Creating a new business unit threatens existing units, changing the organization chart threatens career investments, the need for new skills entails risks for the individuals asked to develop them, and so forth. These threats have a rational basis and need managing. This is where a powerful executive or guiding coalition can help. This coalition can develop agreements and adjustments across the different parts of the organization. They can provide credible reassurance where the threat is more perceived than real, and develop plans to reduce the impact of real threats and risks. And they can negotiate exit strategies and compensation pay-outs where this is the best alternative.

As well as understanding the present organizational context and likely resistance to change, another step is necessary. Leaders also need to understand the scope and scale of the change and the timeline to achieve it. They can then develop an effective change strategy and associated tactics to move from the present state to the desired one. This is an obvious point, but sometimes missed in 'one size fits all' approaches to change management. Different scales and time-frames imply different approaches to strategic change initiatives.[17] For example, large changes with short time-frames are likely to be complex and challenging because many interdependent tasks have to advance in parallel. These dependencies make it hard to coordinate and achieve success and overcome resistance. The short time-frame also heightens perceptions of threat while it limits the time available to address these perceptions through involvement and empowerment. These are some of the reasons large changes with short time-frames are likely to fail. Longer time-frames and smaller changes allow a more sequential approach. This approach has advantages both in showing achievement and overcoming resistance.

In some ways this discussion contradicts Kotter's first step; to have a 'sense of urgency'. However, Kotter's fundamental point is about the need to overcome complacency in the organization. If people remain complacent and happy with the status quo then change may never get off the ground. This is true. The organization needs a convincing and motivating case for change to overcome this complacency. But there are several ways to make this case, and using an urgent message is just one of them. However, it may not always be the right one, especially if urgency turns into haste. Rushing a large-scale change can be counter-productive if people fail to coordinate parallel tasks properly or to address important sources of resistance. Of course, external events such as competitive moves or new market opportunities may dictate urgency. But even here the evidence in Chapter 3 on pioneering versus following demonstrates that speed is not the only way of achieving long-term success. Rather than using a sense of urgency as a blanket prescription, change leaders need to consider the business advantages and risks of different time-frames. Once they have chosen the best time-frame, the guiding coalition needs to work on key people and business units to ensure their commitment to achieving results within that time-frame.

Closely allied to advantage and risk is resource allocation. Basic principles of strategy dictate that leaders should focus on the few key changes that are critically necessary. Also, they should measure how well they are doing using metrics that are directly relevant to these changes. One temptation in major change initiatives is to set too many targets or allow too many subprojects to advance. But asking managers to achieve too many targets or spreading resources too broadly is a risk for change management, just as it is for other areas of business. There is evidence that successful leaders of major change initiatives focus on a few key tasks and performance metrics.[18] However, in selecting these metrics leaders should not overlook Kotter's point on the need for short-term successes. People need evidence the new direction can succeed and their enthusiasm can wane if it takes a long time to achieve their targets.

Integrating all these more recent ideas with Kotter's approach provides a summary of current thinking on change management. This summary has nine principles, which also follow one another in logical sequence. Exhibit 6.1 illustrates these principles.

One final point here is that Kotter's final two steps (consolidating improvements and institutionalizing the new approaches) remain unchanged by recent thinking. That is not surprising, as these steps represent good basic management practice.

1. Identifying the direction for change and documenting the case for it.
2. Given the direction of change, understanding the present organizational context and likely resistance to change, by:
   a. using surveys and qualitative methods to collect information;
   b. paying attention to emotions as well as beliefs.
3. Agreeing on the appropriate scale and time-frame for change, taking into account:
   a. the speed and strength of external events; and
   b. the business risks and returns of various time-frames.
4. Building a powerful guiding coalition to:
   a. advocate the direction and need for change;
   b. overcome structural and economic resistance;
   c. engender the correct degree of urgency in people and units.
5. Allocating resources and rewards for achieving the necessary change, including:
   a. focusing clearly on critical tasks;
   b. selecting a few performance metrics and targets;
   c. creating short-term wins to provide support for change.
6. Developing a strategy and tactics for communicating the direction and need for change, including:
   a. putting out simple and more contextualized messages;
   b. preparing answers to counter arguments;
   c. providing multiple forms of delivery;
   d. publicizing all short-term wins and overall progress.
7. Empowering others to develop solutions through their own insights, considering any alterations to the work environment necessary to achieve this.
8. Consolidating improvements and producing still more change.
9. Institutionalizing the new approaches.

Exhibit 6.1 Nine principles for change management.

COMPARING CHANGE MANAGEMENT AND BREAKTHROUGH INNOVATION

Effective change management is a significant issue for innovations involving new services or business models. These innovations often need employees to alter their ways of thinking and working and can affect people across the organization in many different ways. For example, fewer than 10% of innovations in the service sector are restricted to the service offer itself. Instead 90% of service sector innovations involve process and organizational changes within the firm.[19]

Services are inseparable from their production and delivery procedures and setting up an innovation may need either new procedures or changes to existing ones. Introducing new procedures, changing existing procedures or ensuring the quality of the new service to the customer often need employee training. It may also be necessary to motivate and measure employees' performance in different ways to achieve the innovation objectives. Changes to the organization itself then follow from these procedure, skill or motivation changes. To be successful the innovation may also need the organization's business units to work together in new ways to deliver the service. Similarly innovations in business models may need not only changes in skills, procedures and organization structures but also changes in the way the firm works with external partners. Product innovations can also involve change management especially if their production, distribution or marketing require new skills, procedures or organizational arrangements. Indeed, all three of the challenges from Chapter 1 can involve change management. Project teams in charge of such innovations need good change management skills to ensure success. Innovation involves changing the organization as well as the customer. The vignette *Taking more than one bite from the Apple* shows how one manufacturing company has changed itself to include highly innovative services.

Taking more than one bite from the Apple[36]

Steven Wozniak and Steven Jobs set up Apple Computer, Inc in 1976, after Wozniak designed what was to become the Apple I and Jobs saw the potential of personal computing. In 1977, after the birth of the Apple II – the first computer with a plastic case and colour graphics – the company began to take off. The rest is history and Apple continued to grow year on year, building a reputation as an innovative and different firm throughout the 80s and early 90s.

Growth took a downturn after 1995, however, when Apple had more orders than it could fulfil and Microsoft launched Windows 95. The company declared a loss in the fourth quarter of 1995.

As part of a major shake-up, the company made its first move into service provision, selling computers direct to the consumer on the internet. Within a week of its launch in 1997, the Apple Store was the third largest e-commerce site on the web, and the company had its first profitable quarter in more than a year. The success continued until the second half of 2000, when the company again posted an unprofitable quarter.

In January 2001, Apple moved further into the service sector, with the launch of two new applications. iDVD (a DVD-authoring program) and iTunes (a programme that allows users to encode and listen to MP3 songs and then burn them to CDs). This was part of Apple's corporate strategy to take advantage of the explosion of personal electronic devices such as mp3 players and digital cameras. From May 2001, Apple began opening retail stores to sell Apple computers as well as third-party 'digital lifestyle' products, such as mp3 players.

In October 2001, Apple launched the first generation of iPod – a small hard-drive-based digital audio player. The iPod initially had limited success as a stand-alone product because customers did not have the alternative to download music to the device. Customers could only play a set of songs available at the point of purchase. In the last quarter of 2002, Apple embedded iTunes software in the device to enable music to be downloaded from other sources.

The iTunes music store, which sells individual songs through the iTunes application, was launched in April 2003 to serve the need for a library with quality music. Although the songs could be played only on Macs or iPods, the easy-to-use, no-nonsense music service was seen as a way to enter the digital music market. At launch, the iTunes Music Store was backed by five major record labels and had a catalogue of more than 200 000 songs. The result was almost instantaneous uptake, with sales of more than 2 million songs downloaded in it first week. In October 2003, Apple released iTunes for Windows – a stable, user-friendly Windows version of iTunes.

In its first year, the iTunes Music Store sold more than 70 million songs and had a 70% market share among all legal online music download services.

After Apple launched the iTunes Music Store, the number of iPods sold increased from 140 000 in the fourth quarter of 2002 to 14 million units in the first quarter of 2006. On 26 February 2008, iTunes became the number two music retailer in the US. And on July 10 2008 Apple further extended its services when it launched the App Store for iPods and iPhones. This store offers over 10 000 third-party software applications. In 10 years Apple has executed an incredible transition from products to services, while keeping its reputation as one of the world's best innovators.

Contrasting the nine principles of change management from Exhibit 6.1 with the demands of breakthrough innovations identifies at least five key organizational decisions that need further discussion. These are:

1. the role of the firm's leadership in innovation;
2. the role of the innovation team in change management;
3. the relationship between the team and the rest of the organization;
4. how to manage complex projects involving many parts of the organization;
5. whether the innovation needs a separate business unit.

Each of these decisions is now addressed in sequence, contrasting the change management and innovation perspectives. This contrast helps to point out the additions and adjustments necessary when applying change management principles to innovation projects.

The Role of the Firm's Leadership in Innovation

The first three principles in Exhibit 6.1 mainly concern the direction, scale, time-frame and context for change. For innovation, these have close parallels with the content of the Innovation Charter from Chapter 3. The Charter should outline the strategic directions for innovation, the degree of innovation necessary (which is essentially the mix of projects) and the time-frames available. It should also list the various resources, rewards and support systems available for innovation. The difference is that the second principle also suggests attention to likely resistance, something the innovation literature ignores. However, the innovation team and the gate procedure can easily incorporate the second principle. For example, the team can assess likely resistance and present ideas on how to overcome this to the gate committee.

More importantly, the change principles make a powerful statement about the support for innovation from the leadership of the firm. The Innovation Charter summarizes the direction and case for innovation, but this is simply the written expression of the company leaders. It is the actions and behaviour of these leaders that matter. Here experts on change and innovation agree. This coherence of view is best seen in the fourth and fifth principles (guiding coalition and resources and rewards).

Top-level support for innovation is the main point Kuczmarski makes from his many years of work as an innovation consultant.[20] He argues that, while many elements of successful innovation differ from one company to another, the one common thread is senior management with the right mind-set. In his view the CEO must lead innovation, the executive leadership must support this, and the necessary values and rewards must be put in place throughout the firm. This view has close parallels with the fourth and fifth change management principles above. Academic studies of successful electronics innovators draw similar conclusions.[21] Making plans is important, but successful innovation depends on the commitment, approach and behaviour of leaders.

The Guiding Coalition

Kuczmarski further suggests the senior executive group should include a chief innovation officer and a vice-president of innovation. The role of the chief innovation officer is to achieve the 10-year goals of the firm and to develop an innovation culture across the firm. The role of the vice-president of innovation is to develop and implement short-term innovation strategy. This is remarkably close in thinking to Kotter's fourth principle of building a powerful guiding coalition for managing change, though Kotter recommends a coalition with both leaders and managers. In contrast Kuczmarski sees the vice-president of innovation as managing the various innovation teams, while the other members of the coalition chiefly provide vision and support. The role of this vice-president has something in common with the 'ambidextrous executive' first seen in Chapter 4. However, the ambidextrous executive leads or sponsors innovation teams more than managing them closely. It is also doubtful whether a vice-president for innovation in a large firm could manage all the many projects in the firm's portfolio. Thus the leadership coalition for innovation needs to include several executives who can sponsor projects. However, both these writers agree in arguing for one leadership coalition that guides, encourages and supports. The vignette *Wii changes the rules of the game* describes some of the key people responsible for this innovation, both executives and managers.

Wii changes the rules of the game[37]

Nintendo launched the Wii computer game console during 2006 and has hugely outsold its competitors, Sony's PlayStation3 and Microsoft's Xbox 360. Its success is not because of superior processor technology but a new gaming experience which appeals to customers previously uninterested in this form of entertainment. It is the attitudes of Nintendo's leaders and how they approach innovation that is at the root of the Wii's success.

Nintendo President and CEO Satoru Iwata realized that many non-gamers have an aversion to the look of games controllers lying round their living room, as well as the size and power consumption of traditional consoles. He challenged the Wii developers to solve this problem by literally stacking two DVD cases together and asking them to design a console that was no bigger than them. 'We are not competing against Sony or Microsoft,' said Iwata. 'We are battling the indifference of people who have no interest in video games.'

Shigeru Miyamoto is General Manager of the Entertainment Analysis & Development Division and the creative genius behind many of Nintendo's best-selling games. 'Really, I like the idea of trying to do things differently from other people,' he says. Miyamoto's experience of industrial design (ID) and his policy of recruiting game development team members with an ID background were instrumental in creating the revolutionary movement-sensing remote controller.

One such developer is Kenichiro Ashida who has worked closely with Miyamoto over many years and was a key figure in designing the Wii's controller. 'Although I've specialised in ID since my university days,' says Ashida, 'I'd never encountered ID so closely connected to software until I started here at Nintendo.' According to Miyamoto industrial designers prefer to model physically with their hands, giving them a creative edge which was vital to the Wii's unique controller. When asked why the company was able turn its back on the past and take a different direction with the Wii, Ashida answered simply, 'Isn't it because we're Nintendo?'

Many of the games designed specifically for the Wii, such as tennis and golf, grew out of the possibilities offered by the new controller. 'As the Wii Remote is rod-shaped, it didn't take us long to come up with the idea of making a tennis game,' says designer Keizo Ota. 'Once we'd produced it, it was immediately apparent how well it worked. That's honestly how it happened.' Ota and colleagues, including Katsuya Eguchi and Zenichi Yamashita, pushed the limits of the new controller with new games, which in turn fed back into the design of new control devices for the Wii.

Genyo Takeda is General Manager of the Integrated Research and Development Division. He is largely responsible for many of Nintendo's hardware innovations as well as several game designs. Takeda oversaw and coordinated the whole Wii development process. He realized early on that following the path of 'faster and flashier' graphics would not necessarily have the desired impact on customers. By refusing to follow this path his team was able to concentrate on different technological advances such as chip size. These were important in realizing a finished product conceived from the beginning with its physical appearance in mind. 'Nintendo is a company where you are praised for doing something different from everyone else,' says Takeda. 'In this company, when an individual wants to do something different, everyone else lends their support to help them overcome any hurdles.'

Thus, in a well-run company, many of the general conditions for effective change through innovation are already in place. Each team can then concentrate on making the case for their innovation and the tactics for achieving the changes they need. Thus core teams should build on principles 6 to 9 to develop and carry out a change management campaign for their innovation. However, four important points are made by innovation experts that are not nearly as prominent in the thinking of change experts. These omissions need addressing here.

Managing Failure

The first of these is what Kuczmarski terms the 'art of welcoming risk' or what others call 'tolerating failure'. The latter is the better phrase because the concern here is managing people, not business risk. On the people side, the issue is what to do when the gate committee stops the project before completion or during launch. Even in the most successful companies some innovation projects turn out to be dead-ends and some innovations fail to build momentum in the market. This is often not through any fault of the project team but because of the uncertainty inherent in developing innovations, especially breakthrough ones. However, if the firm's leadership regards the team members as having failed, this will send a powerful and dangerous signal to the rest of the organization. Other employees may start to regard taking part in innovation projects as career-threatening or increasingly focus on less risky or more incremental innovations as the way forward. Hrebiniak provides an example of a successful executive at General Electric who quit because he thought that failure with a difficult project would destroy his career with the firm.[22] Many writers on innovation therefore urge the firm to get the messages on risk and failure right. The guiding coalition needs to make two things clear to all. Firstly, they understand that some projects are more risky than others. Secondly, they will celebrate failures as well as successes. To do this some firms hold burial rituals for cancelled projects.[23] Such considerations are not in the change management literature which assumes that firms do not cancel organizational changes halfway through.

Recognition and Reward Includes Common Fate Incentives

The second point from the innovation literature concerns recognition and reward for involvement in projects. This point is found in the change management literature to a certain extent. If firms do not recognize and reward successful change then it is less likely to occur. However, reflecting their humanistic traditions, change management experts largely focus on individuals. This includes publicly recognizing success, intrinsic rewards, such as enriched jobs, and extrinsic rewards, such as bonuses for reaching objectives. Most authors prefer recognition and intrinsic rewards to economic incentives. In contrast, the innovation management literature, reflecting its connection to new ventures and Silicon Valley, adds an emphasis on both economic rewards and rewards for the team as a whole, rather than the individual. For example, several writers describe the phantom stock option schemes for innovation teams that some leading companies use.[24] These schemes invite the team members to invest in the project and return to them a share of the profits of a successful launch. The key to designing such schemes is to ensure the firm rewards teams with a significant economic incentive determined by the long-run success of the innovation. Done correctly, such schemes can make an important contribution to successful innovation.

Choosing the Right Sponsor

The third point that is the firm's leaders need to agree which executive will sponsor the innovation team. What the firm needs is a sponsor who will advise, mentor and protect the team and who will provide their primary point of contact with the guiding coalition. The choice of a sponsor is clearly an important decision, especially if the innovation cuts across so many organizational boundaries that the choice is not obvious. This is where the ambidextrous executive can play a role. Best practice suggests these executives should be (a) a member of the senior team; (b) have enough breadth of experience and (c) hold a senior position (as a general manager or higher).[25] Best practice also suggests they should sponsor a mix of teams representing a significant part of the firm's innovation portfolio. That will gain the most benefit from cross-fertilization, as well as using these executives well. The latter is an important consideration because ambidextrous executives are rare in most firms. On choosing sponsors, the change management and innovation literatures basically agree, although paradoxically the innovation literature has more specific proposals.

The Dual Responsibility of the Gate Committee

The fourth and final point concerns the way the gate committee connects to the need for innovation leadership and the principles of change management. This is a critical issue because of the dual responsibility of the gate committee. The committee is responsible for supporting and encouraging innovation but it is also responsible for killing bad ideas. There is remarkably little discussion of the organizational implications of this dual role by either experts or academics. Change experts assume all changes are good for the firm and the leadership will not alter its mind halfway. However, the nature of innovation implies the firm does not understand all the outcomes at the start of the project. As the innovation takes shape, and better predictions of likely demand or technical feasibility become possible, the firm may well decide to cancel the project. In addition the gate committee needs to manage the overall portfolio of innovation projects for risk and return. They may decide to cancel a project because of overall firm considerations, not because of the merits of the individual project.

Equally, those who write about best practice in new product development do not say much about the change management implications of gate decisions. Instead they concentrate on whether to have one or several gate committees, who should be members of these committees, and whether membership changes from gate to gate. What this literature does say is that gate committee members should broadly represent the various functions or units of the firm. They should also have enough authority for the scale of decisions they have to make.[26]

Arguably for innovations needing significant change to the organization there should only be one gate committee and some of its members should be from the leadership coalition. That way the nature and scale of change receives careful consideration and, if the committee approves, the necessary backing to give the innovation team the best chance of succeeding. Having a single committee also provides more coordinated management of all the firm's innovation projects. It is hard to imagine a junior committee doing this effectively; just as multiple committees might create problems. Thus, there should be a strong connection between the leadership coalition and the gate committee. Of course in large firms there may need to be more than one committee, reflecting the global organization of the firm. For example, a global division or major subsidiary might need its own coalition and gate committee. However, firms need to minimize the number of these committees and make sure they handle genuinely independent areas of business.

In conclusion, these four points suggest the principles of change management need adjusting for the new world of innovation. Specifically, firms should manage failure well, set up common fate incentives for teams and choose project sponsors with care. They should also make sure there is a strong connection between the guiding coalition and the gate committee.

The Role of the Innovation Team in Change Management

The role of the team in change management starts in Stage 3 – *Business Case* – with a preliminary assessment of the organizational changes the innovation may require. It then continues in Stage 4 – *Development*, where the team conducts a more thorough assessment, and develops a change strategy to implement in Stage 5 – *Commercialization*. There would be little point doing any of this before Stage

3. In the earlier stages the innovation is too ill-defined for the core team to identify the necessary changes and any potential resistance to these changes. Nor would they have good arguments to overcome this resistance. Even during Stage 3 they will not be able to assemble all the evidence or arguments. However, a preliminary assessment is necessary for Gate 3 so the gate committee can judge the relative merits of this innovation against others. The committee also needs to decide whether it is worth investing in the costs and disruption of a more thorough assessment during the next stage. The team can prepare the preliminary assessment from the confidential opinions of senior executives and managers, the thorough assessment will need extensive and public fieldwork within the organization.

During development it becomes clearer what the changes are and the team can start to identify likely sources and types of resistance. They can also begin to assemble the arguments, methods and plans they will use to overcome this resistance. Further, they can target the key people whose support will be necessary and begin to work with them. Essentially during Stage 4 the core team will prepare the ground for commercialization. Once the gate committee gives the go-ahead the team will then carry out their change management plan during Stage 5.

So timing is straightforward, but is it solely the team's responsibility to complete the change management plan? Given the discussion above, the answer to that is surely no. By giving the go-ahead to development the gate committee is saying that it accepts the necessary groundwork for change will occur. By giving the go-ahead to commercialization the gate committee is saying it fully supports the necessary organizational changes. During commercialization the team then has the active backing of the coalition through their sponsoring executive. The team's job is to develop and complete an effective change management campaign that supports the delivery of the innovation.

Is there an argument for having someone other than the core team manage the changes? The answer to this question is most likely not. Having other players would not only complicate an already challenging task but in most circumstances the team should understand the changes better than anyone else. The team is therefore in the best place to develop influential arguments building on its understanding of what the changes need to be. However, one important outcome of placing the team at the centre of change management is that they have the necessary skills. In the new world of innovation project teams need more than just creativity and technical skills. They also need the skills to change their organization, skills which include communication, working with others and consensus-building. If the team lacks these change management skills there is also a role for a facilitative consultant of the kind suggested by Schein, one of the leading experts in this area.[27] This consultant is one who can guide and coach team members on change management principles.

Finally, if major organizational changes are necessary, an autonomous team is best for developing breakthrough innovations. The team's leader – and possibly others in the team – need to have enough status and authority to influence senior managers throughout the organization. And they need to retain independence of thought and action toward the innovation.

The Relationship Between the Team and the Rest of the Organization

Unless the innovation is completely new to the firm the team will achieve success only if they can work effectively with the rest of the organization. Not only will they need other parts of the organization to cooperate in delivering the innovation but they will also need creative ideas from those who have the relevant expertise. This suggests the team also needs members who can identify and work with partners in the main business (or indeed, from other organizations). These members can connect across boundaries and tap into the expertise of others that is necessary for success.

But you need strategy in choosing and investing in these connections. If the team sets up too many connections, then existing organizational practices and priorities may overwhelm the team's efforts to create innovation. If they set up too few they may miss the important ideas or synergies that they can exploit across the organization. Equally, without enough thought they may connect with a powerful manager who wants to block the innovation. Thus several studies identify the need for thought in setting up these links, not only by the team but also by the guiding coalition.[28] This coalition should have the perspective and power to help the team avoid some of these problems. In doing so, the guiding coalition has to balance the team's need for creative autonomy against the organization's need to build on its strengths. Evidence suggests that this balance should favour fewer working relationships rather than many, although the complexity of the project can also influence this conclusion.

How to Manage Large, Complex Projects Involving Many Parts of the Organization

The project management discipline provides the foundation here, including topics such as deciding goals, project scoping, work breakdown, scheduling, resource planning and critical paths. These topics are not discussed here as they are familiar to most managers. For those less familiar with such ideas a good source is the Project Management Institute's *Project Management Body of Knowledge*.[29] Instead here we ask what changes when an innovation project becomes complex and multifaceted? For example, a breakthrough innovation may require a firm to make simultaneous changes to production technology, service standards, financial systems, customer contracts and organizational structures. Each of these might involve one or more projects in its own right. The overall 'project' then becomes more of a programme of many important projects, each with its own team assigned to it, than one stand-alone project and team.

Loch and his colleagues are among the few who have looked at these programmes.[30] They do so for innovations involving complex engineering projects but their lessons apply to service and business model innovations. While they use simulations, their results have striking parallels to studies of real-world programmes. Most of these studies list a litany of problems, including overruns of cost and time, poor quality solutions and even outright failure.[31] The central issue is managing the interdependencies between the various teams in a way that meets the quality target for the final innovation. These interdependencies create a dynamic in which each team tries to solve its own design problems while making these compatible with the decisions of other teams. But with teams progressing at different speeds and focusing on different technical priorities it becomes hard to manage these interdependencies in a coordinated way.

The base case Loch and colleagues use is of teams who solve their problems locally without reference to other teams and who communicate their design decisions to other teams with delays. This base case is remarkably like the way many large organizations work. Here the simulation results show that as the size and complexity of the overall programme increases, severe problems begin to emerge. Because each team is adjusting to the decisions of others with delays, their own designs can often see-saw back and forward. These designs can also begin to diverge from the needs of other teams. In practice, design restarts are often necessary when one team finds that its previous decisions are no longer relevant because of what others have decided. Such restarts delay overall completion as well as wasting time and resources. Sometimes it may become necessary to freeze some parts of the design to progress at all, even though everyone knows that this will result in the final quality of the innovation being lower. Both restarts and freezing are common problems in real-world programmes. The vignette *Difficulties with doors put a spanner in the works for Renault* provides a real example of such problems and the delays that can result.

Difficulties with doors put a spanner in the works for Renault[38]

In October 2001, the car manufacturer Renault started an ambitious project to develop the Laguna II – a car that represented a genuine leap forward in automotive development. The project, which applied a front-loading strategy to creating an innovative car, was part of Renault's strategic effort to match the achievements of its most efficient rivals.

Renault needed the leaders of the project to make substantial use of outsourcing and drastically reduce development costs and lead times. To do this they needed major technical and organizational innovations as well as experience gained in previous projects. These included process innovations to cut production costs, and new materials to reduce the weight of the car and improve its performance. Innovations also included reducing the number of prototypes in the traditional work stream, and reporting and monitoring schemes to guarantee global convergence of the project.

The project ran seamlessly – with good cooperation between the various teams and no issues with budget or schedule. But just a few months before the scheduled launch, and after major investment in tooling, unexpected problems emerged. When the final prototypes became available the car's quality was below target and the core team identified problems in various areas.

One difficult problem was the design of the doors – an area in which the project had made several process innovations. Doors are difficult to produce because of their large size, but because one of their roles is to keep passengers safe, their quality must be beyond reproach. Production engineers had to reset the stamping presses used to create the doors to correct geometrical misalignments and quality problems. Every adjustment made at this stage can introduce new problems, which eventually forced Renault to delay the car's launch by six months.

After launch, independent experts concluded the door design had always involved some risky choices and that several decisions taken during the project had increased these development risks. The innovative design made the doors difficult to produce, and the design team also opted for new metals and stamping technologies. Further, Renault gave a new external supplier total responsibility for the design and production of the stamping presses. The door design specialists at Renault then focused on meeting economic and scheduling requirements rather than design or technology. No one then followed up on reservations about the technologies used by the supplier.

The frequent changes to various door parts also forced project leaders to postpone testing of the final prototypes several times. And while software tools predicted the doors could go out of shape, many engineers questioned these findings as not representative of real production conditions. When everyone saw the final prototypes, Renault's supplier admitted it had not been able to complete all the adjustments to the presses because of these frequent changes.

Project leaders could not find a satisfactory solution to these problems quickly. So they had to send an internal specialist team from Renault to work at the supplier's premises. After months of trial and error and expensive rework, these specialists identified an effective solution.

Fortunately for Renault, despite the final turbulent phase of this project, the Laguna II was ultimately a commercial success.

There are two possible solutions to overcoming these problems. The first is to split, if possible, the overall programme into largely independent sub-programmes. This reduces the size and complexity of the task for the teams in each sub-programme. This approach is seen in software engineering where large software projects are split into smaller ones, or different teams work on different modules of code. There is often an agreed standard on how modules will work together which forms the glue between modules. Where it is possible, such subdivision is desirable as it is the single best way to overcome problems.

On the other hand many programmes do not subdivide easily and here Loch and colleagues look at various methods for improving cooperation among the teams. These methods include: (1) teams that sacrifice their own local performance for bigger gains by another team; (2) communicating rough designs and (3) immediately broadcasting any design decision as it occurs. The first two of these methods concern the rules under which teams work, whereas the third suggests the use of technologies like intranets and wikis. All three dramatically improve final performance by shortening completion time, reducing restarts and improving innovation quality.

Finally, these experts also look at reducing the number of interdependencies that have to be considered. That is, each team pays attention to some but not all the connections in its programme network. The results here imply a trade-off. Reducing the number of connections improves completion time and lessens restarts but also reduces the quality of the final solution. How the core team sets up connections between other teams is thus important to the success of complex programmes. This parallels the advice in the previous section, although it comes from a different perspective. In that section, the concern was resistance to change; here it is carefully reducing the complexity of the problem for a team. On both counts it is important that thought and strategy go into defining the working connections between all the teams that are necessary to complete the programme.

Is a Separate Business Unit Needed?

Chapter 3 briefly raises the controversial topic of whether to develop break-through innovations within existing organizations or separate business units. This is a good point to revisit this topic in more depth. Different experts take differ-ent and sometimes rigid stances on this matter, while the idea of an ambidextrous executive tries to resolve the tension between these extremes.

The strategy and innovation literature sees the decision for a separate unit mainly as one based on the firm's capabilities and culture. Does the existing organization have the capabilities to deliver the innovation? Does the organiza-tional culture support the delivery of the innovation? If the answer to both questions is negative then a separate unit is necessary. Some experts approach the issue from the perspective of knowledge. What part of the knowledge necessary to develop the innovation does the new unit need to borrow from the existing organization? What part does it need to forget? What part must it learn from scratch? Depending on the balance between borrowing, forgetting and learning, and whether the culture and priorities of the existing business make these more or less difficult, a separate unit may be necessary.[32]

However, all of these views make two assumptions that are open to question. The first assumption is that the existing organization is incapable of change. Writers often paint a picture of a big monolith overwhelming the small venture. In contrast, change management experts assume that, while change can be challenging, even large-scale change is possible. Indeed, real organizations change and adapt all the time, often on the small scale but also on the large. The second assumption is that the separate unit can develop breakthrough innovation effectively without drawing extensively on the capabilities of the parent organization. This may well be true for some product innovations. But service or business model innovation may strike a different balance between borrowing and new learning. The strategy literature also treats innovations as in some ways simple projects, which one team or a small start-up can develop. In reality significant innovations now emerge from the complex programmes mentioned before. Again this strikes a different balance between borrowing and new learning.

Service and business model innovations need an extensive range of skills and experience drawn from many parts of the organization. At the minimum this includes skills in marketing, finance, legal, human resources and information technology. Service innovations often need large numbers of people to deliver them, so teams must bring change management, training and job redesign into the picture. To task the innovation team, even in an internal start-up, with the challenge of developing all this without borrowing from the existing organization seems unrealistic. It would not only be uneconomical but also increase the risks of failure by placing too many demands on the innovation team. Thus, these innovations usually draw on the skills, knowledge and resources of the existing organization.

Some circumstances need a greenfield start-up, but these will be exceptional. Two conditions are necessary for such an independent start-up. The first is when the firm's leadership decides not to change the existing organization. They may take such a decision because of business priorities, principally the need to preserve cash flow. Or because the leadership anticipates strong resistance to change and decides it is quicker to build a new organization than change the old. The second is when the innovation team does not need to borrow the existing skills, experience and resources of the organization. If this is the case, this is tantamount to saying the innovation lies in an area that is totally new to the organization in all dimensions. This is a risky venture to undertake. Indeed, the decision to work within the existing organization or to build a separate business unit is essentially one of risk and return. However, to the typical strategy considerations of economic priorities and firm capabilities, the discussion here adds change management. For breakthrough innovations, the firm's leadership needs to take a much broader view of both the necessary capabilities and the scale of the change management challenge.

There is also the issue of timing. The conclusion above is that the core team cannot calibrate the scale of the change management challenge thoroughly until Stage 4. Equally, until the design of the innovation becomes clearer it is difficult to assess whether and what the team needs to borrow from the existing organization. This assessment itself needs cooperation from the rest of the organization, as well as a degree of objectivity in the project team. The dual need for cooperation and objectivity is yet another reason for having an autonomous project team. Thus work on all major innovations should start out as a team project working within the existing organization but distinct and separate from it in reporting and authority. During Stage 4 the team's tasks should include assessing all these issues of change, capabilities and resources. At the Gate 4 decision, before commercialization, the gate committee and firm leadership can then consider whether a separate business unit is necessary for success.

ACTION STEPS: ORGANIZATIONAL PRINCIPLES FOR INNOVATION MANAGEMENT

The principles of change management are clearly relevant to managing innovation but need adapting to account for important differences and key decisions. These adapted principles then become the action steps for managing major innovations, including both breakthroughs and significant incremental innovations.

First, there are preconditions for the success of innovation in the organization. Exhibit 6.2 sets out these preconditions, which are general principles that mainly concern the leadership of the firm. In particular, the messages they communicate to the organization at large and the behaviour they display towards specific innovation projects. These principles should also be in the Innovation Charter.

The CEO, CIO and VP of innovation, together with other senior executives, should:

1. Identify the directions for innovation and present the supporting arguments for these directions.
2. Build a powerful guiding coalition to:
    a. advocate the direction and need for innovation;
    b. overcome structural and economic resistance;
    c. engender the correct degree of urgency in key people and units;
    d. demonstrate their tolerance of failure.
3. Agree on the appropriate scale, time-frame and acceptable risk for the portfolio of innovation projects, considering:
    a. the speed and strength of external events; and
    b. the business risks and returns of various time-frames.
4. Allocate resources and rewards for achieving the necessary innovation, including:
    a. a well-defined process for releasing funds to innovation projects
    b. schemes for recognizing and rewarding both individuals and teams.

Exhibit 6.2   Organizational preconditions for successful innovation.

Second, there are principles that apply to managing specific projects, but these vary according to who is applying them and what stage the project is at. Exhibits 6.3 to 6.6 set out these principles. Exhibit 6.3 is relevant to the leadership of the firm and shows how their role changes between the front-end, development and commercialization. Exhibit 6.4 follows a similar sequence for the project sponsor and Exhibit 6.5 for the gate committee. All these exhibits have some likenesses because they concern the roles and decisions of executives and senior managers.

Exhibit 6.6 is different, because it focuses on the role of the core innovation team itself. This is the logical place for ideas and frameworks about understanding resistance to change, communicating effectively, managing projects and empowering others. The team should be responsible for identifying how to change the organization to support the innovation. Of course, this responsibility is also subject to the approval and support of the team's sponsor, gate committee and guiding coalition.

If this all looks different from best practice in new product development, with its emphasis on flowcharts and technology, then so it should. Major innovations, especially those that go beyond the product, need much more leadership of the organization at large than new product development. One important ingredient of this leadership is changing the organization so the innovation gets the support necessary for its success.

The preconditions in Exhibit 6.2 are common to all successful innovating firms, whether they are product or service firms or large or small ones. Many of the principles in Exhibits 6.3 and 6.4 are also common to successful firms

Front-end (Stages 1 through 3)	Development (Stage 4)	Commercialization (Stage 5)
Choose carefully the project sponsor, team leader and team members in the light of change management and organizational issues as well as their skills in developing innovations.	If the project sponsor asks for it, provide further support to remove organizational roadblocks.	Actively support the change initiative.
Invest in briefing and preparing the core innovation team, including: • team building and training • assessing whether a change consultant is necessary to facilitate their work	Make sure the team's achievements thus far, together with those of others playing a part in the project, get adequate internal publicity and recognition.	Publicize and recognize short-term successes and other achievements.
Carefully delineate the area of the team's autonomy, positioning its work for the rest of the organization and providing advice on how it should build working relationships with other parts of the organization.		Institutionalize the new approaches.
		Reward the team when market and financial objectives are met.

Exhibit 6.3   Guiding coalition's organizational principles for specific innovation projects.

Front-end (Stages 1 through 3)	Development (Stage 4)	Commercialization (Stage 5)
Protect and encourage the core innovation team's creative autonomy.	Support the development efforts of the team, including advice on working relationships and intervening when necessary to remove organizational roadblocks.	Actively support change, including overcoming roadblocks and finding additional resources if necessary.
Provide advice on where ideas and expertise might come from within the organization.	Sharing insights and ideas between innovation teams, including suggesting useful links that can be made between teams and with other parts of the organization.	Identify insights and ideas that are useful to other projects and future initiatives and make sure the organization understands and learns from these.
Encourage and mentor effective teamwork.		

Exhibit 6.4   Organizational principles for the executive sponsor of an innovation project.

Gate 3 (go to Development)	Gate 4 (go to Commercialization)
Consider the core team's preliminary assessment of the scale of change the innovation requires.	Consider the scale of change the innovation requires, and the knowledge, competences and resources necessary to bring it to market successfully.
Provide the resources and support for a more thorough assessment of the scale of change during development. Also for the core team to devise a change management strategy for commercialization.	Decide whether to commercialize the innovation through the existing organization or to set up a separate business unit.
Decide whether a change consultant is needed to facilitate the development and commercialization phases. Similarly, decide whether additional project management expertise is needed for complex projects.	Approve or amend the change management strategy the core innovation team proposes.

Exhibit 6.5 Organizational principles for the gate committee looking at a specific project.

Front-end (Stages 1 through 3)	Development (Stage 4)	Commercialization (Stage 5)
Be sensitive to potential change issues in early work (Stages 1 and 2).	Given the innovation, understand the present context and likely resistance, by: • using surveys and qualitative methods • attending to emotions as well as beliefs.	Implement the change strategy.
Conduct a preliminary assessment of the scale of change the innovation requires (Stage 3). Include this assessment in the business case for development funding.	Develop strategy and tactics for communicating the direction and need for change, including by: • preparing simple and more contextualized messages • providing answers to counter arguments • ensuring multiple forms of delivery.	Plan and create short-term successes.
Develop a plan for assessing change management issues more thoroughly and also include this in the business case.	Provide a full assessment of the scale of change necessary to achieve success for the innovation, including knowledge, competences and resources. Develop a strategy for carrying out the necessary changes. Include both assessment and strategy in the proposal for commercialization funding.	Consolidate improvements and produce still more change.
	For complex projects, split the work into independent projects and establish coordinating rules, including by: • encouraging other teams to communicate rough rather than final solutions • mandating the immediate broadcasting of design decision made by all teams • achieving clarity on compromises between local and global performance.	
	For complex projects, develop working relationships carefully to fit the project structure, including by: • understanding which links need priority attention and which need less • empowering other teams and units to develop solutions through their own insights.	

Exhibit 6.6 Organizational principles for the core innovation team.

regardless of industry or organization. It is only the principles in Exhibits 6.5 and 6.6 whose precise implementation may differ according to circumstances. Specifically, applying these principles may differ according to the degree of innovation, which of the three challenges is most important and the firm's organizational culture. Most of these differences concern managing people and the degree to which change management is necessary.

Breakthroughs Need Expertise in Change and Project Management

It is easy to see that breakthrough innovations need more attention to the steps in Exhibits 6.5 and 6.6 than incremental ones. Incremental innovations stem from what people in the organization already understand, so change management is much less necessary. Communication, project management and empowerment are still important, but here misunderstanding or resistance is less likely. Incremental innovations also build on existing organizational and procedures and so they need fewer changes in the way people work. There are undoubtedly some lessons in these principles for all innovations, especially those around project management, but incremental ones need less effort on the change-related principles.

Where project management may differ between breakthrough and incremental innovation concerns large, complex innovation projects. In particular, how the core team goes about choosing which connections to set up between all the various teams they have working on the project. The fourth principle in the Development column of Exhibit 6.6 suggests the core team should do this with care. Indeed, while many authors recommend setting up connections to all the important areas of the firm, this is not always the best idea. Connections improve communication, especially of rough designs and conclusions, and they generate more perspectives on possible solutions. However, such connections also introduce delays as the core team consults the various areas and their individual projects. And delays can lead to turbulence in the overall project. Hence the need for core teams to set up project links with care. This is true for all complex innovations but breakthrough innovations introduce additional complexities. Firstly, by their nature they are likely to involve areas that are not familiar with working together, which increases the barriers between them. Secondly, by definition all the various teams are working on something of which they have little or no experience. This makes timely receipt of design ideas from other teams more important. For breakthrough innovations delays on critical tasks can thus be more dangerous, leading to restarts and redesigns. The core team needs to ensure the right teams get the right information at the right time. This suggests that core teams should possess or acquire good skills in project management, as well as the necessary depth and breadth of technical knowledge relevant to their project. That will allow them to set up connections in the best way.

At the extreme, some breakthrough projects are so complex that it may be better to reduce their overall complexity by appointing one area to the leadership role.[33] This area is likely to be the one with the biggest role or stake in the success of the innovation. Gate committees decide about putting one area in charge at Gate 3.

The Mix of Challenges Determines the Focus of Change and Project Management

The mix of the three challenges will also have an impact on how sponsors and core teams apply these principles. Customer, development and appropriation challenges each bring their own change and project management demands. Customer innovations often require new mind-sets in marketing and sales, as well as integrating lead users into the project or applying new market research methods. Innovations with a major component of services that need employee–customer interaction will typically need more attention to the change-related principles in Exhibits 6.5 and 6.6. This is especially true for large organizations that must change the skills and behaviour of many service personnel. Development innovations that target performance improvements or technological breakthroughs will need more attention to communication between scientists and technologists. If the innovation requires major changes to manufacturing processes, or the way the firm organizes its back office to deliver services, change management will become more important. Changes to manufacturing might stress retraining production employees, while changes to back-office services might stress IT, analytics and overcoming resistance in service personnel. Similarly, appropriation innovations with new business models will need effort to explain and overcome resistance throughout the organization, not just at the client interface. As well as possibly involving external partners in both the innovation project and changing their way of business.

The specific mix of the three challenges in any innovation project will thus determine the focus of change and project management. Including decisions on who needs to work with whom, how teams communicate ideas, what new skills employees need or where resistance needs to be overcome.

The Existing Organizational Culture Provides the Starting Point

In thinking about changing the organization to deliver an innovation an obvious starting point is the existing culture of the organization. Some organizational cultures are more open to change and innovation than others. Knowing the starting point allows a better evaluation of the degree of change and a good choice of change strategy. Indeed, an assessment of the existing culture is one of the key principles in Exhibit 6.6.

There are many frameworks for examining organizational culture. Three well-known ones are the organizational cultural assessment instrument, Booz Allen's organizational DNA and the cultural web.[34] By applying them to thousands of organizations researchers have built a strong body of evidence. Evidence that shows a minority of firms can change readily, but most need deliberate change management to achieve any change at all.

For example, Booz Allen say the most common culture in their database of firms is one they label 'passive-aggressive'. These cultures represent about 27% of large firms and display quiet but tenacious resistance to directives from their leadership. Developing an innovation with major service or business model changes in such an organization would need major efforts to manage change, as well as subtle and well-conceived strategies of change. In contrast, the 17% of firms with 'resilient' cultures readily cope with change every day. Indeed, these firms, which are often found in high-tech industries, follow many of the organizational principles listed here. Developing a similar innovation in these firms would need little effort in change management and far simpler strategies. To apply the principles in Exhibits 6.5 and 6.6 you have to know what the starting point is. However, for innovation this assessment needs customizing to the specifics of the innovation itself. The toolkit for this chapter includes two tools to do this.

For managing complex innovation projects most of the principles are applicable regardless of culture. However, two principles in Exhibit 6.6 may be harder to achieve in some organizational cultures than others. These are achieving clarity between local and global performance and empowering teams to develop solutions through their own insights. The former concerns a team settling for less in their part of the project so another team has the freedom to achieve more. In non-cooperative organizational cultures this principle will need more effort to set up than in cooperative ones. However, in complex projects where optimizing one part of the project may prejudice greater gains elsewhere this is an important principle to uphold. Some researchers suggest that empowerment is easier to achieve in some organizational and national cultures than others.[35] Where there is an over-reliance on the founder of the firm or a tradition of following authority it may be hard for others to express themselves creatively. It is important for the success of the innovation they do so and again, the core innovation team will need to devote more effort to this.

LINKS TO OTHER TASKS

This chapter has several links to others. The most visible links are the similarities between changing the minds of employees and customers.

Links to Chapter 2 – *Creating Advantage in the Minds of Many* and Chapter 7 – *Building the Market for the Innovation*. An employee and a customer are one and the same person, with the same biases and capacities to make decisions. Thus while the degree of change may be greater when individuals are in their role as employees, the way in which change happens is similar. The ideas of change management, marketing and political campaigning have a great deal in common. In all three, leaders try to change the mind of others through clever persuasion and in all three they meet the forces of resistance. The common theme is building a suitable communication strategy with various messages to deliver to different audiences in different formats. Thus, some parts of Chapter 2 provide scientific backing for the change management strategies described in this one, and both these chapters are relevant to Chapter 7. The latter also explores similar ideas and strategies but with the goal of launching the innovation in the market. Overall, skills in building powerful messages are critical to success in so many aspects of innovation that sponsors and teams must possess or develop them.

Links to Chapter 3 – *Chartering Innovation within the Organization* and Chapter 4 – *Selecting, Preparing and Supporting the Right Team*. The ideas in this chapter, in particular the principles in Exhibits 6.2 through 6.6, provide added support for the recommendations in those chapters. How the organization understands innovation needs to reflect best practice in change and innovation management.

This includes the behaviour of the leadership team and the various procedures that govern developing innovation. Similarly selecting, preparing and supporting the core innovation team needs to reflect this best practice. In many instances, this core team needs change management skills. Intertwined with these skills are those of managing complex projects in large organizations. Breakthrough innovation often requires contributions from many people outside the core team. Being able to empower these people, yet preserve coherence in the project, needs skill but it also requires the right support, governance and core team members.

TOOLKIT FOR CHAPTER 6

This section provides two tools for assessing the scale of organizational change the innovation requires. Assessing the scale of change is an important step in estimating the real cost of the innovation and in developing a change management strategy. This is necessary for innovation ideas that imply large-scale change or where organizational cultures may resist the innovation. Two assessments are necessary, a preliminary one before Gate 3 and a more thorough one before Gate 4. Both are critical to the gate committee's decision to first develop and then commercialize the innovation. As the focus and methods for doing the preliminary and thorough assessments are different two separate tools are necessary.

The toolkit for this chapter might also have included a tool for designing messages about change. However, there is much overlap between ideas on simple change messages and the idea of positioning in Chapter 7. So the reader is referred to that chapter for further discussion.

Tool One: Assessing the Scale of Change for the Go to Development Decision

Background

The core team needs to have a preliminary assessment of the scale of change their ideas imply for their organization. This assessment should include the nature and likely sources of any resistance that may emerge once an innovation moves into development or commercialization. The team conducts the preliminary assessment informally and in confidence. Their conclusions form one part of the business case that goes to the gate committee at Gate 3. This allows the committee to compare the change implications of various projects and evaluate the full costs and benefits of approving development.

Timing

The preliminary assessment should occur towards the end of the front-end, when the innovation team has three or four high priority innovation concepts to consider. These concepts need to have reached the stage at which the team can explain them to other people in an easily understandable manner. Typically, this explanation needs the support of sketches, models or computer representations, as well as verbal and written specifications.

The assessment itself can be part of the more typical discussions that occur between the team and others at this stage. Indeed, in a limited sense, preliminary change assessment is simply the result of being sensitive to certain organizational issues during these discussions. However, the team needs to meet a wider set of people to understand fully the challenge each innovation presents. Being sensitive to change also implies thinking carefully about whose views need checking.

Objectives

The objectives of this preliminary assessment are twofold.

1. Get an understanding of what the consequences of each innovation concept are for various parts of the organization and various levels of employee.
2. Identify the likely sources and nature of any resistance to each innovation concept.

Methods

The team meets the two objectives chiefly through qualitative rather than quantitative information. The overall goal is to produce a dossier of insights, conclusions and recommendations that allow the innovation team to evaluate the scale of change. In most circumstances teams should avoid surveys and questionnaires. Good surveys are hard to design and interpret without expert help. Besides, it is often hard to explain the innovation adequately in a survey. Thus, the method of choice here is one-on-one interviews or small group discussions between the team and other relevant individuals and groups. The innovation team needs to develop a list of topics for these meetings, remembering that they should be about more than just the change assessment. The team also needs to appoint one of its members to guide the discussion and another to record the key points that emerge.

Potential discussion topics include:

- reactions to the innovation concepts (positive first, then negatives);
- the change consequences of each innovation (relating to such aspects as skills, procedures, business priorities and resources);
- what is needed to develop and commercialize each concept, including any changes to organization and people;
- what role participants and their areas might play in development and commercialization;
- the main arguments for and against any changes resulting from these innovations;
- the areas in which there may be resistance from others and suggestions to overcome this.

Alongside discussion topics, the innovation team also needs to develop a plan of whom to talk to. Normally, innovation teams focus on the key people and areas that concern the technical development and delivery of the innovation. However, experience suggests they also need to assess who has formal and informal power in the organization, including those who might see the innovation as a threat. The latter may not even have a technical role in development or delivery. The team also should canvass the views of people in different levels of the organization, including front-line employees in service firms. The team might not need to involve the latter in development but it does need to assess the challenge of changing the skills or procedures at this employee level.

Overall, the schedule of meetings needs careful construction. This schedule also needs the advice and approval of the team's sponsor because of the political consequences that may emerge from the assessment within the firm.

Deliverables

The preliminary assessment provides an evaluation of the organizational changes that will be necessary to make a success of each innovation idea. This evaluation will be one factor in the team's final choice of innovation to propose to the gate committee for development. The team's submission to Gate 3 will include a summary of their discussions. Plus their view on the organizational implications of the innovation they propose. Their submission will also include a plan for doing a more thorough change assessment during development, once the innovation takes final shape. The team will also seek approval to prepare a change management strategy for the commercialization stage.

Tool Two: Assessing the Scale of Change for the Go to Commercialization Decision

Background

During development the innovation will take more definite shape and its organizational implications will become clearer as a result. The team will therefore need to examine the scale of change again, this time for the final innovation they will propose to the gate committee at Gate 4. Gate 4 is the biggest decision gate committees face because the innovation goes 'live' if they approve it. So the committee will need to understand the full organizational implications, costs and benefits of the innovation. Thus the change assessment has to be thorough, and the team should also prepare a change management strategy for the commercialization stage. At this point the assessment should lead to strategies and plans that, if approved, the team will put into effect in the next stage.

Timing

The team should conduct this change assessment and prepare their change strategy towards the end of the development stage. There is no point doing either until the final specification of the innovation is reasonably clear but they also need to allow enough time to do a good job. In particular, this assessment may involve more formal techniques such as surveys which will take several weeks to run and analyse. Equally preparing an effective change strategy will take several discussions, not only within the team but also with other executives, managers and employees.

Objectives

The objectives here are three-fold:

1. Prepare an assessment of all the organizational implications of delivering the innovation, including positive and negative consequences.
2. Propose how the organization will need to change to deliver the innovation successfully, including changes to jobs, skills, reporting relationships and organization charts.
3. Prepare a change management strategy and plan to carry these changes out, including full costs of reorganization, retraining, etc.

Methods

The team will follow two approaches here. The first will be meetings and discussions with executives, managers and employees following a similar agenda and format to the preliminary assessment. Indeed, the only real difference is there will now only be one, final innovation to discuss. However, the second approach, especially in large organizations, may need to be more formal. Methods here can include questionnaire surveys, depth interviews, psychological instruments and observation. They can also include questionnaires or group discussion techniques to assess organizational culture. The team may wish to seek help with these from an internal expert or external consultant.

They may also need this person's help for what follows when they have enough information. To achieve the second and third objectives the team will need to hold internal workshops to consider what the new organization might look like. What organization, skills and mind-sets will deliver the innovation successfully? Once they have a view on those issues they can move to the final step. This is to decide on the overall strategy and specific steps the firm will need to take to move from its present organization to the new one. Here their detailed assessment of likely resistance and possible barriers to change will help them draw up a good strategy and plan.

Deliverables

The team needs to deliver two things to the gate committee. The first is a detailed proposal for what the proposed organization should look like, how it will operate and what sorts of people it needs. The second is their strategy and plan for changing to this organization during the commercialization stage. Together these allow the gate committee to make a good decision on whether the returns from the innovation justify this scale of change.

Key Source for Further Reference: M. Beitler, *Strategic Organizational Change*, Greensboro NC, Practitioner Press International 2006.

CHAPTER 7

BUILDING THE MARKET FOR THE INNOVATION

INTRODUCTION

One of the main themes of this book is that marketing an innovation effectively is just as important as developing the right innovation. Simply because the firm develops a better product or service does not guarantee that it will sell. This is especially true if the innovation customers are to adopt is radically different from the solutions they are familiar with. Chapter 2 sets out the skills, resources and customer insight firms need to persuade customers to adopt a significant innovation. These include recognizing the differences between innovators, connectors and mainstream customers, and understanding how to influence each of them to see the benefits of adoption. Firms can present their message consistently and compellingly by framing the innovation in a positive and relevant way. And then using all the local influences the marketer can access to bring this message to the customer. Marketers also need to be aware of positive and negative influences outside their control. As Machiavelli noted, 'He who innovates will have for his enemies all those who are well off under the existing order of things, and only lukewarm supporters in those who might be better off under the new.'[1]

Indeed, the challenges of marketing a breakthrough innovation are like those of a presidential political campaign, or gaining support for a referendum. The goal is similar – to persuade many people that your case for change is a good one. But there will be people who do not agree with your case, just as in a political campaign. As well unforeseen events such as service or safety problems or attacks by critics may occur that need an effective response or counter-offensive. Firms need a strong public relations capability to handle such events.

Political scientists point out the environment for communication and public relations campaigns is vastly different in the twenty-first century. Many more communication technologies and channels are available. They reach narrower targets and provide much cheaper access to them than the mainstream twentieth century media was ever able to. As a result the numbers of commentators on political events have multiplied and the mainstream media and their associated commentators have lost influence.[2] This is equally true of innovative products and services. A recent conference of the Marketing Science Institute on the new media landscape has detailed the many different ways of reaching consumers. As one speaker put it, there are now 'more colours in the crayon box' of the marketing communications professional.[3] Instead of brands built solely by traditional media, firms now build brands through contact points and experience (Starbucks, Zara), by events or communities (Ducati, Kiehls), through the Internet (Amazon, Google) or by good citizenship and publicity (Virgin). Soon someone will build a new global brand through mobile devices, through online virtual reality games or on a social networking site like My Space.

The striking feature of the new media landscape is the increasing number of commentators and the shift in power from supplier to customer. The commentators now include individual customers reporting on their experiences, offering their opinions or rating products on websites. They also include professional, or self-appointed, experts who blog on particular topics, as well as buying recommendations from both humans and software algorithms. While customers have always trusted the buying advice of family and friends, nowadays we also trust the advice we receive online.[4] This may be because we can hear and judge differing opinions and relate them to our needs. In a few minutes of online browsing we can collect many more of these opinions than hitherto. Finally, the new technologies allow customers to band together to overturn firm decisions or lobby for changes that they think are necessary. For example, in August 2007 several thousand UK students got together through Facebook to lobby and reverse a decision on overdrafts by the HSBC. The vignette *Customer power on the Internet* provides other examples.

Customer power through the Internet[45]

Almost as long as there have been books there have been book reviews, and publishers quickly learned that quoting the best reviews on the jacket helped sell a book. With the arrival of the Internet Amazon went a step further, enabling readers to post their own reviews, exploiting the trend towards peer interaction on the World Wide Web.

Other Internet retailers have developed similar features to sell their goods. Online shoppers can seek out a product and read reviews from customers who have already bought it. Many web stores now use star ratings produced directly by customer feedback. The example of Petco Animal Supplies, an online pet store, shows the power of customer opinion. Their analysis of website sales showed that customers who navigated to the pages of top-rated products converted to a sale at a 50% higher rate than others. When they included customer star ratings in a trial e-mail marketing campaign, they witnessed a click-through rate five times above the usual response.

Although Amazon has attracted criticism for not publishing negative reviews, other retailers have used good and bad reviews to their advantage. Retailers now respond to negative customer reviews by dropping lines from their catalogue and replacing them with higher quality items that sell better. Such a response is not only useful to the retailer, but also to the manufacturer, who can adapt or improve the product in the face of consumer disapproval.

Customer power expresses itself through other less controllable ways on the Internet. People discuss products endlessly on specialist or enthusiast forums or on blogs that can have a worldwide audience. In September 2004, a San Francisco cyclist posted a message on a bike forum that he could open a Kryptonite lock using only a cheap ballpoint pen. The word spread quickly to other online forums and a video displaying the technique appeared on YouTube. The mainstream press then picked up the story and within 10 days of the original posting Kryptonite was forced to announce that it would replace locks at no cost to the customer. The estimated cost to Kryptonite was $10 million, out of annual revenues of $25 million.

The lesson to firms is clear: ignore consumer networking on the Internet at your danger. Customers have always trusted their peers far more than any marketing pitch, but now the word can pass between millions of mouths in a few days.

So, the communication environment into which an innovation campaign now enters is vast, diverse and unpredictable. Local influences in this environment are simultaneously sophisticated and naive, thoughtful and unthinking, spontaneous and structured, authoritative and mistaken. This all gives individual customers far greater choice in the way they receive and experience these influences, who they want to listen to, and how they want to join with other customers to change what firms do.

Because of customer power, this chapter goes beyond the basic principles of launching products and services. It examines how to frame the innovation for different customers, and how to react to competition and independent criticism, and it considers the new media landscape. The chapter is in five sections. The first three of these follow the sequence that a firm must use in building a new market. First, and before launch, the firm must choose the right innovators to target. It must then design an offer that works for these target customers and develop a message that will attract them to this offer. This leads immediately to the second section: how to get sales moving by engaging these innovators through media and other channels of communication. The third section then describes how to appeal to connectors and mainstream customers. If the connectors help spread positive messages then it is far more likely that mainstream customers will follow and the market will reach its true potential. However, if the needs of these mainstream customers are different from those of earlier adopters the firm may need to extend or adapt the innovation for them. The fourth section looks at the action steps that follow from this chapter and the different circumstances that firms may face. One important difference is between firms that pioneer and those that follow. Finally, the fifth section identifies the links between the task of building the market and the tasks in other chapters. The main link is between the lessons from this chapter and the need for many firms to rethink the planning methods and gate criteria they use for innovations. The Toolkit for this chapter includes templates for designing the market and positioning the innovation, and ways to deal with the opposition.

BEFORE LAUNCH

Before launch the three important tasks are choosing the target customers, designing the right offer for them and positioning this offer in their mind so it is attractive. To build a new market the first target customers are the innovators. This is a small segment of most markets (perhaps less than 10% of potential customers) but it is vital to building the market. Unless the innovators adopt the rest will not follow.

Choosing the Target Customer

'Innovator' is a catch-all word for customers who take the risk to adopt a novel product or service they think might add value to their lives or businesses. For specific innovations, the innovation team needs a more detailed description of the customers they expect to be the innovators in their market. This description will follow directly from work they did earlier in development. While working with customers to co-create the innovation (Chapter 5) they develop a description of their likely target customers, including the innovators among them. This description will probably need revisiting because the innovation is now a concrete product or service rather than just an idea, but it can provide the starting point.

The team must now refine this description, check it against all the information they have and rewrite it so it can guide marketing. In some circumstances there may be more than one possible target, especially when the innovation represents a technology with several possible applications. In those circumstances the team may also need to decide their priorities. Which application should come first? Criteria for choosing the priorities should include the market potential of the application and the likelihood that it will be accepted by the innovators. However, remembering the power of social influence discussed in Chapter 2, another might be the impact that a successful launch will have on developing follow-on markets.

The target innovator will have a lot in common with the typical customer for the innovation. Indeed, the basic needs the innovation aims to satisfy will be the same for both. The differences between innovators and mainstream customers lie in the way they approach the adoption decision and the sources of local influence to which they listen. In some markets innovators may be willing to adopt an innovation that is still work in progress or 'first-generation.' In contrast, mainstream customers might prefer to wait for the fully developed second- or third-generation innovation.[5] Equally, the firm and innovation team need to plan for the mainstream market because that is where they will make most money. For all these reasons it is better to write a description of this eventual mainstream market, with the typical customer and their needs, and then specify how the innovators might differ from this. The toolkit for this chapter offers some guidance on this, as well as an example.

Research results also offer guidance on the characteristics which discriminate between innovators and mainstream customers.[6] These span many socioeconomic, personality and communication characteristics. For example, socioeconomic characteristics include those with more education, higher social status or larger resources. Their personality characteristics include items like having greater empathy and a greater ability to deal with abstractions, and being less dogmatic. Communication characteristics include such things as greater exposure to change agents and to mass communication, and seeking information more actively than typical customers. There are many, many more in each category.

The research has three limitations. The first is that these characteristics are proxies for the underlying trait of innovativeness. Chapter 2 shows the innovativeness of individuals depends on the plasticity and stability of their character. Equally, the innovativeness of organizations stems from a complex set of organizational and economic causes. Thus, teams would need extensive research and customized measures to identify innovativeness towards a specific class of products or services. Because such research is typically not available proxies are necessary.

Second, these characteristics define people's tendencies. They identify a set of people who are more likely to innovate than others who are less likely to do so. Whether people actually adopt depends on the benefits of the innovation, and social and other local influences. Thus, these characteristics do not automatically translate into actions when the customer decides to adopt or reject the product.[7]

Third, these characteristics are simply candidates for consideration. The team will need to work out what matters in their market. In particular, they must decide which two or three characteristics are both important and help them develop the offer and the marketing campaign that goes with it. The resulting description needs to be both meaningful for the specific market and actionable for marketing purposes. This in turn requires insight into the market, and analysis and debate among the team. But this step is critical because a clear view of the innovator is a precondition for all that follows, including the next step: designing the right offer.

Designing the Right Offer

To marketing people the offer is more than the core product or service itself. It also encompasses surrounding elements such as pricing, terms and conditions, place of purchase, after-sales support and user communities. In his book *The*

Momentum Effect Larreche points out the key to designing a powerful offer is two-fold. First to increase the benefits the customer perceives in the offer. And second to decrease the costs they perceive in buying and using it.[8] Kim and Mauborgne make a similar point with their grid, 'eliminate-reduce-raise-create', that examines whether parts of the offer add value to the customer.[9] They argue that firms should eliminate or reduce parts that do not add value, thus reducing the firm's costs. And they should raise or create parts that do add value, thus increasing demand.

Customers make their adoption decision through the benefits the product or service provides and not because of its specific features or the way it achieves whatever it does. Thus, a busy household might buy an innovative washing machine because it completes a load quicker (a performance benefit) or because it is easier to use (a convenience benefit). They do not buy it because the machine's motor has specific revolutions a minute or its control panel has a certain design. Rather the household buys because the benefits of the offer meet the needs of their busy lifestyle. The word *perceives* is also crucial. What also matters to their decision is what message they see, hear and remember about the washing machine, not what experts or engineers know about the product. In the cluttered and fragmented information environment of the twenty-first century, with many competing local influences, getting a clear and compelling message through to customers is not easy. However, before looking at that challenge, we need to develop the idea of increasing benefits and lowering costs. Indeed, behind these lies a broader palette of possible offer designs and communication strategies that can help create Larreche's power offer.

From his review of innovation research Rogers sets out five factors that speed or retard the adoption of innovations by the market. These are (1) relative advantage, (2) compatibility, (3) trialability, (4) observability and (5) complexity.[10] An innovation that has more of the first four factors increases the rate of its adoption, while its complexity slows down its adoption.

It has relative advantage in the degree to which people perceive it to be better than the idea it supersedes. It is compatible if people think it fits their values and beliefs, previously introduced ideas, and needs. Many people argue that firms should not launch innovations unless they meet the needs of customers. However, there is a distinction between needs that customers immediately feel and those that are latent and only emerge as customers come to understand the innovation. One role of marketing is to help customers express their latent needs. Relative advantage and compatibility concern the benefits of the offer.

In our hypothetical washing machine its relative advantage might be the benefit of its performance and its compatibility might be its convenience.

The innovation has trialability when potential customers can experiment without buying the innovation. This speeds adoption but is more important for innovators than mainstream customers. While innovators have no experience or precedents they can use to judge the innovation, mainstream customers have access to information from other customers. Trialability is thus another way to reduce the perceived costs of the innovation to the innovators.

The innovation has observability in the degree to which its results are visible to others. Note that it is the results that matter most, not simply observing the existence of the product or service. Observable innovations do better than ones where the results are less visible. Observability also reduces the customer's perceived costs of both evaluating the innovation (because others clearly value it) and it reduces risk (because it works for others).

Like compatibility, complexity also concerns how difficult the innovation is to understand or use, but it falls into the costs rather than benefits side of the equation. In general, people do not like complexity and they take a long time to develop an understanding of the innovation, if indeed they ever bother to do so. So complexity typically slows down adoption.

Are these five factors enough to encourage adoption? Economists would add a sixth, risk. This could be both economic risk (monetary loss) and social risk (status loss), depending on the nature of the innovation. As we saw in Chapter 2, risk triggers emotions that influence the eventual decisions of customers to adopt or reject. Risk is therefore an important part of the perceived costs of the innovation.

Rogers also makes a good point in noting that for an actual innovation it is necessary to develop an exhaustive list of benefits and costs. Most of these will fall under the six headings described above, but there may also be others specific to the innovation. Techniques such as voice-of-the-customer and means–ends chains (Chapter 5) can help here. Because the innovation team needs to pay as much attention to perceived costs as to benefits, the six factors therefore help the team to cover both aspects.

For designing a power offer, marketers should try to increase their customers' perceptions of the relative advantage and compatibility of the innovation, while decreasing perceptions of its complexity and risk. They should do whatever they can to increase its trialability and observability and in this way they should maximize the chances of rapid adoption.

We have not addressed the problem of getting a message through to the target customer in the cluttered and fragmented information environment of the twenty-first century. In the most common scenario the innovation will have several benefits, both new and existing. It may also have several costs and typically many more features that underpin both benefits and costs. Trying to communicate all this complexity is difficult, if not impossible, and doing so risks rejection because people abhor complexity.

For that reason, marketing professionals focus on choosing the key points they want to get across in their early campaigns. Once they can attract the attention of the target customer, they can start engaging with them and encouraging them to gain a deeper understanding of the innovation. Developing a message which gets this early attention is what psychologists and political scientists call 'framing' and marketing professionals call 'positioning'.

Positioning the Offer in the Mind of the Customer

To get attention marketing messages focus on the two or three important points that need communicating about the innovation. These points will include what is better about the offer and they need to be relevant to the target customer. The standard tool for selecting these points used by marketers in mature, competitive markets is the *positioning triangle*. The three corners of the triangle represent:

1. The frame of reference: defining what the product or service is.
2. The point of parity: the firm's brand delivers the main benefit of such a product or service.
3. The point of difference: why the target customer should prefer this brand to others.[11]

Since this tool is well-known, and has a sound basis in psychology, it is a suitable place to start examining the challenges of positioning innovation.

Choosing the Frame of Reference and Point of Parity

For an incremental innovation the choice of frame is the existing product or service category. This would also be the case for a business model innovation providing a lower cost alternative for customers. The marketer's attention is then free to move to the other points of the triangle. Rogers sees positioning as a compatibility issue in which the firm tries to fit the innovation into the existing values, practices and needs of the target customer. That lessens customer resistance and speeds up adoption because it is easy for customers to understand the innovation and fit it into their life (B2C) or business operations (B2B). In his view, therefore, the firm should try to understand how the innovation links to the ideas these customers already have. The ideal marketing message will then be one that shows how the innovation is both similar to, and different from, these existing ideas. He gives an example of an antibiotic innovation that is similar to previous drugs in the category but, unlike the previous products, has no unpleasant side effects. Here the frame of reference is clearly the existing product category and all the ideas customers have in their minds about that category.

It is probable that most innovations are incremental substitutes for existing products and services. Unfortunately, it is also true that marketing professionals and academics pay inadequate attention to understanding what customers have in their minds before the launch of the innovation. This is far more complex, diverse and subtle than most assume.[12] The first step in choosing a frame of reference and positioning message is, therefore, a thorough understanding of what is in the mind of the target customer. This is true for breakthrough innovations as well, including non-customer innovations.

However, for breakthrough innovations choosing the frame of reference is often a far less obvious and a more difficult decision for the marketer. Take for example, the Roomba made by the firm iRobot. Is it a vacuum cleaner or a robot? In fact, it is both, and has the goal of removing the drudgery of cleaning the floor from people's lives. The Roomba is also not a straightforward incremental innovation (which would be a vacuum cleaner with a better design and more powerful suction). For successful use it requires significant change in the behaviour of the customer. Most people clean where the dirt becomes visible and are happy when the biggest piles of dirt are gone. In contrast, Roomba achieves a high standard of cleanness over several days or weeks rather than in one cleaning session. To understand and appreciate this difference most customers need to try one in their homes. iRobot needs to get the customers' attention so they understand how the Roomba cleans, thus setting up the right conditions for a successful *extended* trial. Otherwise customers may return the product the first time the Roomba ignores a pile of dirt. The first step is to define the innovation in their minds.

It is a challenge to choose the right frame of reference for the Roomba because potential customers have two sets of ideas already well-entrenched in their minds. One set is about vacuum cleaners. These are noisy, people need to push them, and the cord always tangles around something. They go where the dirt is visible, everyone owns one and has a favourite brand, and they are cheap. The Roomba is not like this.

The other set of ideas is about robots. These look like people, work hard and can be useful. Depending on the customer's cultural background they can also be either heroes or monsters. But they are clearly complex and expensive, no one has one in their home and there are no established brands. The Roomba is not like this either.

So should iRobot try to build a new set of ideas in the customers' minds? That would be expensive and difficult, and it runs against the evidence that human beings link new ideas to existing ones.[13] Or should it try to use the positives in both existing sets, while trying to de-emphasize or erase the negatives? iRobot takes the second course of action, defining Roomba as a 'vacuum-cleaning robot' with the tagline 'maintains cleaner floors every day' to draw attention to its different way of cleaning.[14] If the potential customer becomes interested they can then get more details about the specific value of this innovation for them. In this case the friendly name 'Roomba' de-emphasizes the negatives. Names are important in most B2C and some B2B markets. They also link to existing associations either through their meaning (for example here, 'room') or because they link to previous brands of the firm. For example, the name of the Roomba's floor-washing sibling, the Scooba builds on the previous introduction of the Roomba.

Indeed some research shows that B2C customers infer the degree of innovation from the similarity of the innovation's name to those of any predecessors.[15] If the name is completely new they anticipate greater innovation, and therefore greater risks and rewards. If the name is similar they anticipate less innovation, and therefore lower risk and reward. This suggests that significant innovation should have a new name, so priming the customer to look for the major changes and weakening any links to the past that might raise their resistance to change. In contrast, names for incremental innovations can usefully build on previous associations. This reduces the potential for an innovation to raise unrealistic expectations and uses previous success to encourage people to adopt it.

Once the team chooses the frame of reference selecting the point of parity is usually simple. The innovation has to deliver the main benefit that customers expect from this definition of the product or service. Thus the Roomba has to clean floors, Apple's iPod must deliver music and First Direct's Monilink must provide mobile banking services. In a B2B setting, CoreMedia's MultiDRM platform must protect digital content for mobile operators and Atlas Copco's Silenced SmartRig must drill holes in the ground for construction companies. Indeed, the point of parity is nearly always a benefit that customers know and understand. The real question is how the innovation does this better and differently.

Selecting the Point of Difference

Given the frame of reference and point of parity, the point of difference is the benefit that will motivate the potential customer to learn more about the innovation. This benefit should set the innovation apart from its predecessors, if any, and overcome the status quo bias. To do that it needs to be relevant and important to the potential customer. Choosing this benefit sounds like a simple decision but for two reasons it is often not.

First, there are often many potential points of difference to choose from in major innovations. For example, customers can describe contraceptives on up to 30 factors. No short message can convey that number of factors, so the choice of which one to stress is critical in getting the attention of the potential adopter. When the Copper T intrauterine device became available in Asia in the mid-1970s consumer research identified three potential benefits. These are long lifetime, reliability in preventing pregnancy and little interference with sexual activity.[16] Since other contraceptive technologies are also reliable and do not interfere with sexual activity, its long lifetime became the key point of difference. Copper T's promoters used this point to get across the superiority of their innovation. The Copper T has since gone on to become the most widely used reversible contraception method worldwide.

This is an early example of using positioning research to good effect. But it also highlights one problem in choosing the right point of difference: there are often too many possibilities from which to choose. Various research methods from Chapter 5 can help the core team here. In particular, choice experiments show what matters to the customer.

Typically incremental innovations have fewer candidates for the point of difference. Such innovations build on and incorporate the important benefits of the previous technologies and often have only a few novel benefits to promote. Choosing which is important to the target customer as a result is simpler. For example, Akzo Nobel's Interplate Zero is a water-based preconstruction paint primer for use by shipbuilders during fabrication and assembly.[17] Like several other primer technologies it offers good corrosion protection and resistance to construction and assembly damage. However, the advantages of this innovation are that it is more environmentally friendly. The shipbuilder also does not need specialized spraying equipment to apply it and can weld soon after priming. Depending on what the target segment values, the point of difference can either be environmental suitability or faster and simpler construction.

Second, experts point out that adopting certain innovations may mean the customer must give up something the current technology provides.[18] For example, adopting an electric car like the Tesla Roadster allows customers to be environmentally friendly but they lose out on driving range, easy refuelling and passenger space. Since cognitive psychology tells us that typical customers evaluate losses over gains by a factor of three, the point of difference has to overcome a large hurdle. Tesla stresses the stunning performance advantage that electric motors have over petrol engines through their high torque at low revolutions (delivering zero to 100 km/h in four seconds). For some customer segments this may be a telling point.[19]

Business model innovations providing low cost alternatives also take something away from the customer. However, this is not an issue for positioning, because the target segment does not value what the firm takes away and in any event the point of difference is typically low price. Both RyanAir ('the low fares airline') and Formula 1 Hotels ('sleep well at the best price') strip away benefits from the traditional offer. Thus they provide the essential benefits of the frame of reference at the lowest price.

Since positioning the innovation is so important, the toolkit for this chapter provides a simple positioning template and worked example. This example also shows that teams need to consider positioning before they fix the final design of the innovation.

ENGAGING THE INNOVATORS

Once the team decides how to position the innovation the next logical step is to develop an awareness-building campaign. Done well such a campaign leads to the first adoption of the innovation by innovators (some experts also call adoption a trial, a first purchase or market penetration). This important step is one most marketing managers are familiar with. However, while it is a necessary step it is not a sufficient one. To build a market successfully the firm also needs to start a virtuous circle in motion. Each of these topics is now discussed in turn.

Building Awareness and Getting Adoption

Customers adopting an innovation go through two stages: becoming aware and then deciding whether to adopt.[20] Reality is messier than this, but the distinction is useful, particularly because different types of influence often have greater or less impact at each stage. For example, media campaigns often have the greatest impact in creating awareness, whereas local influences often become more important for getting adoption. Dividing adoption into the two stages thus helps to structure the firm's campaign design. Research and experience also provides some useful generalizations about the overall characteristics of the two stages. These can help to understand the challenge of getting the necessary adoption.

Generally the potential market gets to know about the innovation long before adoption, particularly by mainstream customers, starts happening.[21] Thus, a period of slow sales growth often characterizes the start of the new market until the mass of customers reach some tipping point and sales sharply increase. Before the tipping point the level of adoption is around 2% of the potential market.[22] Afterwards it often climbs more rapidly to 50%, although this is lower in developing countries.[23] Chapter 2 shows that this tipping point occurs when the experience of the innovators and connectors legitimizes the innovation in the eyes of the mainstream customers. Firms, including competitors, also respond to this shift in demand by designing variants of the innovation that appeal better to mainstream customers.[24] It is notable that for significant innovations the time between introduction and the tipping point is often six to 10 years, although this varies by product and country.[25] The change in annual sales growth at this point of take-off can be considerable. Annual growth rates can shift from around 30% during the early phase, to 400% during take-off and 45% from there to peak sales.[26]

A competing explanation for the rapid increase in sales that managers sometimes put forward revolves around price. In this version, the high early price of the innovation restricts it to certain customers and it is only when the price becomes more affordable that sales take off. However, recent research has shown that falling prices are more likely to be a result than a cause of the increasing demand from mainstream customers.[27] Price plays a role, but this role is smaller than managers often think. This conclusion is also consistent with research that shows the level of adoption across countries varies much more than can be explained by differences in income levels in these countries.[28]

The entry of competitors is an important added factor in building momentum and sales. The entry of the pioneer alerts other firms to the opportunity, even if they were not aware of it before. Once they conclude that a mass market will emerge they seek to establish their own presence in it. Indeed, research shows other firms beginning to enter the market three to four years before the tipping point.[29] In one sense this is harmful to the pioneer who will lose their market share as a result. However, in another sense it is helpful. The arrival of other firms, each with their own variant, further legitimizes the innovation in the eyes of mainstream customers. It also shapes the opinion of other commentators (such as journalists and bloggers) who provide reviews or opinions. And, because these firms must differentiate themselves from the pioneer, customers gain more choices. Thus, while the pioneer loses their monopoly, the size of the market expands dramatically, partially because of the entry of these other firms.

Social influence thus often spreads in an environment of several competing firms. Because this environment is different from when the pioneer was speaking to the market alone, at this point the marketing campaign should also change. Everything we have considered above suggests that marketing the innovation consists of a series of campaigns, rather than just one launch campaign. Further proof of this conclusion is that market building typically occurs over several years. The information environment, the state of knowledge of the customer and the competition changes markedly over such a time period. As a result, each individual campaign should aim to achieve an objective that is relevant to the particular state of the market, while logically building on the previous campaign. This seems obvious, but marketing professionals often focus on the yearly plan. For major innovations, firms need at least a three-year marketing plan.

The right positioning message by the pioneer is central to building awareness in the market. It is difficult to make people aware of something that is ill-defined or unclear. This message is also central in getting the innovators to adopt and thus start the market moving. In some ways marketing to innovators is more like the traditional view of marketing. In that view, innovators are a distinct market segment addressed by firms mainly through controllable media channels. The innovators give more weight to such messages than others do and can make their mind up without social reassurance.[30] But more choice and positive social influence is central to the tipping point, when real market demand builds. Since firms cannot control which other firms enter or not, the question now turns to how they can best stimulate positive social influence. Before we address this topic in the next section, two qualifications must be made to the account above.

First, there is a common assumption that overall adoption in the market follows an S-shaped or logistic pattern. Academics and professionals share this assumption and build forecasting models around it. However, it is wrong. Recent research done for the National Bureau of Economic Research (USA) shows that 115 major technological innovations across 150 countries followed no such pattern.[31] The problem is that many previous researchers used the wrong data, namely data on sales rather than adoption. Sales data include later purchases by the same customer and multiple purchases by the same customer at the same time. Including these extra sales inflates the seeming level of adoption and leads to the wrong conclusion. When the National Bureau researchers correct the data for these problems, the adoption patterns of major innovations are idiosyncratic. They reflect many causes such as the different nature of the technologies themselves, the history of their evolution, varying levels of competition and customer behaviour. This suggests that, rather than expecting a smooth growth path, strategic marketing plans should incorporate flexibility for different outcomes and timing of events.

Second, our view of how awareness and adoption occurs is distorted in other ways. We know far more about successful innovations than about failures, as people do not document or research the latter. There is anecdotal evidence for innovations that fail through poor design or choice of name, or confusing or inconsistent positioning in the early stages. Also for those that lack enough variants for mainstream segments. This picture is far from complete. There are gaps in our knowledge even for successful innovations. Those that people study tend not only to be major successes but are also found at the more expensive end of the scale. For cheaper innovations, chiefly entertainment, information and supermarket products, the time to the tipping point is much shorter (possibly two years for entertainment or information products and less for supermarket products). This suggests that a good strategy for these products may be to encourage adoption by giving away (in some sense or other) the first product. That turns out to be useful when the firm makes most money through repeat purchases (for example, razor blades) or follow-on revenues (for example, licensing fees on games for a game console maker).

The Virtuous Circle

How best can firms stimulate positive social influence? Having the right innovation that meets the needs of the target customers is clearly a precondition for this. Having the right positioning message is also a precondition. This message must not only attract customers to buy the innovation but it must also set their expectations about how the innovation should perform when they use it. The innovation should clearly meet or exceed those expectations if it is to have any chance of producing positive social influence. But, supposing the innovation and message are right, what more can the firm do to ensure success?

The answers to this question are in fact, well-known, but often people do not associate them with innovation. These answers come from customer relationship management (CRM), particularly our growing understanding of the connection between customer satisfaction, retention and advocacy. In the CRM view, building a market and brand consists of more than the first transaction between customer and firm. It entails the relationship that follows from that first purchase. If firms manage their relationship with each customer correctly, they will satisfy and retain those customers for future purchases. By doing this well they can also create customer advocates for their innovation. This creates a virtuous circle created by two powerful forces.

The first is that customer advocates can be convincing salespeople for the innovation, who are more convincing than any other source of local influence. Not only do these advocates influence the decisions of potential adopters, but these in turn pass on the advocate's message to others in their network. Thus each person who interacts with an advocate can influence people who are two or three steps removed from them in this network. That exerts a powerful leverage on future adoption, not only by persuading others to adopt but also in making the overall social climate support the innovation. It is better that those who are not yet, or who may never be, customers support the innovation rather than oppose it.

The second force is that this social influence is free. While the firm still needs to manage its relationships to create advocates, which has costs, this form of marketing turns out to be more efficient than other types. In addition, a firm

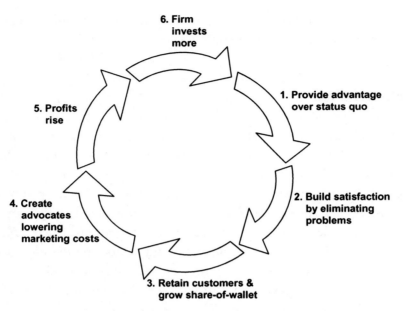

Exhibit 7.1   The Virtuous Circle for Engaging Innovators.

that can create advocates is by definition doing a good job in retaining customers. As in many industries it is cheaper to retain customers than to attract new
ones, a firm that retains customers cheaply and attracts new ones partially through
efficient social influence sets up a virtuous circle. This makes it increasingly successful and profitable. Exhibit 7.1 summarizes this circle.

These ideas are especially relevant for the tipping point for innovations that
involve frequent purchases, generate extra sales through add-ons or services, or
require frequent service interactions. At the tipping point the firm that does the
best at creating advocates is likely to emerge as the leader, whether it is the
pioneer or a later entrant. More customers will adopt their variant of the innovation so it will grow more rapidly than that of other firms. And the greater
profitability that results from the circle will allow them to reinvest into keeping
and extending their leadership.

There is a qualification to all this. As Larreche points out, most firms do
not create advocates or even keep enough existing customers.[32] Instead they have
what others call a 'leaky bucket'. As fast as new customers buy, existing customers become dissatisfied and leave after one or two purchases. Larreche talks about
the need for vibrant satisfaction and vibrant retention – that is the need for
strong, positive emotional engagement by the customer with the innovation.

This is a key point. Emotions are an essential part of all decisions, including decisions to adopt or reject innovations. Advertising, social and other local influences can also produce positive emotions towards the innovation. This is important in encouraging innovators and others to adopt. However, *experience* of the product or service is much stronger than any of these influences. Experience with the innovation can strengthen and deepen positive emotions, but dissatisfaction can turn them into negative ones. These negative messages spread through social influence just as widely, if not more widely, than positive ones. Thus, the gap between a firm that achieves vibrant satisfaction and retention and one that creates dissatisfaction and loses customers can widen rapidly and irrevocably. The attractiveness and profitability of the first will rise strongly, while the other will struggle at increasing cost to attract, let alone keep, enough customers to survive.

How, then, can a firm achieve vibrant satisfaction and retention? The right innovation and right message are preconditions for this. Beyond these the firm needs an effective strategy and management in three areas: setting the right goal, detecting and removing sources of dissatisfaction, and customer recovery.

Setting the Right Goal

The goal of the innovating company should have two facets. First, it must aim to attract adopters who get true satisfaction from the innovation and are willing to buy it again or deepen their involvement with it in some other form. Second, it must attract adopters who make an emotional engagement with the innovation and are willing to recommend it to others. These two facets underpin Larreche's useful definition of vibrancy. It orients the firm to the customer and the state of mind they want that customer to have.

To achieve goals requires measurement and to measure these two facets is not as easy as it first looks, nor as precise as managers might like. For example, there is a wealth of emotional difference between customers who tick the 'satisfied' box on a questionnaire and ones who tick 'completely satisfied'. The connection between satisfaction and retention is often nonlinear so retention rates start to climb dramatically only with delighted customers.

The best goal is therefore to move as many adopters as possible into the 'completely satisfied' category. That maximizes retention and customer lifetime. What should the target be for retention rates? Larreche argues for 90% because of the exponential impact of retention on the firm's customer base. Annual retention rates of 80% sound good, but mean the typical customer lasts only four years. Raising retention from 80% to 90% more than doubles the life of this typical customer.[33]

However, even high retention rates may not be a good indicator of customers' emotional engagement and therefore of the leverage the firm can gain from social influence. Are completely satisfied customers passive or do they actively encourage others to adopt? This line of thinking leads some firms to use recommendation measures like the Net Promoter Score. This classifies customers into detractors and promoters to see where the balance lies between positive and negative word-of-mouth.[34] While these are not the ultimate question, as some believe,[35] they provide a useful indicator of the likelihood and directionality of the social influence in the market. However, social influence does not always work through word-of-mouth and in any event what people say in questionnaires is not always what they do. Besides, the impact of any recommendation that an adopter makes also depends on the receptivity of the person who receives it. Both satisfaction and recommendation scores are simply indicators, not precise measures or ends in themselves. Managers need to balance them with qualitative and diagnostic information so they can take suitable action if they believe there are problems.

Detecting and Removing Sources of Dissatisfaction

One obvious action is to try to remove any source of dissatisfaction with the new product or service. Designing and launching an innovation, especially a breakthrough innovation, is always difficult and it is unlikely the firm will get everything right first time. The launch team should set up all the possible channels of communication they can to detect any problems and fix them as quickly as possible. Speed is critical in the introductory phase because negative social influence spreads at least as quickly and as far as positive influence. Thus the impact of any source of dissatisfaction that lasts for a few months will multiply itself several fold in the market. A proactive strategy for listening to customers, retailers, third-party commentators and others can help here. So can systematically researching the customer experience of the early innovators. Launch plans should include these actions, with the necessary procedures and budgets for product or service adjustment.

Recovering Customers with Grievances

Detecting and removing sources of dissatisfaction, with the aim of improving the innovation for all customers, must be a part of launch strategy. But what of the specific customers who are unhappy with their purchase or experience? If the firm does not manage these properly they may create detractors who will slow or stop adoption by others. As they are identifiable individuals with a specific problem or grievance, action should be possible. Firms should make sure there are ways for employees to look for, identify and respond to customers who are unhappy. They should make it easy for customers to bring their problems or grievances to the firm. In the early stages the firm might directly follow up the innovators to check their experience. In later stages this may become more difficult, because of the number of customers. In this case the launch team can use sample surveys to identify problems among specific categories of customer, leading to advisory messages for everyone in that category. For this to be possible the firm needs to follow good CRM practice and to get basic data on all its customers. The team needs to build all such actions into the launch strategy, with procedures and budgets, as before.

Recovering Innovators with Grievances has High Pay-Off

This is all beginning to sound expensive. A firm that actively searches out and fixes customer problems and grievances could spend a lot of money. Some customers may abuse the firm. Some may not only expect the firm to fix their problem but also to provide fair compensation for any aggravation or loss. The CRM literature argues that firms should be selective and focus only on the customers who are, or can be, profitable.[36] In fact, it is not inconsistent to respond to customer problems as well as focusing on profitability. The issue is return on investment over the medium to longer term. In the growth stages of the new market, effective customer recovery has a high pay-off. Not only is the firm more likely to keep these customers for the future, they are less likely to become detractors. If the firm manages the incident well, they may even become advocates for the innovation. Thus the flow-on effects are both significant and positive. Ignoring the problem, or handling the incident poorly, creates negative flow-on effects of equal or greater size. The gap between the two in terms of return in investment is often great.

Note that this gap will narrow when the market becomes mature. The firm may then have to become more selective in weeding out or changing the terms and conditions of unprofitable customers. However, that is outside the scope of this book.

Dealing with Opposition

As well as building awareness, adoption and the virtuous circle, the pioneering firm will also need to manage any opposition to the innovation. 'Opposition' here means the sceptics and critics who will emerge once the firm launches the innovation. It does not mean the competing products or services that other firms may launch subsequently. As outlined above, these often lead to an expansion of sales and can be positive for both customers and firms. Sceptics and critics, on the other hand, can be a problem.

Many experts and managers view launch campaigns as injecting a message into a passive and uninformed audience. This hypodermic needle model of communication is wrong. In reality, the audience is active and already holds many opinions on topics relevant to the innovation. Some members of this audience are not afraid to voice their opinion, either locally by word–of–mouth or more broadly through reviews, blogs and social network sites. Others write professional critiques of the innovation for independent media outlets. Thus, a better way to think about the launch campaign is that it will interact in some way with the existing beliefs of the audience. The innovating firm defines the agenda for this interaction through its choice of positioning message, but what happens depends on how this message resonates with the audience.[37] How credible, for example, are its claims that the point of difference improves on the status quo? Do these benefits meet an important need of the customer? If the firm chooses its message with a thorough understanding of what customers currently believe, the message will resonate with many customers. And will provide an early platform for success with the innovators in the audience.

But the issues the firm faces in dealing with the opposition are more complex than just choosing the right positioning message. These issues have to do with the diversity of opinion and the dynamics of opinion formation. Even with a good positioning that engages the innovators effectively, sceptics and critics may still emerge from the rest of the audience. Left unchecked, their influence may grow and retard adoption of the innovation. Around the year 2000 several firms tried to combine GPS location and mobile phone technology with various monitoring devices and services. The firms created these innovations to monitor patients at home or enable parents to find their children – both worthwhile goals addressing important customer needs. However, in the USA strong opposition arose around privacy concerns, and several vocal critics of these innovations emerged, ranging from the rational to the excessive.[38] While these innovations may have failed for many reasons, clearly for a time the media debate over privacy drowned out any message about their potential benefits. Innovation teams need to anticipate and think proactively about countering opposition like this, in a manner more akin to political campaign managers than traditional marketing managers. Especially as critics can now exert influence through blogs and social network sites as well as traditional media.

Critics can launch potentially damaging attacks in two principal areas. First, they can undermine the positioning claims. For example, they can argue the point of difference is not important to most customers or the innovation has drawbacks. The latter can be hard to deal with, as the first generation of an innovation is often not perfect, especially for mainstream customers. Second, they can raise an argument against the innovation on an issue that has nothing to do with the positioning claims. The privacy concerns above are one example of this.

The solution to this problem is influencer management. This involves identifying individuals or third-party organizations that can potentially influence the outcome, and working out how to persuade them to support the innovation. Innovation teams can often achieve this simply by telling them about the innovation (before launch) and opening a discussion around any issues they have. This works when the potential influencer has no strong motive to oppose the innovation. However, if they do have such a motive the innovation team needs to anticipate and neutralize the attacks.

The key to identifying such opponents is Machiavelli's question: who gains most from the status quo? If there is likely to be such a critic the team has to consider how they will respond to this opponent's arguments. Possible strategies include ignoring the attack, directly addressing the criticisms or switching the debate to another topic. Which strategy is best depends on circumstances, especially on the level of adoption. The strongest defence against such opposition is to show that many customers are gaining real benefit from the innovation. The toolkit for this chapter provides one tool that can help with some of the issues in dealing with opposition.

GAINING MOMENTUM AND REACHING OUT TO THE MAINSTREAM

Assuming the innovators are adopting, the virtuous circle is in motion and there is no damaging opposition, what next? The pioneering and other firms will want to reach sales take-off as soon as possible. If the virtuous circle is working some innovators will become advocates and this will start positive social messages flowing to the rest of the market. What then needs to happen is for momentum to build in the market. That happens first through the connectors.

Amplifying the Message through Connectors

By themselves the innovators will not exert enough influence to achieve market take-off. There are simply not enough of them in any local network. What enables take-off is for the connectors to provide the bridges for social messages to reach mainstream customers. Like the innovators, connectors are more open to new ideas. However, they have better personal networks than the typical innovator. Thus if the connectors hear about an innovation that *works* they will share the message with many others, as well as add force to the message through their own adoption.

But to connectors, like mainstream customers, all innovations are *social* goods. Connectors also need to be comfortable there is enough positive common knowledge that they can pass on the message or adopt the innovation themselves. And they first need to reach the point where they are ready to listen to the messages coming from innovators and others. However, because of their openness to innovation their thresholds for listening to other people and to the firm's advertising are lower than mainstream customers. Thus for an innovation that provides a significant advantage to the innovators, it should not take as much to convince them the claim of the firm is true. In this case the connectors will want to share the message with others. What, then, can the innovating firm do to further encourage the connectors and reach take-off more quickly?

Encouraging Positive Common Knowledge

The firm cannot directly target these influential customers. In most circumstances it is impossible to know in advance who will be influential for a specific innovation (Chapter 2). Because as a group, connectors are socially active, they are also harder to reach through traditional media or telephone selling. Instead, the firm must be present in all the sources of media that they might use, including the full gamut of new media, and get the real benefits of the innovation across to people like them. In addition, as the focus moves to the tipping point, the innovating firm needs to use its marketing activities to build up common knowledge. The new media provide more opportunities for this than traditional ones because they encourage social networks. Because common knowledge stems from strong links between people, part of this marketing activity needs a local focus. The goal here should be to encourage many small networks of people with similar interests to develop their own common knowledge of the innovation.

Extending the Innovation to Key Mainstream Segments

At this point in the launch of the innovation, the connectors are spreading the message of change, adopting the innovation and some becoming advocates themselves. Common knowledge is shifting from 'I don't think this innovation is for me' to 'I believe many people I know and trust are going to adopt'. So what about the mainstream customers? In fact, the story for the mainstream market is simply one of small networks repeated many times. Provided enough small networks develop positive common knowledge, mainstream customers should follow the innovators and connectors. However, as Moore notes in *Crossing the Chasm*, there is critical change in the innovation that needs to happen if this is to occur.[39]

In many circumstances, the needs of mainstream customers are more diverse than those of the earlier adopters. These customers are also often less willing to accept any mismatch between their needs and the innovation's benefits. Because of their higher plasticity, innovators and connectors are more open when trying the innovation out and learning about how it meets their needs. Mainstream customers are less open and are more inflexible in wanting products to fit what they see as their needs. Similar comments are true for innovations sold to B2B customers. In B2B markets, mainstream customers are more fixed in their organizational cultures than innovators. So they need something that works for them and their more rigid procedures or organization. For both B2B and B2C markets, this diversity of needs and more rigid nature of mainstream customers creates Moore's 'chasm' between the early and mass market.

The typical way to cross this chasm is to extend and adapt the innovation to meet the needs of the mainstream. Moore points out that this involves applying traditional marketing techniques and recommends firms 'segment, segment, and segment'. So, the innovation often extends from a single product or service to a range of variants for different sets of needs. That way the different mainstream customers get what they want.

The danger is the firm may lose focus and spread itself too thinly at this point. So Moore recommends the firm first tries to establish a dominant position in one or two bounded mainstream segments. After they achieve dominance in these they can target other segments. However, he also notes that choosing these segments is not easy. The firm needs to balance several factors well. These factors include the messages coming from earlier adopters, the needs of the various mainstream segments and the firm's ability to deliver variants that meet these needs. Moore's work focuses on high-tech products but is consistent with theoretical research on the diffusion of innovations. His advice also receives support from research showing that careful diversification is the key to growth.[40] So the points he makes are useful for many products and services.

An interesting example of how an innovation can successfully change into variants for different segments is *Cirque du Soleil*. This innovation is definitely not high tech, although it is a breakthrough. But the conclusions on reaching out to the mainstream remain the same. Exhibit 7.2 shows how the *Cirque* adapts their basic idea into shows with different themes for different market segments. Many people know that *Cirque du Soleil* grew to be a billion-dollar business at a time when audiences for traditional circuses were declining. The names on the exhibit refer to various shows, each with its own unique twist on the basic format. In the early years there was one show, by 2000 there were six.

As more and more customers adopt, marketing the innovation becomes increasingly like traditional marketing. Adapting the innovation itself also becomes more and more incremental as the firm attacks each successive mainstream segment. So, the strategic emphasis of the firm switches from acquiring customers and building sales to keeping customers and protecting their market share. What was a Blue Ocean has now become a Red Ocean. As this is no longer the subject of this book, no more is said on these topics here. But we need to reinforce the point that the last step in the innovation sequence is important. Put crudely, mainstream customers are where most of the money is. Firms that

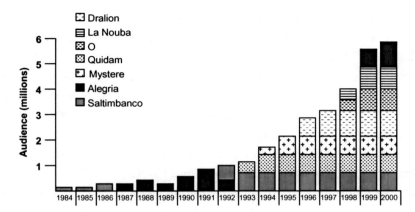

Exhibit 7.2 *Cirque du Soleil* broadens its appeal.

Source: C. Kim, R. Mauborgne and B. Bensaou, Teaching note to accompany the case, *Even a Clown Can Do It: Le Cirque Recreates Live Entertainment,* Fontainebleau, France: INSEAD Euro-Asia Centre, 2002. Estimates based on available company information. Reprinted by permission of C. Kim, R. Mauborgne and B. Bensaou.

fail to make the transition from the early to the mass-market stages of the innovation life cycle risk losing major opportunities. From their historical research Golder and Tellis have found that having a 'vision of the mass market' is an important characteristic of firms that endure over decades.[41] Vision of the mass market is the firm's ability to foresee all the mainstream segments to which they can successfully bring a variant of the innovation. The vignette *Ampex: the Cinderella who missed the ball* shows the opportunities that firms can lose if they lack this vision.

Ampex: the Cinderella who missed the ball[46]

If you ask most people who invented video recording technology they will most likely answer Sony, or JVC, or perhaps Philips. The name Ampex is unlikely to come up unless you ask a retired broadcasting technician.

But it was Ampex who were the true originators of video recording, unveiling their VRX-1000 machine to an astonished audience of TV professionals in 1956. Despite its expense ($45 000) the VRX-1000 quickly became a fixture in TV studios around the world. And Ampex became the leading provider of video recording technology to professional broadcasters for many years to come.

Other electronics manufacturers saw an immediate opportunity to develop a video recorder for the consumer market. Shortly after VRX-1000's launch, Sony had built its own version. Like the Ampex machine it was the size of a roll-top desk, 'as heavy as an anchor', and hugely expensive to produce. Instead of launching this machine, Sony challenged its developers to produce a version for a tenth of the cost, and once they had achieved this to develop a version for a tenth of that again.

Around twenty years later Sony, JVC and Philips launched their consumer recorders, triggering a war which would end in victory for the VHS format. Despite its technical expertise and its jealous defence of its original patents, Ampex was conspicuously absent from that war.

It seems hard to believe that Ampex did not consider the mass-market potential. It would have known that others were seeking to exploit it from the early attempts to license their patents. Clearly though, Ampex did not seriously research the possibilities. Its few tries at consumer video products were woeful failures. In 1963 it produced the first ever home video recorder in the Signature V. But the waist-high, three metre-long, 900lb cabinet, selling at $30 000, was hardly likely to find a place in every home! In the early 1970s Ampex collaborated with consumer electronics partner Toshiba to develop the InstaVision home video camera and recorder, but they repeatedly postponed the launch and the partners eventually scrapped the project.

Although Ampex had the technology, the consumer electronics companies had what Ampex lacked – a vision. Their vision was of a video recorder in every home. They set a price point which would realize that vision and worked tirelessly to create the product. And they, not Ampex, reaped the rewards of video technology.

ACTION STEPS: RETHINKING BUSINESS PLANNING, DEVELOPING MANAGERS FOR THE NEXT STAGE

Successfully building a market for an innovation has many critical facets. These spread over three phases and typically take several years for most major innovations. In the first phase, before launch, the core team needs to design the right offer and positioning for the innovator segment they target. This phase is part of developing the innovation, coming towards the end of Stage 4 in the stage–gate sequence. One of the final tasks of the team in Stage 4 is to plan the launch campaign.

The second phase starts with building awareness and getting innovators to start adopting. It goes on to using the virtuous circle of satisfaction, retention and advocacy to build momentum through social influence. The second phase also includes defusing any opposition to the innovation, while welcoming the entry of competing firms. This phase equates to Stage 5 – *Commercialization.* This chapter gives Stage 5 a much broader scope than the typical approach to product development does. Commercialization is not just about marketing and operations, it includes taking a long-term view of the market and handling the external politics of innovation and competitive strategy.

The third phase includes amplifying the message through connectors, using local marketing to encourage positive common knowledge, and eventually adapting the innovation to key mainstream segments. This phase matches to Stage 6 of the new stage–gate. Stage 6 does not appear in most books or in firms' procedures, but it is essential for long-run profitability.

Rethinking Business Planning

Such a long-term, complex and uncertain process does not suit traditional business planning with its emphasis on annual plans and fixed budgets. Yet a firm can do much to reduce this complexity and uncertainty with more effective approaches to planning. Discovery-driven planning (Chapter 3) can help during Stage 4. Developing a long-term, more strategic plan for the new business can help in Stages 5 and 6.

The business plan for Stages 5 and 6 should take an overall perspective on building the new market, including introduction, take-off and the mass market. For most major innovations this implies a long-term view, perhaps over a five-, seven- or even 10-year horizon. This is longer than the typical planning horizon of many firms. However, it is important to take that view and to work back from it to all the steps the firm needs to take to maximize its mass-market opportunity. Scenario planning can help here, both to reduce the number of uncertainties and to test the robustness of the strategy the firm chooses.

This will be a 'go-to-market' strategy and plan that paints the big picture. It sketches out the general direction and major campaigns the firm needs, and the intermediate milestones and long-term objectives the firm should achieve. Detailed plans are likely to focus on the more immediate future, although this future may be over a two- or three-year horizon rather than a typical budgetary year. Both the immediate and long-term plans should be flexible and include possible contingencies and funding provisions. It is not easy to predict how markets for major innovations will develop or when events such as competitor entry or market take-off will occur. Firms should therefore not miss opportunities or run into problems because they apply restrictive financial policies. As a result this plan needs approval by the firm's leadership.

Developing Managers for the Next Stage

The core innovation team, with the support from their sponsoring executive and gate committee, are the people who should get this approval. But who should carry out the business plan? And what are the implications of its distant time horizon for team members and personnel policies?

It is not hard to see the core team is in the best place to carry out the business plan because of their deep knowledge of the potential market. They understand their customers and the innovation, and they know what the firm needs to do to launch it successfully. However, reaching market take-off may take several years. The problem is most managers change their jobs every two or three years, so team members may move on before sales reach take-off. From a management development perspective such a turnover is natural and valuable. It allows the team members to apply the skills they have developed during the project to other parts of the business. It also gives other people opportunities to move into these roles, learn and develop. But the potential loss of continuity before the mass market develops is a significant risk for the firm. If new managers come in without the deep knowledge the original team has, the innovation effort may falter or fail.

Chapter 6 recommends the core team is responsible for carrying out any change management strategy necessary during commercialization. Delivering major innovations to the market, especially those involving service or business models, often needs the organization to change significantly. Again, it is the team that best understands how to do this. Further, if they took external collaboration within the firm seriously, as Chapter 4 recommends, they also have the personal connections that enable them to change it successfully. If new managers come in without this knowledge, or with weaker connections, the change strategy may also falter or fail.

This suggests there is a natural limit to the team members' involvement. The core innovation team should be responsible for successfully changing the organization and successfully engaging the innovators. Losing team members before the firm achieves these twin objectives is dangerous.

By agreeing to be part of an innovation team, individuals must therefore accept responsibility for building the business for at least one or two years after launch. However, it is unrealistic to expect all team members to stay in their roles for much longer than this. Some may, and perhaps become senior managers of the new business, which is also an important step toward preserving continuity. But many team members will move on to new jobs.

Thus, a crucial role for the team is to ensure they have equally knowledgeable and influential managers to succeed them when this happens. This they can achieve by identifying high-potential junior or middle-level managers for the new business. Once the team identifies these managers, they also have to involve, educate and mentor them so this next generation is ready for the challenge of the mass market.

Exactly how teams carry out the ideas in this chapter, including business and succession planning, will differ according to circumstances. While there are many possible differences, three are especially important. These are the degree of innovation, whether the innovation involves a network product or service, and whether the firm is the pioneer or a follower.

Breakthroughs Take Time

The more radical the innovation is to customers, the greater the timescale of change needed. Innovations that require great changes from the status quo take more time for mainstream customers to accept, as well as more effort from the suppliers. This conclusion chiefly concerns innovations that present a significant customer challenge, especially those that tap latent needs. These require changes in the way customers think and extensive efforts to build the new market. In contrast, it does not take as long to build the market for innovations that present development or appropriation challenges. Here both customers and firms have prior knowledge they can use in decisions. Non-customer innovations are a mixed case, depending on how latent the needs of the target non-customer are. If the innovation addresses an obvious barrier to consumption adoption may be more rapid; if the need is more latent it will take more time.

Similar comments apply to B2B versus B2C markets. B2B markets often rely more on personal selling and, if adoption requires a group decision, B2B customers are also more deliberate in their buying. As well as needing different marketing tactics to influence adoption, this more deliberate style often slows down the rate at which B2B markets adopt. Different countries also take a longer or a shorter time to achieve take-off. However, here this is less to do with the customer. It is mainly because communication and business infrastructures differ greatly between countries, speeding or retarding adoption as a result.[42]

Is the Innovation a Network Product or Service?

These are mostly seen in communications and information technology industries. For network innovations the customer benefits in a different way to the typical innovation. As other people adopt they receive added benefits from being able to interact with them. This includes benefits like wider access to other people (for example, in mobile telephones or electronic payment systems) or being able to share with others more easily (for example, Microsoft PowerPoint or CAD/CAM files). Thus, as the number of adopters increases so do the overall benefits of the innovation to each customer. In general, added benefits like these make the innovation gain acceptance faster and more robustly, in a way that is less likely to slow down or fail.[43]

However, there is an important qualification to this where two or more incompatible standards or technologies compete for the new market. The common view of such markets is that the technology that builds its base of adopters quickest will end the winner. What may happen is often more subtle than this, depending on the social connectivity of the market.[44] Where there are strong connections between all the potential customers, the technology that gets biggest fastest does indeed take all the market. But where the market consists of weakly linked clusters of potential customers the two technologies can coexist. Examples of the latter include Apple's stronghold in graphic design coexisting with the PC's dominance in general business applications.

Firm Characteristics

This chapter describes how to build the market from the launch of the innovation to its acceptance by the mainstream. This perspective is that of the pioneering firm. However, not all firms will pioneer the market: indeed most will follow. So how might the ideas above adapt to the case of the follower? This depends on when the follower enters the market, and what the market looks like then. Research suggests that most enter after the pioneer engages the innovators but two or three years before market take-off. Thus, the typical follower enters knowing the innovators have found the innovation worthwhile and that positive social influence is spreading.

Their challenge is thus different from that of the pioneer. It has three main elements. First, the followers must learn about the market, especially what innovators think, and use this knowledge to improve on the innovation. There is no point launching something that is inferior to the pioneer's product or service. Second, followers must decide what the positioning message for their innovation is, especially the point of difference. The pioneer has already shown the market that the innovation delivers the main benefit customers expect, and to do so they probably also chose the most useful point of difference. So what can the follower do if the best message is already in the market?

Followers who improve the innovation have created one obvious point of difference. However, with the mass market about to take off, followers also need to consider whether their improvement should focus on one or two mainstream segments. In short, the best strategy of the follower is likely to be focus. Followers should use the experience of the pioneer to improve the innovation, but they should design this improvement with certain mainstream segments in mind.

The third element of the follower's challenge is then simply to follow the principles of good marketing. They need to build their reputation in the new market so their product or service becomes part of common knowledge. Then the follower needs to engage these mainstream segments as they reach their point of take-off.

LINKS TO OTHER TASKS

This chapter builds on the ideas in Chapter 2 – *Creating Advantage in the Minds of Many*. Chapter 2 discusses the different types of customer and the role of local influences, especially other customers, in motivating adoption. This chapter applies those ideas to building the market for the innovation, chiefly through effective strategy, marketing and planning. This chapter also builds on the ideas of Chapter 5 – *Co-Creating the Innovation with Customers* – and Chapter 6 – *Changing the Organization to Deliver the Innovation*. Unless the firm partners with the right customers to develop the innovation it is unlikely to develop one that has the right benefits. Equally, unless the firm can change its organization to deliver these benefits effectively, the new market is unlikely to appear. But this chapter also has implications for others. The most important of these are the methods of Chapter 3 – *Chartering Innovation within the Organization*.

Links to Chapter 3. There are many flaws in the way that firms currently think about business plans and gate criteria. Chapter 3 details some of these and recommends improvements. However, from the discussion above we can add to this list. Business plans need to take a long-term perspective, and reflect the realities of building new markets. Business plans also need to address management development and succession, and work with change management strategies for the organization. Equally, gate criteria need to recognize both the nature of market building and the uncertainties in planning over these time horizons. For example, rather than have a global criteria for market potential, as many do, firms need to break down this potential into innovators, connectors and mainstream customers. More realistic time-frames and scenarios also need placing around these potentials. For instance, what is the market potential in the first three years? How might this change if the connectors decide early (or late)? Similarly there is an argument for including in the gate criteria the ability of the innovation or firm marketing to support positive common knowledge.

The next chapter looks at these and other important questions and issues. Chapter 8 – *Putting it All Together* – seeks to bring together all the action steps from the preceding chapters into an overall framework.

TOOLKIT FOR CHAPTER 7

This section provides three tools for building the market for the innovation. The first is a simple planning template for designing this market. This helps the team create a vision of what the market might look like if they are successful. Working back from that vision then gives them insight into several important decisions during the business case, development and commercialization stages. The second tool is a template for a positioning statement. This also looks simple but it is not. Much thought and effort needs to go into getting the right positioning, and the team can only achieve this if they have the right innovation design. So this tool is useful during both development and commercialization. As both tools are best seen through examples, a short case study accompanies each. The third tool is advice on dealing with opposition from professional or amateur commentators, whether this criticism comes through traditional or new media. Handling criticism well is crucial when the firm introduces the innovation.

Tool One: Designing the Market

Having a vision, even a rough one, of the eventual size and composition of the market is important to many decisions the core innovation team will need to make. The exhibit below provides a simple template, where the team needs to fill in the details.

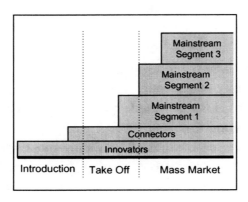

These details include the expected duration of each phase (introduction, take off and mass-market development) and the potential sales from each segment (innovators, connectors and various mainstream segments). Also, they need to write brief descriptions of each of these segments. Note this template is for an innovation where customers, once they adopt, buy again regularly. This is the case for many products and services, both B2C and B2B. For innovations like consumer electronics or capital equipment, where there is a long period between purchases, the template needs adjusting. For such innovations, hills of varying height and duration replace the rectangles.

Whatever the precise form, this vision of the future market aids discussions among the core team and clarifies what they seek to achieve. It also ensures they take a long-term perspective and realize that most of the revenue potential lies several years after launch.

An example may help here. Take a firm launching an innovation for Alzheimer's patients and their relatives. This innovation might combine medical monitoring and global positioning system (GPS) location devices, and a call centre or web services.[47] Here the innovation team might first describe the typical user and customer (where the latter might be a relative or caregiver rather than the patient). They need to describe the users' full set of expressed and latent needs, and any obvious segments of the market whose priorities might differ from the typical case. Here these mainstream segments might include patients prone to falling, those who become lost, or those with other medical conditions. This description essentially sketches the full potential of the Alzheimer's market and assumes the firm will subsequently develop second or third generations of the innovation to satisfy all segments of the market. To this the team might also usefully add any other applications of their technology beyond Alzheimer's but a logical and related extension of it.

Then the team focuses on segments whose needs the first generation product will best satisfy and identify who the innovators in those segments might be. In the Alzheimer's example these innovators might be caregivers with patients most prone to falling (strong needs). They could be caregivers with busy lifestyles (strong constraints) or simply those with a strong interest in technological solutions (predisposed to innovation). Finally, the team would list the characteristics of these innovators that best discriminate between them and typical customers. Together, this approach provides a broad vision of the mass market and a clear starting point – the innovators most likely to accept the current product design.

Tool Two: Positioning Statement for Innovators[48]

To stand any chance of success the core team needs to position the innovation clearly in the minds of innovators. And while this is the job of marketing professionals, it is also clear they cannot succeed unless the design of the innovation provides the right platform for an effective positioning. Design and positioning are two sides of the same coin because they both reflect the needs of the customer. Thus innovations that firms co-create with customers are more likely to provide both the right platform and an effective positioning.

It is best to explain all these points, and the positioning tool itself, through an example, in this case the Palm Pilot 1000. The Palm Pilot was launched in 1996 and went on to become the world's first truly successful personal digital assistant (PDA). The Pilot was not the first PDA; others had tried before including Apple (Newton), Motorola (Envoy) and Tandy (Zoomer). However, a combination of expense, poor software, hard-to-use interfaces and unclear positioning prevented any of them selling in significant numbers. In contrast Palm shaped the Pilot by asking Newton and Zoomer buyers what they hoped a PDA would do for them. Thus Palm co-created the Pilot with innovators, resulting in a more usable and less expensive but fully-featured product. The benefits and features of the Pilot included shirt-pocket size, information management software, PC connectivity, intuitive interface, integration with Microsoft Office, extendible architecture, Graffiti handwriting recognition, Windows and Macintosh compatibility and a $299 price point. All of these benefits and features innovators obviously need (since they helped design them) but which will best convince potential innovators to adopt?

The exhibit below provides a template for positioning innovations. This is a simple tool, but it is an important one. Following best practice and psychology it focuses attention on a clear message with three main facets. These are the frame of reference and two claims the firm should make. First, the innovation delivers the most important benefit of this frame. Second, the claim of advantage the firm is making to overcome the status quo. However, because customers are in general sceptical, both these claims should also have evidence in their support.

Positioning Statement for Innovators

Amongst _____,

The frame of reference

The _____,

Name of innovation

Delivers _____, AND

Single most important benefit of the frame of reference

Because _____,

Single most important evidence for this claim

Is the _____,

Single most important claim for advantage over the status quo

Because _____,

Single most important evidence for advantage

And inferring from Palm's advertising and packaging in 1996, this is what their positioning statement might have looked like.

Positioning Statement for PDA Innovators

Among *personal digital assistants* (frame of reference),

The *Palm Pilot 1000,*

Delivers *staying organized,* (main benefit)

Because *it contains a planner, journal, notes, address book and calendar in a shirt-pocket size device* (evidence for benefit), AND

Is *always in touch with your PC* (advantage over status quo),

Because *of HotSync technology* (evidence of advantage)

The genius of Palm and the Pilot 1000 lies in the choice of PC connectivity as the point of advantage over the status quo. The innovators of 1996 were people who had to travel away from their office or workplace. Replacing a paper diary or organizer with a PDA was a nice, but not compelling, idea until Palm gave them connection back to their workplace. As a result Palm sold one million units within 18 months.

Positioning statements are an important part of core team discussion and business planning. They look deceptively simple but, as this example proves, their impact is great. For that reason they need serious thought and debate among the team. Just imagine Palm had not included HotSync technology in the final specification, or had chosen to advertise another benefit? Their story might have been completely different.

Tool Three: Dealing with Opposition[49]

Be Prepared

It is always better to prepare for criticism than to be wise after the event. A well-planned public relations strategy is crucial to launching any innovation, and complements 'above the line marketing' in important ways.

Your strategy will ensure there is a solid body of key writers, opinion formers and analysts who had privileged access to your innovation before launch and are ready to report on their positive experience. It will also keep a flow of communication throughout the launch to prevent a vacuum of comment developing, that critics may fill rather than supporters. All this is credit in the bank to offset any negativity that may appear.

Store any negative opinions that surface during the innovation testing phase as well as the positive ones. You can use these later to show that you were aware of features that some people did not like. Explain how you addressed these complaints or decided to follow an alternative design for justifiable reasons. Work these into Q&As and position statements that aim to second-guess all possible objections to your innovation.

Keep Yourself Informed

Responding to criticism from whatever quarter is often a judgement call, but you can make better judgements by knowing your media channels thoroughly. Watch closely all the relevant media outlets: trade publications, columns and sections in the press, websites, enthusiasts' blogs and message boards. It is essential that you are aware of any criticism as soon as it appears. Delay in responding to a problem can be damaging.

Respect your Audiences and Engage Them Appropriately

Marketing and PR have to work much more *with* customers in the twenty-first century, not at them. People are taking more control over their sources of information, and are more savvy about firms and the media talking to them – and much less tolerant of them.

It is a grave mistake to dismiss the criticisms of a blogger as simply one unhappy customer. Many blogs are the mouthpieces of recognized experts in a field, read not only by their peers, but also by journalists who pick up stories from Internet forums. Such journalists can then redistribute the perceived flaws of your innovation through mass media channels.

Even if a blogger is no more than an ill-informed amateur it would be rash to ignore their criticisms. If they were a customer on the end of a telephone, no sensible organization would treat them dismissively. In reality this is a customer service issue, except that this customer has the power to damage your reputation more widely than most.

The following advice applies to adverse reaction in any influential media, old or new, professional or amateur:

- Respond to their article or blog as quickly as possible.
- Be polite – don't try to be clever or sarcastic – it will backfire.
- Correct any factual errors in their criticism.
- Rebut constructively any comments you feel are unfair.
- Be honest, and accept criticism when it is fair.
- Tell the writer (and their readers) that you are open to receiving comments directly.

Consider inviting key bloggers to take part in testing, or pitch to them in the same way you would to a key journalist. They can just as easily become evangelists as critics, spreading the word about your innovation to an audience which trusts their opinion much more than yours. They may not have the 'authority' of a traditional media outlet behind them, but they may be just as influential.

CHAPTER 8

PUTTING IT ALL TOGETHER

INTRODUCTION

This chapter summarizes and integrates the ideas and conclusions in the book. It contains the main steps that firms need to take to improve their management and development of innovation. To do this, the chapter omits much of the logic, justification and details of the argument in the preceding chapters. Here the focus is on a few important conclusions that are broadly applicable across firms.

The chapter has three sections. The first provides recommendations for better practice in six key areas. These are co-creation, market design, the Innovation Charter, the core team, organizing for change and building new markets. This section also includes exhibits that allow the reader to cross-reference these recommendations to the relevant discussion in Chapters 3 through 7. And the section ends with an exhibit that summarizes how the various tools from each chapter support innovation. The second section examines the ways innovation teams may need to adapt these recommendations to the different circumstances in which they find themselves. This includes the magnitude of innovation the firm's leadership demands, which of the three challenges in Chapter 1 is most important, and the firm's stance towards pioneering or following. The third and final section then reflects on the two objectives of the book. The final conclusion is that firms need to change their management practices and embrace more breakthrough innovation.

TOWARDS BETTER PRACTICE

Advances in our understanding of the way customers adopt innovations have important outcomes on the way firms should innovate. Exhibit 8.1 summarizes these advances.

The firm needs to have a clear understanding of its starting and ending point. The pioneer has significant power to shape the new market by developing and framing an offer that is attractive to customers. Firms can create advantage in the minds of many. To do so they must understand what people are thinking today and what the future possibilities are. What might customers in the future see as valuable to them? How can the firm best frame this advantage to get sales moving? Since there are always many future possibilities, the firm must also decide what shape of new market best meets their strategic goals. What revenues and profits does the firm require? Which business model makes most sense? And so on.

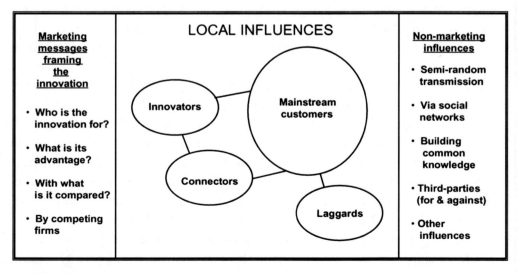

Exhibit 8.1 The new model of adoption.

Understanding these starting and ending points allows the firm to develop an innovation that can build the market they want. This is not the entire story, nor does the pioneer have complete power. Much more needs to be done to attract mainstream customers and build the mass market. And competitors will surely enter if this market looks attractive to them. The mass market that results will probably not look like the one the innovation team describes to their leaders at the start of the project. And evidence suggests many pioneers will not keep market leadership once others enter. But the pioneer is uniquely placed to design the market and set the rules for both customers and competitors. Further, if they are skilful enough to lead their innovation into the mass market, pioneers can hold onto their leadership and make significant returns.

So the two foundations of effective development are for the firm to understand their customers and see the desired end point. But to break from past practices, and incorporate the latest thinking, it is best to think of these as co-creating the innovation and designing the new market.

Co-Create the Innovation with the Right Customers

Customer involvement has always been a major part of good development practice. Leading firms involve customers, in some way or other, from their first analysis of customer needs to their final forecast of launch demand and beyond. This dialogue between firm and customer helps identify the innovation design that will be the best and ensures the innovation will deliver what customers expect. However, firms often treat customers as passive and external sources of advice, and fail to see them as equal partners in the development project itself.

The new approach respects and values customers as co-creators of the innovation. Some firms now pay a great deal of attention to the way their customers use and experience products and services, and involve them proactively in the actual design of concepts and prototypes. Various new methods and approaches are now available for doing this. These include methods for eliciting latent needs, lead-user workshops and choice experiments, among others.

However, the new model of adoption shows that different types of customers should play different roles at different times during development. Broad samples of customers are useful in the early stages, chiefly to understand the nature and intensity of unmet needs. However, the innovators and connectors, who are more open to new ideas, are easier to involve productively in creating solutions for meeting these needs. They can co-create innovations and their views are influential in the market place. When a prototype is ready, the views of innovators are also useful in gauging early acceptance by the market and in guiding the further development of the innovation.

Mainstream customers should also play a major role, but firms should consult them later when a more concrete innovation prototype is available. The role of the mainstream customer in co-creation is to corroborate the viability of the final innovation. Also, to suggest where changes or variants of the innovation might better fit the needs of different mainstream segments.

Not only does co-creation help to identify the best design for the innovation, it also provides much insight into building the new market. Knowing the views of innovators, connectors and various mainstream segments enables the firm to understand how the market might or might not develop. It also leads to decisions on the best ways of influencing a positive outcome.

Thus, to make co-creation work effectively, firms need to align the new methods and approaches with the new model of adoption. Customer understanding in and of itself is not enough: this understanding has to reflect the way that customers will adopt the innovation once the market starts.

Design the New Market

The firm should define the innovation project to reflect the revenue and profits it needs to meet its strategic goals. The revenues and profits, in turn, depend on the profile of the new market the firm wants to build, the position it wishes to achieve in this market, and the business model it selects. They also depend on how much the firm is willing to invest to reach sales take-off. Since the pioneer is best placed to make choices like these, it needs to determine what market it wants. This then allows the firm to specify the design of the innovation (and associated strategies and marketing campaigns) that will give it the best chance of building the market it wants.

Various methods and approaches can help the firm to think about the market they desire and how they might build it. These include the strategy canvas, scenario generation and discovery-driven planning. All these provide useful insights and background information for market design. However, here too there must be a break with past practices. In the past firms used methods like these chiefly to prepare the launch campaign. Instead, firms now need also to paint a picture of what the mass market might look like and when it might happen. In doing so, they need to recognize the slow introduction period, the likely entry of competition, and the sales take-off to the mass market. They also need to think about what the size and characteristics of mainstream segments might be and in what sequence these will develop. This vision focuses the firm on the real revenue potential and helps clarify what it wants to achieve. Working back from this vision to the present also sheds added light on what might be the best innovation to introduce and who might accept it most readily. Finally, at the launch the team needs a clear profile of the selected innovators, and a road map for building the largest possible market five or 10 years into the future.

As before, having vision in and of itself is not enough. A useful vision has to reflect the way customers will adopt the innovation, how competitors will react to the new market, and the right time horizon.

Co-Creation and Design are Complementary

Customers need advantage if they are to change from the status quo, but equally the firm needs certain revenues and profits to build the new market and satisfy its shareholders. Partnership with the right customers at the right time therefore goes alongside strategic planning, and both must inform and influence each other. This interplay can be of great benefit to both sides. The customers get an innovation that improves their life or business while the firm has a better chance of meeting strategic and financial goals. And the more that both co-creation and market design incorporate the advances in our understanding of innovation, the more likely it is that both goals will be met.

Cross-References to the Two Key Consequences of the New Model

Exhibit 8.2 provides cross-references to the sections of the book that deal with methods for co-creation and market design. Also to sections discussing the major improvements that firms can make in the way they involve customers or think about future markets.

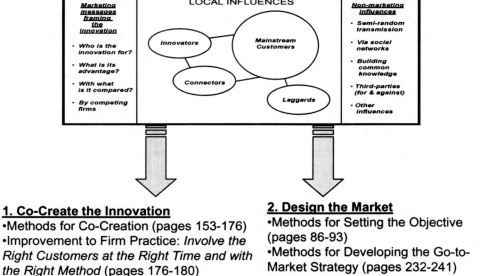

1. Co-Create the Innovation
•Methods for Co-Creation (pages 153-176)
•Improvement to Firm Practice: *Involve the Right Customers at the Right Time and with the Right Method* (pages 176-180)

2. Design the Market
•Methods for Setting the Objective (pages 86-93)
•Methods for Developing the Go-to-Market Strategy (pages 232-241)
•Improvement to Firm Practice: *Plan for the Mainstream Market from the Start* (pages 257-258)

Exhibit 8.2   Cross-references to the two key consequences of the new model.

Incorporate Advances in the Innovation Charter

The Innovation Charter is an important way of ensuring the firm designs the right innovations and markets. This charter follows from the firm's purpose and strategic plan and defines the portfolio of innovation projects the organization seeks. It also sets out the stage–gate method and decision–making criteria so all involved understand these. In essence, the Charter provides all employees with a clear direction and transparent governance. The direction includes the types of innovation the firm seeks, its goals and objectives for innovation, and what the firm seeks to leverage or develop through innovation. Governance includes key steps such as forming gate committees and selecting executive sponsors, team leaders and members for specific projects. It also sets out how project teams will agree on their objectives with the leadership. However, to succeed the Charter also needs to incorporate both the new world of innovation and the new model of adoption.

The stage–gate methods and gate criteria firms use need to recognize the specific organizational impacts of service and business model innovation.

Innovation is often as much about organizational change as it is about developing the innovation itself. An important part of the work of innovation teams and gate committees is thus considering the form of organization that will best deliver each innovation, and how to go about changing the firm to achieve this. Ensuring the Charter is clear about how to do this provides a good foundation for successful change.

Equally, stage–gate methods and gate criteria also need to recognize the new model of adoption. Setting up the project needs great attention, as does the critical transition from the early market of innovators to the mass market of mainstream customers. Gate criteria should reflect current knowledge about adoption and market dynamics, alongside more traditional criteria. Likely competition needs more serious analysis, as does the decision whether to pioneer the new market or simply follow others. Incorporating such advances in understanding in the Charter will improve your chance of designing the right innovations and building new markets successfully.

Invest in Core Teams that can Lead the Organization

Firms need to set up their core innovation teams correctly. That means selecting team leaders with care, thinking through whom they should report to and carefully selecting the other team members according to the project's needs. It also means giving the members enough support, training and resources to become an effective team. The need to select teams carefully applies to all innovations, even incremental ones. However, the changing nature of innovation makes team selection and project setup so critical to success that firms and their leaders should invest significantly more time in this. Innovations that cross firm silos, that change the way the organization works, or whose markets will take years to build, all require teams that can *lead* as well as develop.

Contemporary innovation teams need to work extensively with the rest of the organization, often across many countries. They may have to lead and manage many subprojects, perhaps involving hundreds or thousands of other employees. Thus the idea the innovation team is mainly inwardly focused, creatively developing the innovation behind closed doors, is wrong. The core team spends as much or more time on external relations as it does within its own group. They have to spend time identifying the resources they need, securing agreement that they can access these resources and then leading the work of the people assigned to the task. Their project is often massively complex, requiring skilful leadership, coordination and project management across many activities.

To be effective in this new world, especially during the early stages of development, the core team needs the right executive sponsor and team leader. An important consideration in selecting both is their ability to gain support for the project from the rest of the organization. The core team leader also needs the mental flexibility to use the seven styles of innovation leadership well, if they are to get the best out of their team. [Ambassador, business strategist, team coach, creativity facilitator, explorer, project manager and change agent.] These seven styles accurately reflect the leadership challenges of the new world of innovation.

The other team members should also have leadership and relationship-building skills, as well as the expertise and experience that is relevant to the particular innovation. Developing good teamwork during the project setup is best done with support from executives with an experience of innovation, as well as professional trainers. Firms need to invest time, experience and resources in their core teams if they are to maximize their chance of success.

Organize for Change

The other consequence of the new world of innovation, especially innovations in services or business models, is that the organization itself often has to change to deliver the innovation effectively. There are general preconditions for success with innovation: what the firm's leadership communicates about the innovation and how they behave toward specific projects and teams. Done effectively, this gives force to the Innovation Charter. However, in the contemporary world, organization and organizational change figure much more prominently in the work of both executives and core innovation teams.

The guiding coalition for innovation in the firm, executive sponsors of projects and gate committees all need to play a role in bringing projects to completion. These roles differ and change according to the stage the project is at. But these days all three need to consider not only the innovations that teams propose, but also the organizational implications of these innovations. Issues of organizational structure, managerial and employee roles, skills and incentives, and new procedures, processes and mind-sets become more important.

The innovation team itself is central here. They understand in depth and detail what it will take to deliver the innovation. They are also in the best position to understand any resistance to change that may come from other managers or employees. The team is also closest to the problems they may face in communicating the necessary changes effectively, managing projects with organizational implications or empowering others to make these changes. The team itself should therefore be responsible for identifying how to change the organization to support the innovation. And, subject to the approval of the team's sponsor, gate committee and guiding coalition, they should be responsible for carrying out these changes.

In short, innovation development typically now needs much more leadership of the organization at large than was the case in the past. One important ingredient of this leadership is changing the organization so the innovation gets the support necessary for success.

Build Your Market Using a Long-Term Perspective

Successfully building the market for a major innovation goes through three phases and typically takes several years. In the first phase, before launch, the core team must design the right offer and develop the right positioning for the innovator segment they select. The second phase starts with building awareness and organizing trials among the innovators, using the virtuous circle of innovator satisfaction, retention and advocacy to build momentum through social influence. The third phase includes adapting the innovation to mainstream segments and using connectors and local marketing to encourage these segments to form positive common knowledge. Such a long-term, complex and uncertain process does not suit traditional business planning, with its emphasis on annual plans and fixed budgets. Nor does it suit the short-term thinking about career development and managerial succession often seen in firms. To be successful with major innovation, firms need to address both these issues.

First, they need a plan to build the market that takes a long-term perspective, including the introduction and market take-off, and crossing the chasm to the mainstream. For major innovations this implies a five-, seven- or even 10-year time horizon. This plan will sketch out the general direction, major campaigns and the intermediate milestones and long-term objectives the firm needs to achieve. It also complements and builds on any change strategy needed to complete, develop or launch the innovation. Detailed plans then focus on the more immediate future, with two-year to three-year horizons. Both the immediate and long-term plans should be flexible, including possible contingencies and funding provisions.

Second, firms need to plan who will manage the launch of the innovation and build the new market. Here the innovation team should be responsible for both changing the organization and engaging the innovators. Losing team members through promotion or job rotation before the firm achieves those twin objectives is dangerous, because knowledge and understanding is lost in this way. However, it is unrealistic to expect all team members to stay in their roles for much longer than one or two years after launch. Thus, another important task for the innovation team is to identify and mentor managers to succeed them.

Cross-References to Key Advances in Practice

Exhibit 8.3 shows which section of the book contains the key materials that support the improvements in practice toward innovation charters, core teams, change management and building markets. The idea here is not to cross-reference all the materials in the book. Rather it is simply to note where the reader can find further discussion of these specific topics.

Incorporate Advances in the Innovation Charter	*Invest in Core Teams that can Lead the Organization*	*Organize for Change*	*Build Your Market Using a Long-Term Perspective*
Innovation is a strategic programme	Embed the project at the top level through the right sponsor	Build a guiding coalition that supports innovation and change	Position the innovation to best advantage
pages 59-61	*page 121*	*pages 201-206*	*pages 237-241*
How stage-gate methods should be improved	Choose a team leader with mental flexibility	The core team should manage change	Engage the innovators
pages 77-83	*pages 122-124*	*pages 207-209*	*pages 241-250*
Examples of the new stage-gate method and proposed criteria	Select an effective and externally focused team	How to manage large, complex projects involving many parts of the organization	Reach out to mainstream customers
pages 84-85	*pages 125-129*	*pages 210-213*	*pages 252-256*
Template for an Innovation Charter	Invest in developing teamwork	Organizational principles for innovation management	Plan long-term and develop managers for the next stage
page 87	*pages 129-135*	*pages 215-219*	*pages 257-259*

Exhibit 8.3 Cross-references to key advances in practice.

How the Tools Support Innovation

Exhibit 8.4 links the tools proposed in each chapter to the stages of development. This shows how each tool supports each stage. Some tools support a single stage. Some tools support several stages as the core team's understanding improves and they refine their assumptions and specifications for the innovation. Note the exhibit stops at Stage 5 – *Commercialization*. Once the innovation is on the market and sales and customer data becomes available, more typical marketing and business methods take over. Further, while several of the tools such as the strategy canvas or choice experiments are clearly also useful for Stage 6 – *Broaden to the Mass Market* – this is several years into the new market's future.

The other perspective that is useful here is how the tools support the six areas of improvement to practice noted above. This is straightforward because the tools follow the chapters shown in Exhibit 8.4. For example, the tools in Chapter 4 support building an effective core team, while those in Chapter 5 support co-creation. Similarly, the tools in Chapter 6 support organizational change and those in Chapter 7 support both market design and taking a long-term perspective. The only extra comment that needs making concerns the tools

CHAPTER	TOOLS	STAGES				
		1.Project Set Up	2. Idea Generation	3. Business Case	4.Innovation Development	5.Commercialization
3	Strategy Canvas	▓				
	Scenario Generation	▓				
	Discovery-Driven Planning	▓	▓	▓	▓	
4	Team Selection Guide	▓			▓	
	First Meeting Agenda	▓				
	Team Climate Inventory	▓	▓	▓	▓	
5	Voice-of-the-Customer	▓			▓	
	Identifying Lead Users & Innovators		▓	▓	▓	
	Choice Experiments			▓	▓	
6	Scale of Change (Preliminary)			▓		
	Scale of Change				▓	
7	Designing the New Market		▓	▓	▓	
	Positioning Statement for Innovators				▓	
	Dealing with Opposition					▓

Exhibit 8.4 How the tools support innovation.

of Chapter 3. These support the Innovation Charter mainly by helping the core team define an objective that reflects both customer and firm goals.

FLEXIBILITY IN VARIOUS CIRCUMSTANCES

While the previous section offers recommendations that are applicable to most firms, these recommendations need adapting to the particular circumstances in which their core teams find themselves. While several contingencies have been mentioned in the preceding chapters, here we address three important ways in which practice may need to differ according to circumstance. These are the magnitude of innovation the firm requires, which of the three challenges is the most important and the firm's competitive stance.

Breakthrough Innovations

Innovations that require a breakthrough on one or more of the three dimensions of innovation need autonomous teams and different rules. Innovations along the customer dimension also need different approaches to co-creation and market design.

New Rules

Firms need to be flexible in approaching and organizing for different types of innovation. Incremental innovation fits normal business methods, whereas breakthrough innovations need different rules, different people and a degree of protection from the mainstream business. Achieving this flexibility is mainly the job of the leadership through their communication, behaviour and support for the Innovation Charter. The Charter itself should also distinguish between different types of projects. However, firms also need to apply different stage–gate methods for breakthrough innovations than for incremental ones. The stages and gate criteria remain essentially the same, but the firm places its attention and resources differently.

First, forming the right team is more critical to the success of breakthrough innovation projects than to incremental ones. Developing breakthroughs often needs company-wide cooperation and change, which the right team members can make easier. Second, the stages and gates critical to eventual success also depend on the nature of the innovation. Breakthrough innovation takes managers beyond their existing knowledge and so, in the early stages, they need to pay extra attention to creating and screening ideas. In contrast, the later stages are on some dimensions more critical for incremental than breakthrough innovations. Incremental innovations face incumbent competitors who are able to compete in similar ways to the innovating firm. The firm therefore needs to be sure it has an advantage over its competitors before the innovation advances to development or launch. Finally, for launching breakthrough innovations, especially those involving new services or business models, the firm often needs to put more resources into employee training. This is less the case for incremental innovations.

Autonomous Teams

Innovations the existing organization may resist, fail to understand or fail to prioritize require an organizational solution outside the normal ways of doing business. For breakthrough innovations an autonomous multifunctional team is likely to be the best solution. Here the firm assigns full-time core team members to the team who report to the team leader. The strongest influence on the career progress of individual members is thus the team's performance and their own part in it. This encourages them to be loyal to the project and the team leader rather than to functions or business units. And it creates a focus on the priorities of the project rather than on existing business. In tandem, the executive sponsor needs to nurture the new idea while working with fellow executives to ensure support is forthcoming from the rest of the business.

In contrast, the best solution for incremental innovations is likely to be the standard or heavyweight multifunctional team. These are innovations that build on current ways of doing business and that people in the existing business will understand. In these teams the functions or business units of each member still have the strongest influence on their career and most still formally report to their functional boss. However, there are fewer issues of conflict or resistance because the innovation extends existing business. Thus, people in those functions or units will more readily see working on the project as a legitimate task and not a threat.

For complex projects, project management during the development stage needs extra consideration. Complex projects involve many other people outside the core innovation team. While the common solution for these is to set up working relationships with all the important areas of the firm, this may not always be the best idea. In project management all working relationships have their positive and negative sides. They improve communication, especially of rough designs and conclusions, and they provide more perspectives on possible solutions. But such connections also introduce delays as the core team and other parts of the project consult with one another. These delays can result in instability when the various parts of the project are out of synchronization. Thus the core team needs to consider and plan for how it will organize the project, including setting up connections and delegating responsibility.

Co-Creation and Market Design

Innovation breakthroughs along the customer dimension require special approaches to co-creation and market design. In incremental innovations the firm already knows who the customers are, and these customers already understand much about the innovation. In business model breakthroughs customers are often familiar with the underlying product or service, and only have to grasp a change to delivery methods or pricing terms. And breakthroughs on the development dimension typically also improve performance on a feature that customers understand. For these latter cases, customers will grasp the benefits (or lack of benefits) of the innovation idea or prototype easily, building on their existing experience. But this is far less true for breakthroughs in customer benefits. Here most customers need information and time to understand these benefits and become persuaded of their worth. For these breakthroughs it is often less clear to the core team which customers they should target at the launch, and who will provide the most valuable mainstream segments when the market takes off.

So, in the early stages of development the team needs to keep an open mind on defining the customer, and observe or question broad samples of customers. Remember that many important innovations come from outside the firm's existing customer base, including lost customers, competitors' customers and non-customers. The team may also need to use new and less direct research methods to understand the needs of these customers. To create ideas they may need to draw lead users from analogous markets or involve relevant experts from outside the firm. In later stages, the team will also need to pay more attention to informing mainstream customers about the innovation before they get their opinions.

In defining customers' needs the team has to build a vision of the future market. For breakthrough innovations, this vision should include all the possible applications of the innovation they can anticipate. Plus the innovators and mainstream customers they associate with these applications. The team may subsequently recommend their firm focuses on one area, but if it does so, everyone will be fully aware of what the next steps in building business beyond this area might be.

Challenges and Solutions

Breakthroughs on each of the three dimensions of customer, development and appropriation have different implications for leadership, personnel and procedures. These implications lie mostly in the areas of team membership, gate criteria and organizational culture.

Team Membership Should Reflect Focus

Innovations can focus on customers by meeting their latent needs, delivering value to some underserved segment or creating some new experience. Alternatively, they can focus on development by achieving a technological breakthrough to improve the product's performance or by changing the organization to deliver a new service. Lastly, they can focus on appropriation by changing the business model or the way in which supply and distribution works, to reduce price, improve profitability or change the power structures. Each of these three dimensions sets up a different challenge and so requires different teams.

Innovation teams whose primary focus is on the customer, with less need for technological breakthroughs, organizational or business model change, will have more customer-facing members. Innovation teams whose primary emphasis is on technological breakthroughs will have more members with technological expertise. Equally, teams aiming to deliver a new service may focus more on organizational change than on the market or technology. In the last case team members with change management experience and expertise are needed.

Similarly, innovations that pose an appropriation challenge will need some team members who are familiar with industry structures and competition, and possibly with skills in understanding the mind-set of other players and negotiating with them.

The difficulty here is that neither gate committee nor team may know the balance to make between these three dimensions at the start of the project. Indeed, if both parties keep an open mind about how to reach the firm's objective they should not decide on this balance too early. But if the balance changes later, this has implications for team membership. So there needs to be some degree of flexibility in the team membership, while preserving the team's continuity and consistency of purpose by having a stable group of core members. The logical point to review and change team membership is at Gate 3 – before development starts.

The Gate Criteria Should Reflect Focus

Chapter 3 sets out 12 key gate criteria for gate committees to apply at the five gates. All these criteria are important and potential innovations need to meet at least some acceptable level on all of them. However, from Gate 3 onwards, gate committees and teams need to pay extra attention to where their main challenge lies. If the challenge lies with the customer, the criteria for customer and market issues assume more importance. If the challenge lies with development, the criteria for technical feasibility or organizational change assume more importance. And if the challenge lies with appropriation, the criteria for strategy and external partners assume more importance. Whichever is the case, the team will need to devote time and resources to ensuring that they make useful assessments of the relevant criteria. In turn, committees will need to devote time to corroborating the team's work, and in deciding whether the team's solution meets the main challenge.

Attend to the Organizational Culture

Innovations delivering new services that need employee–customer interactions should typically give more attention to organizational change. This is especially true for large organizations that must change the skills and behaviour of many service personnel. Similarly, new business models will need efforts to explain and overcome resistance throughout both the organization and its external partners. The content and goals of the change strategies will differ according to the specific challenge, but achieving change needs effort and knowledge of the organizational culture. In contrast, developing and delivering new products will typically need less effort or knowledge of the firm's culture. The main issue in achieving the desired organizational change is the existing culture of the organization. Some organizations are open to change and innovation; others are less so.

Unfortunately, many large firms have cultures which display resistance to directives from their leadership. Developing an innovation needing major service or business model changes in such an organization need major efforts to manage the change and well-conceived strategies for doing so. In contrast, a minority of firms have cultures which readily cope with change. Developing a similar innovation in these firms would need little effort in change management and far simpler strategies for doing so. Similar remarks apply to managing complex projects: some cultures make this easy, non-cooperative or authoritarian cultures make this hard. So, to assess the degree of challenge, teams and gate committees also need to be accurate and honest about the (organizational) point from which they start.

Decide Whether to Be a Pioneer or a Follower

To be a pioneer means to be the first firm to build a new market. To be a follower means to enter the market after the pioneer. The typical follower will enter after the pioneer has successfully engaged the innovators but two or three years before the market takes off. So the follower enters knowing the innovators find the innovation worthwhile, and that positive social influence is spreading. Followers take less risk than the pioneers and are in a good position to capitalize on the mainstream market. But they miss the opportunity to be first in the customer's mind, as well as the early revenues from the new market.

A firm's decision to pioneer or follow can be an ad hoc one, driven by circumstances such as technological opportunities or a response to the moves of competitors. Or it can be part of the firm's overall strategy and thus stated in the Innovation Charter. The point here is not to debate what firms should decide in particular circumstances. Rather, the relevant issue is what the implications of either strategy are for developing innovations.

The decision to pioneer a new market heightens the need for the team to understand how to build markets. They have two significant opportunities. Firstly, to shape the way the market evolves, and secondly to keep leadership once the mass market takes off. However, to be successful in both, the team has to take a much longer term view of strategy and planning than is often the case. The firm's leadership should support them to do this with their policies and decisions, the resources they devote to pioneering projects and their approach to career planning. Similarly, the team has to take a sophisticated and subtle approach to customer research, using the ideas of Chapter 5. Otherwise it will not develop the right innovation for the innovators, or it may fail to seize the opportunities in the mainstream market. Pioneering also makes organizational change more difficult, as there is no example to point to when trying to convince others. Both these points on research and change also need support from the leadership, as well as gate committees that are sensitive to these issues.

The decision to follow the pioneer raises different challenges. Followers need to learn and improve the innovation while staking out a different position to the pioneer, often by focusing on specific mainstream segments. In one sense this is easier: customers are better informed for followers than they are for pioneers and thus market research is more accurate. Besides, take-off to the mass market is closer and easier to predict, and others in the organization can readily see the opportunity. However, in another sense it is not easier. The pioneer may have staked out the best position in the market and the follower is not alone. Other firms can now see the opportunity just as clearly as your firm. An effective follower needs to move quickly, to learn the new market, to choose its focus and to develop and bring its own variant to the market. Both the leadership and gate committees need to fast-track follower projects to ensure quick and effective decisions and mobilize the necessary resources without delay. Pioneers should not be slow or ponderous, but followers need to be fast and agile.

It is likely that many firms will end by both pioneering and following. They may have a general stance towards pioneering or following, but events in the market may make them adjust this stance. This is especially the case if the stance is to be a pioneer. Leading firms are often working on similar lines of development and competitive intelligence is not perfect. Teams may think they are pioneering, only for competitors to catch them out by launching first. Leaders and gate committees therefore have to handle both strategies. They should also prepare to switch a project from one mode to the other, just as teams should incorporate such possibilities into their scenarios and planning.

FINAL REFLECTIONS

The first objective of this book was to address the changing nature of innovation. By now it can be seen the pressure to create greater value, and the switch in emphasis from products to services and business models, requires a new and different approach to that of the past. Co-creation has replaced traditional market research. Market design has replaced market analysis. Core teams that lead and change organizations have replaced cross-functional teams. Strategies and contingency plans straddling many years have replaced the typical launch plan. This approach to innovation management is markedly different from that of the past and represents a major challenge for many organizations. Yet leading firms are already achieving great success using one or more elements of the new approach.

In addition, the recipe for success is simple, needing only three basic steps. First, the firm needs to build the coalition of senior executives that will guide and support innovation. Second, it needs to write and put into practice an Innovation Charter that reflects the ideas in this book. Third, it needs to develop a better appreciation of how to build new markets among its executives and managers. All three steps require effort and insight, especially in tailoring practices to the firm's purpose and culture, but all three can be done if the will to do so exists.

The second objective of the book was to provide an integrated and practical approach to bringing innovation to the market. The most critical tasks in innovation management are the five this book focuses on. If the firm can charter innovation effectively, invest in the right teams and co-create with customers, it is more likely to be able to identify and develop good innovations. If it can also change itself to deliver the resulting innovations well, and build new markets with a long-term vision, then it will be better able to capitalize on these innovations.

The tools associated with each chapter should help in turning these ideas into practice. There are enough to cover the scope of the five tasks adequately, but not too many to make the job excessively complex. Most of them are also tools that managers can learn and apply themselves. Finally, by discussing how firms may need to adapt these ideas to various circumstances, the author also hopes to have provided enough guidance for managers to start their own projects. There is no one magic formula for innovation projects. Projects need setting up and carrying out differently according to how big a breakthrough the firm requires, which of the three challenges – appropriation, customers or development – is most important, and the firm's competitive stance.

Clearly many firms can do better at innovation than they are doing at present. They can reduce the number of innovations that fail in the market and shift the balance of their efforts towards more breakthroughs. Studies conflict on what this balance currently is and in any event they focus mostly on products rather than on the new world of services and business model innovation. My intuition is that most global firms are good at significant incremental innovations and this is what they do most of the time. It is not true that most innovation is minor or trivial. Where the real challenge lies is in increasing the proportion of successful *breakthrough* innovations. If this is 15 to 20% of all innovation now, then huge returns will accrue to those raising these proportions to 25 or 30%. These returns not only profit firms but society in general. While incremental innovation provides benefits, it is breakthrough innovations that dramatically improve the quality of peoples' lives and raise the productivity of economic endeavours. Human progress depends, in large part, on firms doing a better job at innovation.

GLOSSARY

Adopt/Adoption The customer buying the innovation for the first time.

Ambidextrous executive An executive who can manage breakthrough and incremental projects simultaneously.

Appropriation How a business extracts profit from the innovation through its business model.

Architectural disruption An innovation that reinvents an existing business model. Also called a format innovation and often associated with low-cost suppliers.

Autonomous team A team whose members' career advancement depends more on the team leader than their current boss.

B2B/B2C Business-to-business or business-to-consumer markets. The main difference is between group and individual buying decisions.

Business model The way a business configures its activities, and those of its partners, to deliver value and make a profit.

Choice experiment A market research method that uses the principles of experimental design to get accurate evaluations of what the customer values.

Co-creation Working with customers as partners in developing an innovation.

Common knowledge The knowledge about the innovation in a social group. Not only of what others think about the innovation, but also what other people know about what other people know.

Connectors Customers with greater numbers of social connections who form a bridge between innovators and the mainstream.

Crossing-the-chasm The challenge firms face in moving from selling to the innovators to selling to the mainstream market.

Discovery-driven planning A business planning method that continually tests and refines the assumptions behind the new business.

Executive sponsor An executive who champions, mentors, and protects an innovation team.

Framing How the firm describes the innovation to the customer, especially which advantages it highlights.

Guiding coalition The executives who promote, support, and direct the firm's innovation programme.

House of Quality A method for relating the technical features of the product or service to customer needs, and deciding the design targets for the innovation.

Information acceleration Providing information to customers during market research, simulating the environment in which customers will decide once the firm launches the innovation.

Innovation Creating and delivering a new product, service, or business model to the market. And the actual product, service, or business model itself.

Innovation Charter A written description of the firm's goals and governance systems for innovation.

Innovators Customers who are open to new ideas and less influenced by social opinion. Some writers use the term 'early adopter' but this tautologically confuses an inclination with behaviour.

Laddering A market research technique for connecting product or service features with the benefits to, and higher goals of, customers.

Lead user A customer who is ahead of their peers in thinking about possible innovations and who can benefit significantly from better solutions. Also one who has the expertise and creativity to help in co-creation.

Local influences All the sources of information and influence the customer receives while making their adoption decision. Includes supplier, peer and third-party sources, and traditional and new media.

Mainstream customers The typical customer, less open to new ideas and needing social confirmation to adopt. The majority in most markets, both B2B and B2C.

Market design A picture of the market the firm wishes to create, including the size and timing of revenues from various customer segments.

Multifunctional team A team which draws it members from the various functions or business units of the firm. Comes in two sorts, lightweight and heavyweight, according to the seniority of the leader. But note the team member's career advancement may still depend on their current boss rather than the team leader.

Non-customer innovation An innovation which seeks to extend a technology or service to a segment of customers who are unable or unwilling to use it in its existing form. See also *Crossing-the-chasm*.

Positioning Marketing's version of framing. This includes identifying the category the firm wishes to associate the innovation with, proof the innovation delivers the main benefit of that category, and the advantage the firm thinks will overcome the status quo bias.

Project objective A short statement of what the firm expects an innovation project to achieve. Usually expressed as what the innovation will provide to the customer.

Scenario A logical story about what an alternate future looks like and how it comes about.

Stage-Gate A sequential procedure for developing innovations, breaking development into clear stages, and providing for regular review and go/no go decisions.

Status quo bias   The bias mainstream customers have against change, driven by their perception that they will lose more than they gain.

Strategy Canvas   A visual depiction of how the innovation will deliver value in a different way to existing products or services.

Virtuous circle   The idea that improving customer satisfaction not only results in more business from existing customers but also, through customer advocates, lowers the costs of winning new ones. This increases profitability and allows firms that are doing a good job to pull away from their rivals.

Voice-of-the-customer   A market research technique built around depth-interviews by innovation team members. The goal is to identify and prioritize all possible customer needs.

X-team   An externally oriented innovation team. That is, one that devotes as much time to working with the rest of the organization as it does to its own internal deliberations.

NOTES

CHAPTER 1: THE THREE CHALLENGES OF BUSINESS INNOVATION

1. C. Kim and R. Mauborgne, *Blue Ocean Strategy*, Boston, Harvard Business School Press, 2005.
2. R. Garcia and R. Calantone, 'A Critical Look at Innovation Typology and Innovativeness Terminology', *Journal of Product Innovation Management*, March 2002.
3. A. Afuah, *Business Models*, New York, McGraw-Hill/Irwin, 2004.
4. C. Hipp, B. Tether and I. Miles, 'The Incidence and Effects of Innovation in Services', *International Journal of Innovation Management*, December 2000.
5. B. Jaruzelski, K. Dehoff and R. Bordia, 'The Booz Allen Global Innovation 1000', *strategy + business*, Winter 2005.
6. N. Mourkogiannis, *Purpose*, New York, Palgrave Macmillan, 2006.
7. P. Lencioni, *The Five Dysfunctions of a Team*, San Francisco, Jossey-Bass, 2002.
8. T. Kelley with J. Littman, *The Ten Faces of Innovation*, London, Profile Books, 2006.
9. J. Kotter, *Leading Change*, Boston, Harvard Business School Press, 1996.
10. P. Golder and G. Tellis, *Will and Vision*, New York, McGraw-Hill, 2002.

CHAPTER 2: CREATING ADVANTAGE IN THE MINDS OF MANY

1. J. Gourville, 'The Curse of Innovation', *Harvard Business School Marketing Research Paper 05-06*, June 2005.

2. P. Smethers and A. France, *Five Myths of Consumer Behavior*, Seattle, Consumer Ease Publishing, 2007.

3. E. Rogers, *Diffusion of Innovations*, New York, Free Press, 2003.

4. G. Moore, *Crossing the Chasm*, New York, HarperBusiness, 1991.

5. S. Pinker, *How the Mind Works*, London, Penguin Books, 1999.

6. D. Kahneman and A. Tversky, 'Prospect Theory', *Econometrica*, March 1979.

7. E. Rogers, *Diffusion of Innovations*, New York, Free Press, 2003.

8. J. Gourville, The Curse of Innovation, *Harvard Business School Marketing Research Paper 05-06*, June 2005.

9. C. Kim and R. Mauborgne, *Blue Ocean Strategy*, Boston, Harvard Business School Press, 2005.

10. Z. Katona, J. Lajos, A. Chattopadhyay and M. Sarvary, 'Category Activation Model', *Working Paper*, INSEAD, 06.

11. E. Glaeser, 'Psychology and the Market', *National Bureau of Economic Research Working Paper 10203*, December 2003.

12. C. Camerer, G. Lowenstein and D. Prelec, 'Neuroeconomics', *Journal of Economic Literature*, March 2005.

13. T. Wilson, D. Lisle, J. Schooler, S. Hodges, K. Klaaren and S. LaFleur, 'Introspecting about reasons can reduce post-choice satisfaction', *Personality and Social Psychology Bulletin*, March 1993.

14. D. Wegner, *The Illusion of Conscious Will*, Boston, MIT Press, 2002.

15. M. Hsu, M. Bhatt, R. Adolphs, D. Tranel and C. Camerer, 'Neural Systems Responding to Uncertainty in Human Decision-Making', *Science*, December 2005.

16. P. Costa and R. McCrae, 'Four Ways Five Factors are Basic', *Personality and Individual Differences*, June 1992.

17. R. Reimann, A. Angleitner and J. Strelau, 'Genetic and Environmental Influences on Personality', *Journal of Personality*, September 1997.

18. S. Yamagata, A. Suzuki, J. Ando, Y. Ono, N. Kijima, K. Yoshimura, F. Ostendorf, A. Angleitner, R. Riemann, F. Spinath, J. Livesley and K. Jang, 'Is the Genetic Structure of Human Personality Universal?' *Journal of Personality and Social Psychology*, June 2006.

19. R. Depue and P. Collins, 'Neurobiology of the Structure of Personality', *Behavioral and Brain Sciences*, June 1999.

20. C. DeYoung, 'Higher-Order Factors of the Big Five in a Multi-Informant Sample', *Journal of Personality and Social Psychology*, December 2006.

21. D. Midgley and G. Dowling, 'A Longitudinal Study of Product Form Innovation', *Journal of Consumer Research*, March 1993.

22. A. Caspi, 'The Child is Father of the Man', *Journal of Personality and Social Psychology*, January 2000.

23. M. Kirton, 'Adaptors and Innovators in Organizations', *Human Relations*, April 1980.

24. Y. Benson, S. Oreg and T. Dvir, 'CEO Values, Organizational Culture and Firm Outcomes', *Journal of Organizational Behavior*, July 2008.

25. A.-L. Barabasi, *Linked*, New York, Plume 2003.

26. M. Granovetter, 'The Strength of Weak Ties', *American Journal of Sociology*, May 1973.

27. M. Gladwell, *The Tipping Point*, New York, Little, Brown and Company, 2000.

28. E. Keller and J. Berry, *The Influentials*, New York, Free Press 2003.

29. J. Denrell and G. Le Mens, 'Interdependent Sampling and Social Influence', *Psychological Review*, April 2007.

30. M. Chwe, 'Cultures, Circles and Commercials', *Rationality and Society*, February 1998.

31. M. Chwe, 'Communication and Coordination in Social Networks', *Review of Economic Studies*, January 2000.

32. C. Roch, 'The Dual Roots of Opinion Leadership', *Journal of Politics*, February 2005.

33. E. Arnould, L. Price and G. Zinkhan, *Consumers*, New York, McGraw-Hill/Irwin 2003.

34. M. Newman and J. Park, 'Why Social Networks are Different from Other Types of Networks', *Physical Review E*, May 2003.

35. P. Morrison, D. Midgley and J. Roberts, 'The Effect of Network Structure in Industrial Diffusion Processes', *Research Policy*, December 1992.

36. D. Watts and P. Dodds, 'Influentials, Networks and Public Opinion Formation', *Journal of Consumer Research*, December 2007.

37. E. Glaeser, 'Psychology and the Market', *National Bureau of Economic Research Working Paper 10203*, December 2003.

38. E. Glaeser, 'Psychology and the Market', *National Bureau of Economic Research Working Paper 10203*, December 2003.

39. T. Farley, *Mobile phone history*, available at: http://www.affordablephones.net/HistoryMobile.htm (23 February 2008). T. Farley, *History of cellular phones*, available at: http://www.affordablephones.net/HistoryCellular.htm (23 February 2008). Cell phone history, *Original structure*, available at: http://library.thinkquest.org/04oct/02001/original.htm (23 February 2008). Global Source Marketing, *History of cell phones*, available at: http://www.global-source-mkt.com/cellphonefacts.html (23 February 2008). Gartner, *Gartner says mobile phone sales will exceed one billion in 2009*, available at: http://www.gartner.com/press_releases/asset_132473_11.html (20 February 2008). EarthVision Cellular, *The wireless industry – an overview of the cellular phone service in America*, available at: http://www.cellularphonenews.com/ebook/overview.html (23 February 2008).

40. LG Electronics, *Achievements: Digital appliance*, available at: http://us.lge.com/aboutus/achievelist/list/achieve_Digital%20Appliance.jhtml (5 March 2008). LG Electronics, *With Unique, Innovative Features, LG Improves Household in 2007*, available at: http://uk.lge.com/about/press_release/detail/PRE%7CMENU_5484_

6.jhtml (5 March 2008). LG Electronics, *Light wave oven*, available at: http://my. lge.com/proddivergent.do?categoryId=060601&modelCategoryId=&parentId=0606 (5 March 2008). LG Electronics, *LG SolarDOM®*, available at: http://sg.lge.com/ products/mobile/mobil/sidemenu.do?action=filedown&group_code=060505&list_ code=PRD_BROC&page=1&filepath=/download/product/1123731143096_01_ Solardom(1).pdf&filename=Solardom(1).pdf& (5 March 2008). LG Electronics, *Much more than white goods*, available at: http://us.lge.com/aboutus/pressdetail/detail/ press_Home%20Appliances_180_3.jhtml (5 March 2008).

41. Wikipedia, the free encyclopedia, *Digital audio player*, available at: http://en. wikipedia.org/wiki/MP3_player (24 February 2008). dabs.com, *Digital audio/video players (mp3/mp4): compare product*, available at: http://www.dabs.com/compare.aspx? &ql=4PK0&ql=4PJR&ql=45DH&ql=4Q3M&ql=43N3&NavigationKey=11212& ExposedRefinement=11006&CategorySelectedId=11212 (24 February 2008). Creative, *Creative introduces the world's first 32GB flash memory-based portable media player with the latest credit card-sized Zen™*, available at: http://asia.creative.com/corporate/ pressroom/releases/welcome.asp?pid=12867 (24 February 2008). S. Hansell, Technology: Battle of form (and function) in MP3 players, *New York Times*, 4 October 2004, available at: http://query.nytimes.com/gst/fullpage.html?res=9C00E3DE1138 F937A35753C1A9629C8B63&sec=&spon=&pagewanted=all (24 February 2008). R. Wray, Stun gun has a pop at MP3 market. *Guardian*, 8 January 2008, available at: http://www.guardian.co.uk/business/2008/jan/08/technology.gadgets?gusrc= rss&feed=networkfront (24 February 2008).

CHAPTER 3: CHARTERING INNOVATION WITHIN THE ORGANIZATION

1. B. Jauruzelski, K. Dehoff and R. Bordia, 'Money Isn't Everything', *strategy + business*, Winter 2005.
2. B. Jaruzelski and K. Dehoff, 'The Customer Connection', *strategy + business*, Winter 2007.
3. R. Garcia and R. Calantone, 'A Critical Look at Innovation Typology and Innovativeness Terminology', *Journal of Product Innovation Management*, March 2002.
4. J. March, 'Exploration and Exploitation in Organizational Learning', *Organization Science*, February 1991.
5. R. Moss Kanter, 'Innovation: the Classic Traps', *Harvard Business Review*, November 2006.
6. N. Mourkogiannis, *Purpose*, New York, Palgrave Macmillan, 2006.
7. M. May, *The Elegant Solution*, New York, Free Press, 2007.
8. N. Mourkogiannis, *Purpose*, New York, Palgrave Macmillan, 2006.
9. C. Christensen, *The Innovators's Solution*, Boston, Harvard Business School Press, 2003.

10. M. May, *The Elegant Solution*, New York, Free Press, 2007.

11. N. Harper and P. Viguerie, 'Are You Too Focused?' *The McKinsey Quarterly*, August 2002.

12. K. Goffin and R. Mitchel, *Innovation Management*, Basingstoke UK, Palgrave Macmillan, 2005.

13. R. Cooper, *Winning at New Products*, Cambridge MA, Basic Books, 3rd edn, 2001.

14. B. Jauruzelski, K. Dehoff and R. Bordia, 'Money Isn't Everything, *strategy + business*', Winter 2005.

15. R. Cooper, *Winning at New Products*, Cambridge MA, Basic Books, 3rd edn, 2001.

16. A. Griffin, *Drivers of NPD Success*, Chicago, Product Development and Management Association, 1997.

17. S. Hart, E. Hultink, N. Tzokas and H. Commandeur, 'Industrial Companies' Evaluation Criteria in New Product Development Gates', *Journal of Product Innovation Management*, January 2003.

18. J. Morone, 'Technology and Competitive Advantage', *Research Technology Management*, March–April 1993.

19. P. Carbonnel, A. Rodriguez Escudero and J. Munuera Aleman, 'Technological Newness and Impact of Go/No-Go Criteria on New Product Success', *Marketing Letters*, July/October 2004.

20. I. Alam, 'Innovation Strategy, Process and Performance in the Commercial Banking Industry', *Journal of Marketing Management*, November 2003.

21. V. Jolly, *Commercializing New Technologies*, Boston, Harvard Business School Press, 1997.

22. T. Kuczmarski, *Innovation*, Chicago IL, NTC Publishing Group, 1996.

23. D. Teece, 'Profiting from Technological Innovation', *Research Policy*, December 1986.

24. P. Golder and G. Tellis, *Will and Vision*, New York, McGraw-Hill, 2002.

25. W. Boulding and M. Christen, 'First-Mover Disadvantage', *Harvard Business Review*, October 2001.

26. C. Bart, 'Product Innovation Charters', *R&D Management*, January 2002.

27. R. Cooper, *Winning at New Products*, Cambridge MA, Basic Books, 3rd edn, 2001.

28. C. Kim and R. Mauborgne, *Blue Ocean Strategy*, Boston, Harvard Business School Press, 2005.

29. P. Schoemaker, *Profiting from Uncertainty*, New York, Free Press, 2002.

30. R. Gunther McGrath and I. MacMillan, 'Discovery-Driven Planning', *Harvard Business Review*, July–August 1995.

31. E. von Hippel and J. Churchill, video on 3M lead user studies available at: http://userinnovation.mit.edu/videos/Breakthrough.mpg (14 September 2008).

32. S. Hart, E. Hultink, N. Tzokas and H. Commandeur, 'Industrial Companies' Evaluation Criteria in New Product Development Gates', *Journal of Product Innovation Management*, January 2003.

33. *Sources*: A. Leiponen and C. Helfat, 'Innovation Objectives, Knowledge Sources, and the Benefits of Breadth' *Working Paper, London, London Business School*, 2005. Available at: http://www.london.edu/assets/documents/PDF/Helfatpaper.pdf (10 March 2008). Saint-Gobain, *Objectives*, London, Saint-Gobain, 2004. Available at: http://www.saint-gobain.com/en/html/innovation/objectifs.asp (10 March 2008). Demohouse, *Objectives*, Petten, Demohouse, 2005. Available at: http://www.demohouse.net/home/objectives/ (11 March 2008).

34. *Sources*: C. Bart, Product Innovation Charters, *R&D Management*, January 2002. IBM, *Who Innovates? IBM Research*. Available at: http://www.research.ibm.com/resources/innovate.shtml (27 February 2008). IBM, *IBM Charter for iSeries Innovation*. Available at: http://www-03.ibm.com/servers/uk/eserver/iseries/charter/index.html (27 February 2008). IBM, *iSeries Initiative for Innovation*. Available at: http://www-03.ibm.com/servers/uk/eserver/iseries/innovation/index.html (27 February 2008). IBM, *History of IBM: 1880*. Available at: http://www-03.ibm.com/ibm/history/history/decade_1880.html (27 February 2008).

35. M. Abramovici and L. Bancel-Charensol, 'How to Take Customers into Consideration in Service Innovation Projects', *The Services Industries Journal*, January 2004.

36. *Sources*: Siemens, *Siemens – global network of innovation*. Available at: http://www.siemens.com/Daten/siecom/HQ/CC/Internet/About_Us/WORKAREA/about_ed/templatedata/English/file/binary/Long%20Portrait_1244581.pdf (24 February 2008). Siemens, *Annual report 2007*, Munich, Siemens AG, 2007. Available at: http://w1.siemens.com/annual/07/pool/download/pdf/e07_00_gb2007.pdf (24 February 2008). Siemens, *Strategy & vision*, Munich, Siemens AG, 2008. Available at: http://w1.siemens.com/innovation/en/strategie/innovation_strategy/index.htm (18 February 2008). Siemens, *Pictures of the future – strategic planning for the future at Siemens*, Munich, Siemens AG, 2008. Available at: http://w1.siemens.com/innovation/en/strategie/method.htm (18 February 2008). Siemens, *Pictures of the future*, Munich, Siemens AG, 2008. Available at: http://w1.siemens.com/innovation/en/strategie/results_future_study/index.htm (18 February 2008). Siemens, *Transportation*, Munich, Siemens AG, 2008. Available at: http://w1.siemens.com/innovation/en/strategie/results_future_study/transportation.htm (18 February 2008).

CHAPTER 4: SELECTING, PREPARING AND SUPPORTING THE RIGHT TEAM

1. J. Katzenbach and D. Smith, *Wisdom of Teams*, New York, NY, Collins 2006.

2. R. Cooper, *Winning at New Products*, Cambridge, MA, Basic Books, 2001; J. Maxwell, *The 17 Indisputable Laws of Teamwork*, Nashville Tennessee, Thomas Nelson 2001.

3. V. Govindarajan and C. Trimble, *10 Rules for Strategic Innovators*, Boston, MA, Harvard Business School Press, 2005; M. Tushman and C. O'Reilly, *Winning through Innovation*, Boston MA, Harvard Business School Press, 2002.

4. R. Moss Kanter, 'Innovation', *Harvard Business Review*, November 2006; K. Goffin and R. Mitchell, *Innovation Management*, Basingstoke UK, Palgrave Macmillan, 2005; Chapter 10 by S. Markham and P. Holahan in K. Kahn, G. Castellion and A. Griffin (eds), *The PDMA Handbook of New Product Development*, Hoboken NJ, John Wiley & Sons, Inc, 2005.

5. D. Ancona and H. Bresman, *X-Teams*, Boston MA, Harvard Business School Press, 2007.

6. A. Griffin, 'PDMA Research on New Product Development Practices', *Journal of Product Innovation Management*, November 1997.

7. S. Wheelwright and K. Clark, *Revolutionizing Product Development*, New York, Free Press, 1992.

8. R. Cooper, *Winning at New Products*, Cambridge MA, Basic Books 2001.

9. R. Leenders, J. Kratzer, J. Hollander and J. van Engelen, Chapter 6 in P. Belliveau, A. Griffin and S. Somermeyer (eds), *The PDMA Toolbook 1 for New Product Development*, New York, John Wiley & Sons, Inc, 2002.

10. S. Wheelwright and K. Clark, *Revolutionizing Product Development*, New York, Free Press, 1992.

11. K. Goffin and R. Mitchell, *Innovation Management*, Basingstoke UK, Palgrave Macmillan, 2005.

12. C. Christensen, *The Innovator's Solution*, Boston MA, Harvard Business School Press, 2003.

13. V. Govindarajan and C. Trimble, *10 Rules for Strategic Innovators*, Boston MA, Harvard Business School Press, 2005.

14. M. Tushman and C. O' Reilly, *Winning through Innovation*, Boston MA, Harvard Business School Press, 2002.

15. M. Tushman, W. Smith, R. Wood, G. Westerman and C. O'Reilly, 'Innovation Streams and Ambidextrous Organizational Designs', *Harvard Business School Working Paper*, February 2004.

16. M. Berg Jensen, B. Johnson, E. Lorenz and B. Lundvall, 'Forms of knowledge and modes of innovation', *Research Policy*, June 2007.

17. Y. Doz, J. Santos and P. Williamson, *From Global to Metanational*, Boston MA, Harvard Business School Press, 2001.

18. S. Heck and T. Grewal in K. Kahn, G. Castellion and A. Griffin (eds), Chapter 11, *The PDMA Handbook of New Product Development*, Hoboken NJ, John Wiley & Sons, Inc, 2005.

19. R. Leenders, J. Kratzer, and J. van Engelen, Chapter 5 in P. Belliveau, A. Griffin and S. Somermeyer (eds), *The PDMA Toolbook 2 for New Product Development*, Hoboken NJ, John Wiley & Sons, Inc, 2004.

20. M. Csikszentmihalyi, *Creativity*, New York, HarperCollins, 1996.

21. D. Ancona and H. Bresman, *X-Teams*, Boston MA, Harvard Business School Press, 2007.

22. A. Orban and C. Miller, Chapter 4 in A. Griffin and S. Somermeyer (eds), *The PDMA Toolbook 3 for New Product Development*, Hoboken NJ, John Wiley & Sons, Inc, 2007.

23. G. Altshuller, *Creativity as an Exact Science*, New York, Gordon and Breach, 1984.

24. Y. Wind and C. Crook, *The Power of Impossible Thinking*, Upper Saddle River NJ, Wharton School Publishing/Pearson Education, 2005.

25. C. Rabe, *The Innovation Killer*, New York, Amacom, 2006.

26. B-C Lim and K. Klein, 'Team Mental Models and Team Performance', *Journal of Organizational Behavior*, June 2006.

27. K. Goffin and R. Mitchell, *Innovation Management*, Basingstoke UK, Palgrave Macmillan, 2005; R. Moss Kanter, 'Innovation', *Harvard Business Review*, November 2006.

28. P. Lencioni, *Overcoming the Five Dysfunctions of a Team*, San Francisco, Jossey-Bass, 2005.

29. J. Katzenbach and D. Smith, *Wisdom of Teams*, New York, Collins, 2006.

30. J. Mueller, 'Why Individuals in Larger Teams Perform Worse', *Wharton School Working Paper*, June 2006.

31. M. Tushman, W. Smith, R. Wood, G. Westerman and C. O'Reilly, 'Innovation Streams and Ambidextrous Organizational Designs', *Harvard Business School Working Paper*, February 2004.

32. T. Kuczmarski, *Innovation*, Chicago IL, NTC Publishing Group, 1996.

33. D. Ancona and H. Bresman, *X-Teams*, Boston MA, Harvard Business School Press, 2007.

34. J. Buijs, 'Innovation Leaders Should Be Controlled Schizophrenics', *Creativity and Innovation Management*, June 2007.

35. R. Moss Kanter, 'Innovation', *Harvard Business Review*, November 2006.

36. J. Katzenbach and D. Smith, *Wisdom of Teams*, New York, Collins 2006.

37. P. Lencioni, *The Five Dysfunctions of a Team*, San Francisco, Jossey-Bass, 2002.

38. P. Lencioni, *Overcoming the Five Dysfunctions of a Team*, San Francisco, Jossey-Bass, 2005.

39. S. Fisher, T. Hunter and W. MacRosson, 'A Validation Study of Belbin's Team Roles', *European Journal of Work and Organizational Psychology*, June 2001.

40. R. Leenders, J. Kratzer, J. Hollander and J. van Engelen, Chapter 6 in P. Belliveau, A. Griffin and S. Somermeyer (eds), *The PDMA Toolbook 1 for New Product Development*, New York, John Wiley & Sons, Inc, 2002.

41. N. Anderson and M. West, 'Measuring Climate for Work Group Innovation', *Journal of Organizational Behavior*, May 1998.

42. M. Csikszentmihalyi, *Creativity*, New York, HarperCollins, 1996.

43. P. Koen, T. Holcombe and C. Gehres, Chapter 6 in A. Griffin and S. Somermeyer (eds), *The PDMA Toolbook 3 for New Product Development*, Hoboken NJ, John Wiley & Sons, Inc, 2007.

44. *Sources*: M. Tushman, W. Smith, R. Wood, G. Westerman and C. O'Reilly, 'Innovation Streams and Ambidextrous Organizational Designs', *Harvard Business School Working Paper*, February 2004. G. Pisano, CIBA Vision, Harvard Business School Case, March 1996. CIBA Vision, *Milestones*, Duluth GA, CIBA Vision, 2008. Available at: cibavision.com/about_worldwide/milestones.shtml (10 March 2008).

45. *Sources*: Visitask, 'The benefits of a kick-off meeting'. Available at: http://www.visitask.com/project-kick-off-meeting.asp (28 August 2008). M. Sisco, 'A well-planned kickoff meeting sets the tone for a successful project', *TechRepublic*, 6 June 2002. Available at: http://articles.techrepublic.com.com/5100-10878_11-1038879.html?tag=rbxccnbtr1 (28 August 2008). M. Sisco, 'Follow these steps to conduct an effective project kickoff meeting', *TechRepublic*, 13 June 2002. Available at: http://articles.techrepublic.com.com/5100-10878_11-1038766.html?tag=rbxccnbtr1 (28 August 2008).

46. *Source*: N. Anderson and M. West, *The Team Climate Inventory*, Windsor UK, Assessment Services for Employment, NFER–Nelson, 1994. (Manual and Users' Guide).

CHAPTER 5: CO-CREATING THE INNOVATION WITH CUSTOMERS

1. Marketing Science Institute, *Conference on Innovation and Co-Creation*, Seattle, June 2008.
2. B. Jaruzelski and K. Dehoff, 'The Customer Connection', *strategy + business*, Winter 2007. R. Cooper, *Winning at New Products*, Cambridge MA, Basic Books, 3rd edn, 2001.
3. J. Gourville, 'The Curse of Innovation', *Harvard Business School Marketing Research Paper 05-06*, June 2005.
4. E. von Hippel, *The Sources of Innovation*, New York, Oxford University Press 1988.
5. G. Lilien, P. Morrison, K. Searls, M. Sonnack and E. von Hippel, 'Performance Assessment of the Lead User Idea-Generation Process for New Product Development', *Management Science*, August 2002.
6. M. Schrage, 'My Customer, My Co-Innovator', *strategy + business*, August 2006.
7. E. Rogers, *Diffusion of Innovations*, New York, Free Press, 2003.
8. G. Katz, Chapter 7 in P. Belliveau, A. Griffin and S. Somermeyer (eds), *The PDMA Toolbook 2 for New Product Development*, Hoboken NJ, John Wiley & Sons, Inc., 2004.
9. G. Katz, Chapter 7 in P. Belliveau, A. Griffin and S. Somermeyer (eds), *The PDMA Toolbook 2 for New Product Development*, Hoboken NJ, John Wiley & Sons, Inc., 2004.
10. T. Kelley, *The Ten Faces of Innovation*, London, Profile Books, 2006.

11. G. Zaltman, *How Customers Think*, Boston, Harvard Business School Press, 2003.

12. G. Katz, Practitioner Note, *Journal of Product Innovation Management*, January 2004.

13. E. von Hippel and R. Katz, 'Shifting Innovation to Users Via Toolkits', *Management Science*, July 2002.

14. T. Kelley, *The Ten Faces of Innovation*, London, Profile Books, 2006.

15. T. Grimm, *User's Guide to Rapid Prototyping*, Dearborn MI, Society of Manufacturing Engineers, 2004.

16. M. George, *Fast Innovation*, New York, McGraw-Hill, 2005.

17. T. Kelley, *The Ten Faces of Innovation*, London, Profile Books, 2006.

18. J. Louviere, D. Hensher and J. Swait, *Stated Choice Methods*, Cambridge UK, Cambridge University Press, 2000.

19. G. Urban, J. Hauser, W. Qualls, B. Weinberg, J. Bohlmann and R. Chicos, 'Information Acceleration', *Journal of Marketing Research*, February 1997.

20. G. Urban, B. Weinberg and J. Hauser, 'Premarket Forecasting of Really-New Products', *Journal of Marketing*, January, 1996.

21. S. Thomke and A. Nimgade, Innovation at 3M, *Harvard Business School Case Number 9699012*, August 1998.

22. *Sources*: UMTS World, *UMTS/3G history and future milestones: the early days*, available at: http://www.umtsworld.com/umts/history.htm (10 March 2008). Wireless Watch, *Vodafone policy shift evidence of European 3G failure*, available at: http://www.theregister.co.uk/2006/08/07/3g_woes/ (10 March 2008). Wearden G. *UK faces 3G failure*, available at: http://news.zdnet.co.uk/communications/0,1000000085,2086061,00.htm (10 March 2008). BBC. *3G phones 'bad value' says Which*, available at: http://news.bbc.co.uk/1/hi/talking_point/4061541.stm (10 March 2008).

23. *Sources*: Friendly Robotics website, available at: http://www.friendlyrobotics.com (27 February 2008). Probotics, *RoboMower model history: 1999–2005*, available at: http://www.probotics.com/robomower/model-history.htm (27 February 2008). D. Brinn, *Israeli lawn-mowing robot makes the cut*, Jerusalem, Israel 21c, 2005. Available at: http://israel21c.com/bin/en.jsp?enDispWho=Articles%5El1021&enPage=Blank Page&enDisplay=view&enDispWhat=object&enVersion=0&enZone=Health& (27 February 2008). CJ Murray, 'Mowing on autopilot', *Design News*, June 2006. Available at: http://www.designnews.com/article/CA6344241.html (27 February 2008).

24. *Sources*: National Statistics, *MRSA: deaths continue to rise in 2005*, available at: http://www.statistics.gov.uk/CCI/nugget.asp?ID=1067&Pos=1&ColRank=1&Rank=208 (23 February 2008). Health Protection Agency, *Staphylococcus aureus*, available at: http://www.hpa.org.uk/infections/topics_az/staphylo/default.htm (23 February 2008). Health Protection Agency, *MRSA: Information for patients in hospital*, London, HPA, 2006. Available at: http://www.hpa.org.uk/publications/2006/mrsa/MRSA_leaflet.pdf (23 February 2008). Health Protection Agency, *Staphylococcus aureus bacteraemia laboratory reports and methicillin susceptibility*, London, HPA, 2005. Available

at: http://www.hpa.org.uk/infections/topics_az/staphylo/lab_data_staphyl.htm (23 February 2008). Department of Health, *A simple guide to MRSA*. London: DoH, 2005. Department of Health, *Winning ways: working together to reduce healthcare associated infection in England. A report from the Chief Medical Officer.* London, DoH, 2003. J. Elliot, *Simple band could cut hospital bugs.* London, BBC, 2007. Available at: http://news.bbc.co.uk/1/hi/health/6917334.stm (23 February 2008). Anonymous, Award: Christian Fellowes/Ryan Kerstein, Imperial College School of Medicine, *Engineer Online 2007*. Available at: http://www.theengineer.co.uk/Articles/300368/The+Graduate+Innovator+Award.htm (23 February 2008). Department of Health, *Clean, safe care: reducing infections and saving lives.* London, DoH, 2008. Available at: http://www.clean-safe-care.nhs.uk/ArticleFiles/Files/CleanSafeCare_ReducingInfections AndSavingLives_Strategy.pdf (23 February 2008). Anonymous, *Super-bug saviours*, Newcastle-upon-Tyne, HERO, 2007. Available at: http://www.hero.ac.uk/uk/business/archives/2007/super_bug_saviours_Jun.cfm (23 February 2008).

25. E. Enkel, J. Perez-Freije and O. Gassman, 'Minimizing Market Risks through Customer Integration into New Product Development', *Creativity and Innovation Management*, December 2005.

CHAPTER 6: CHANGING THE ORGANIZATION TO DELIVER THE INNOVATION

1. R. Kanter, B. Stein and T. Jick, *The Challenge of Organizational Change*, New York, Free Press, 1992.

2. J. Kotter, *Leading Change*, Boston MA, Harvard Business School Press, 1996.

3. G. Neilson and J. McGrath, 'Exercising Common Sense', *strategy + business*, November 2007.

4. E. Schein, *Process Consultation Revisited*, Reading MA, Addison-Wesley 1999. M. Beitler, *Strategic Organizational Change*, Greensboro NC, Practitioners Press International, 2006.

5. W. Bridges, *Managing Transitions*, Cambridge MA, De Capo Press 2003.

6. H. Gardner, *Changing Minds*, Boston MA, Harvard Business School Press, 2004. P. Rogers, M. Gunesekera and M. Yang, 'Rhetorical Tools for Communicating Strategic Change', *Working Paper 1079, Ross School of Business*, University of Michigan, April 2007.

7. J. Kotter, *The Heart of Change*, Boston MA, Harvard Business School Press, 2002.

8. H. Gardner, *Changing Minds*, Boston MA, Harvard Business School Press, 2004.

9. E. Schein, *Process Consultation Revisited*, Reading MA, Addison-Wesley, 1999.

10. M. Beitler, *Strategic Organizational Change*, Greensboro NC, Practitioners Press International, 2006.

11. K. Cameron and R. Quinn, *Diagnosing and Changing Organizational Culture*, Reading MA, Addison-Wesley, 1999.
12. G. Neilson, B. Pasternack and K. Van Nuys, 'The Passive–Aggressive Organization', *Harvard Business Review*, October 2005.
13. K. Cameron and R. Quinn, *Diagnosing and Changing Organizational Culture*, Reading MA, Addison-Wesley, 1999.
14. Q. Huy, 'Emotional Balancing of Organizational Continuity and Radical Change', *Administrative Science Quarterly*, March 2002.
15. D. Rock and J. Schwartz, 'The Neuroscience of Leadership', *strategy + business*, May 2006.
16. S. Kerr, 'On the Folly of Rewarding A, While Hoping for B', *Academy of Management Executive*, February 1995.
17. L. Hrebiniak, *Making Strategy Work*, Upper Saddle River NJ, Wharton School Publishing/Pearson Education, 2005.
18. A. Hartman, *Ruthless Execution*, Prentice-Hall/Pearson Education, 2004.
19. C. Hipp, B. Tether and I. Miles, 'The Incidence and Effects of Innovation in Services', *International Journal of Innovation Management*, December 2000.
20. T. Kuczmarski, *Innovation*, Chicago IL, NTC Publishing Group, 1996.
21. M. Jelinek and C. Schoonhaven, *The Innovation Marathon*, Oxford UK, Basil Blackwood, 1990. D. Jung, C. Chow and A. Wu, 'The Role of Transformational Leadership in Enhancing Organizational Innovation', *Leadership Quarterly*, August–October 2003.
22. L. Hrebiniak, *Making Strategy Work*, Upper Saddle River NJ, Wharton School Publishing/Pearson Education, 2005.
23. K. Goffin and R. Mitchell, *Innovation Management*, Basingstoke UK, Palgrave Macmillan, 2005.
24. T. Kuczmarski, *Innovation*, Chicago IL, NTC Publishing Group, 1996. K. Goffin and R. Mitchell, *Innovation Management*, Basingstoke UK, Palgrave Macmillan, 2005.
25. M. Tushman, W. Smith, R. Wood, G. Westerman and C. O' Reilly, 'Organizational Designs and Innovation Streams', *Harvard Business School Working Paper*, No. 07–087, May 2007.
26. R. Cooper, *Winning at New Products*, 3rd edn, Cambridge MA, Basic Books, 2001.
27. E. Schein, *Process Consultation Revisited*, Reading MA, Addison-Wesley 1999.
28. C. Fang, J. Lee and M. Schilling, 'Exploration and Exploitation', *Working Paper No. 2007-01, KAIST Business School*, Korean Advanced Institute of Science and Technology, March 2007. N. Siggelkow and D. Levinthal, 'Temporarily Divide to Conquer', *Organization Science*, November–December 2003.
29. Project Management Institute, http://www.pmi.org.
30. J. Mihm, C. Loch and A. Huchzermeier, 'Problem-Solving Oscillations in Complex Engineering Projects', *Management Science*, June 2003.

31. M. Tatikonda and S. Rosenthal, 'Technological Novelty, Project Complexity and Product Development Project Execution Success', *IEEE Transactions on Engineering Management*, February 2000.

32. V. Govindarajan and C. Trimble, 'Building Breakthrough Businesses within Established Organizations', *Harvard Business Review*, May 2005.

33. J. Mihm, C. Loch and A. Huchzermeier, 'Problem-Solving Oscillations in Complex Engineering Projects', *Management Science*, June 2003.

34. K. Cameron and R. Quinn, *Diagnosing and Changing Organizational Culture*, Reading MA, Addison-Wesley, 1999. G. Neilson, B. Pasternack and K. Van Nuys, 'The Passive-Aggressive Organization', *Harvard Business Review*, October 2005. G. Johnson and K. Scholes, *Exploring Corporate Strategy*, 5th edn, Edinburgh, Pearson Education, 1999.

35. D. Jung, C. Chow and A. Wu, 'The Role of Transformational Leadership in Enhancing Organizational Innovation', *Leadership Quarterly*, August–October 2003.

36. Glen Sanford, *Company History*, available at http://www.apple-history.com (27 February 2008).

37. *Sources*: Nintendo.com *Iwata Asks* ... http://www.nintendo.com/wii/what/iwataasks/volume-1/part-1. CNNMoney.com *Wii will rock you* Jeffrey O'Brien, 4 June 2007 available at http://money.cnn.com/magazines/fortune/fortune_archive/2007/06/11/100083454/index.htm. MTV, interview with Shigeru Miyamoto, March 2005, quoted at http://www.n-sider.com/personnelview.php?personnelid=170.

38. *Source*: F. Aggeri and B. Segrestin, 'Innovation and Project Development', *R&D Management* 2007, 1:37–47.

CHAPTER 7: BUILDING THE MARKET FOR THE INNOVATION

1. N. Machiavelli, *The Prince, transl.* N. Thomson, New York, Dover Publications, 1992.

2. J. Blumler, 'The Third Age of Political Communication', *Journal of Public Affairs*, August 2001.

3. J. Nueono, 'Beyond Hype', Marketing Science Institute Conference on the New Media Landscape, Barcelona, May 2008.

4. M. Toscano, 'The Human Factor of Interactive Media', Marketing Science Institute Conference on the New Media Landscape, Barcelona, May 2008.

5. G. Moore, *Crossing the Chasm*, New York, HarperBusiness, 1991.

6. E. Rogers, *Diffusion of Innovations*, New York, Free Press, 2003.

7. D. Midgley and G. Dowling, 'Innovativeness', *Journal of Consumer Research*, March 1978.

8. J.-C. Larreche, *The Momentum Effect*, Upper Saddle River NJ, Wharton School Publishing, 2008.

9. C. Kim and R. Mauborgne, *Blue Ocean Strategy*, Boston MA, Harvard Business School Press, 2005.

10. E. Rogers, *Diffusion of Innovations*, New York, Free Press, 2003.

11. K. Keller, B. Sternthal and A. Tybout, 'Three Questions You Need to Ask About Your Brand', *Harvard Business Review*, September 2002.

12. B. Dattee and H. Weil, 'Dynamics of Social Factors in Technological Substitutions', *Working Paper 4599-05, MIT Sloan School of Management*, August 2005.

13. Z. Katona, J. Lajos, A. Chattopadhyay and M. Sarvary, 'Category Activation Model', *Working Paper, INSEAD*, April 2006.

14. Available online at http://www.irobot.com (11 June 2008).

15. M. Bertini, J. Gourville and E. Ofek, 'The Branding of Next Generation Products', *Working Paper 07-003, Marketing Science Institute*, 2007.

16. J. Harding, *Population Council Copper-T Study in Korea*, New York, Population Council, 1973.

17. Available online at http://www.internationalpaints.com (11 June 2008).

18. J. Gourville, 'The Curse of Innovation', *Research Paper 05-06, Harvard Business School Marketing*, June 2005.

19. Available online at http://www.tesla.com (11 June 2008).

20. C. Van den Bulte and G. Lilien, 'Two-Stage Partial Observability Models of Innovation Adoption', *Working Paper, Wharton School*, February 2004.

21. E. Rogers, *Diffusion of Innovations*, New York, Free Press, 2003.

22. P. Golder and G. Tellis, 'Will It Ever Fly? Modeling the Takeoff of Really New Consumer Durables', *Marketing Science*, Summer 1997.

23. D. Talukdar, K. Sudhir and A. Ainslie, 'Investigating New Product Diffusion across Products and Countries', *Marketing Science*, Winter 2002.

24. G. Moore, *Crossing the Chasm*, New York, HarperBusiness, 1991.

25. D. Chandrasekaran and G. Tellis, 'A Critical Review of Marketing Research on the Diffusion of New Products', *Working Paper MKT 01-08, USC Marshall School of Business*, April 2008.

26. P. Golder and G. Tellis, 'Cascades, Diffusion, and Turning Points in the Product Lifecycle', *Working Paper 03-004, Marketing Science Institute*, 2003.

27. R. Agarwal and B. Bayus, Market Evolution and Sales Takeoff of Product Innovations, *Management Science*, August 2002.

28. D. Comin and B. Hobijn, 'Five Facts You Need To Know About Technology Diffusion', *Working Paper 11928, National Bureau of Economic Research*, June 2006.

29. R. Agarwal and B. Bayus, 'Market Evolution and Sales Takeoff of Product Innovations', *Management Science*, August 2002.

30. E. Rogers, *Diffusion of Innovations*, New York, Free Press, 2003.

31. D. Comin and B. Hobijn, 'Five Facts You Need To Know About Technology Diffusion', *Working Paper 11928, National Bureau of Economic Research*, June 2006.

32. J.-C. Larreche, *The Momentum Effect*, Upper Saddle River NJ, Wharton School Publishing, 2008.
33. Available online at http://www.themomentumeffect.com (10 July 2008).
34. Available online at http://www.satmetrix.com (10 July 2008).
35. F. Reichheld, *The Ultimate Question*, Boston MA, Harvard Business School Press, 2006.
36. W. Reinartz and V. Kumar, 'The Mismanagement of Customer Loyalty', *Harvard Business Review*, July 2002.
37. S. Iyengar and A. Simon, 'New Perspectives and Evidence on Political Communication and Campaign Effects', *Annual Review of Psychology*, 2000.
38. Y. Moon, 'Digital Angel', Case 9-502-021, *Harvard Business School*, March 2002.
39. G. Moore, *Crossing the Chasm*, New York, HarperBusiness, 1991.
40. N. Harper and S. Viguerie, 'Are You Too Focused?' *The McKinsey Quarterly*, June 2002.
41. G. Tellis and P. Golder, *Will and Vision*, New York, McGraw-Hill, 2002.
42. G. Tellis, S. Stemersch and E. Yin, 'The International Takeoff of New Products', *Working Paper 02-121, Marketing Science Institute*, 2002.
43. M. Dhrehman, J. Oechssler and A. Roider, 'Herding with and without Payoff Externalities', *Discussion Paper 5310, Centre for Economic Policy Research*, October 2005.
44. E. Lee, J. Lee and J. Lee, 'Reconsideration of the Winner-Takes-All Hypothesis', *Management Science*, December 2006.
45. *Sources*: Internet Retailer.com 'The Power of customer reviews', Mary Wagner, February 2008. Available at: http://www.internetretailer.com/article.asp?id=25215. 'Twist a Pen, Open a Lock', Leander Kahney, *Wired*, 17 September 2004. Available at: http://www.wired.com/culture/lifestyle/news/2004/09/64987. 'Why there's no escaping the blog', David Kirkpatrick, *Fortune*, 10 January 2005. Available at: http://money.cnn.com/magazines/fortune/fortune_archive/2005/01/10/8230982/index.htm.
46. *Sources*: G. Tellis and P. Golder, *Will and Vision*, McGraw Hill, 2001 http://www.bbc.co.uk/dna/h2g2/A3224936; http://news.bbc.co.uk/1/hi/entertainment/tv_and_radio/1182165.stm; http://www.cedmagic.com/history/ampex-signature-v.html; http://www.fundinguniverse.com/company-histories/Ampex-Corporation-Company-History.html. B. Prasad and S. Ganesan (eds), *Advances in Concurrent Engineering*, Oakland CA, CRC Press, 1997.
47. Y. Moon, 'Digital Angel', Case 9-502-021, *Harvard Business School*, March 2002.
48. *Sources*: Palm Pilot 1000 retrospective, Palminfocenter.com, March 2006. http://www.palminfocenter.com/news/8493/pilot-1000-retrospective. Palm – historical timeline available at http://www.palm.com/us/company/corporate/timeline.html. A. Butter and D. Pogue, *Piloting Palm*, New York, John Wiley & Sons, Inc., 2002.
49. *Sources*: Public RelationSHIPS, Edelmann & Technorati, Winter 2006. R. Sachs, 'Using the Media to Introduce New Products', RMR & Associates, Inc. available at http://www.rmr.com/marketingtips.asp?nid=358&lid=1.

INDEX

Index compiled by Annette Musker